Reading R. S. Peters T

The Journal of Philosophy of Education Book Series

The Journal of Philosophy of Education Book Series publishes titles that represent a wide variety of philosophical traditions. They vary from examination of fundamental philosophical issues in their connection with education, to detailed critical engagement with current educational practice or policy from a philosophical point of view. Books in this series promote rigorous thinking on educational matters and identify and criticise the ideological forces shaping education.

Titles in the series include:

The Good Life of Teaching: An Ethics of Professional Practice
Chris Higgins

Reading R. S. Peters Today: Analysis, Ethics, and the Aims of Education
Edited by Stefaan E. Cuypers and Christopher Martin

The Formation of Reason
David Bakhurst

What do Philosophers of Education do? (And how do they do it?)
Edited by Claudia Ruitenberg

Evidence-Based Education Policy: What Evidence? What Basis? Whose Policy?
Edited by David Bridges, Paul Smeyers and Richard Smith

New Philosophies of Learning
Edited by Ruth Cigman and Andrew Davis

The Common School and the Comprehensive Ideal: A Defence by Richard Pring with Complementary Essays
Edited by Mark Halstead and Graham Haydon

Philosophy, Methodology and Educational Research
Edited by David Bridges and Richard D Smith

Philosophy of the Teacher
By Nigel Tubbs

Conformism and Critique in Liberal Society
Edited by Frieda Heyting and Christopher Winch

Retrieving Nature: Education for a Post-Humanist Age
By Michael Bonnett

Education and Practice: Upholding the Integrity of Teaching and Learning
Edited by Joseph Dunne and Pádraig Hogan

Educating Humanity: Bildung in Postmodernity
Edited by Lars Lovlie, Klaus Peter Mortensen and Sven Erik Nordenbo

The Ethics of Educational Research
Edited by Michael Mcnamee and David Bridges

In Defence of High Culture
Edited by John Gingell and Ed Brandon

Enquiries at the Interface: Philosophical Problems of On-Line Education
Edited by Paul Standish and Nigel Blake

The Limits of Educational Assessment
Edited by Andrew Davis

Illusory Freedoms: Liberalism, Education and the Market
Edited by Ruth Jonathan

Quality and Education
Edited by Christopher Winch

Reading R. S. Peters Today

Analysis, Ethics, and the Aims of Education

Edited by
**Stefaan E. Cuypers and
Christopher Martin**

WILEY-BLACKWELL

A John Wiley & Sons, Ltd., Publication

This edition first published 2011
Originally published as Volume 43, Supplement 1 of *The Journal of Philosophy of Education*
Chapters © 2011 The Authors
Editorial organization © 2011 Philosophy of Education Society of Great Britain

Blackwell Publishing was acquired by John Wiley & Sons in February 2007. Blackwell's publishing program has been merged with Wiley's global Scientific, Technical, and Medical business to form Wiley-Blackwell.

Registered Office
John Wiley & Sons Ltd, The Atrium, Southern Gate, Chichester, West Sussex, PO19 8SQ, United Kingdom

Editorial Offices
350 Main Street, Malden, MA 02148-5020, USA
9600 Garsington Road, Oxford, OX4 2DQ, UK
The Atrium, Southern Gate, Chichester, West Sussex, PO19 8SQ, UK

For details of our global editorial offices, for customer services, and for information about how to apply for permission to reuse the copyright material in this book please see our website at www.wiley.com/wiley-blackwell.

The right of Stefaan E. Cuypers and Christopher Martin to be identified as the author of the editorial material in this work has been asserted in accordance with the Copyright, Designs and Patents Act 1988.

Wiley also publishes its books in a variety of electronic formats. Some content that appears in print may not be available in electronic books.

Designations used by companies to distinguish their products are often claimed as trademarks. All brand names and product names used in this book are trade names, service marks, trademarks or registered trademarks of their respective owners. The publisher is not associated with any product or vendor mentioned in this book. This publication is designed to provide accurate and authoritative information in regard to the subject matter covered. It is sold on the understanding that the publisher is not engaged in rendering professional services. If professional advice or other expert assistance is required, the services of a competent professional should be sought.

Library of Congress Cataloging-in-Publication Data

Reading R. S. Peters today : analysis, ethics, and the aims of education / edited by Stefaan E. Cuypers, Christopher Martin.
  p. cm. – (Journal of philosophy of education)
  Includes bibliographical references and index.
  ISBN 978-1-4443-3296-4 (pbk.)
  1. Education–Philosophy. 2. Peters, R. S. (Richard Stanley), 1919- I. Cuypers, Stefaan E., 1958- II. Martin, Christopher.
  LB1025.2.R397 2011
  370.1–dc22
                              2011013209
A catalogue record for this book is available from the British Library.

This book is published in the following electronic formats: ePDFs (9781444346466); Wiley Online Library (9781444346497); ePub (9781444346473); Kindle (9781444346480)

Set in 9 on 11 pt Times by Macmillan India Ltd.
Printed in Malaysia by Ho Printing (M) Sdn Bhd
01 2011

Contents

Notes on Contributors

Robin Barrow is Professor of Philosophy of Education at Simon Fraser University, where he was Dean of Education for over ten years. He was previously Reader at the University of Leicester. His recent publications include *Plato* (Continuum) and *An Introduction to Moral Philosophy and Moral Education* (Routledge) and, as co-editor, *The Sage Handbook of Philosophy of Education* (Sage). In 1996 he was elected a Fellow of the Royal Society of Canada.

Stefaan E. Cuypers is Professor of Philosophy at the Catholic University of Leuven, Belgium. He works in philosophy of mind and philosophy of education. His research interests are autonomy, moral responsibility and R. S. Peters. He is the author of *Self-Identity and Personal Autonomy* (Ashgate, 2001), the co-author, together with Ishtiyaque Haji, of *Moral Responsibility, Authenticity, and Education* (Routledge, 2008) and an invited contributor to *The Oxford Handbook of Philosophy of Education* (2009), edited by Harvey Siegel.

Mike Degenhardt taught philosophy of education at Borough Road and Stockwell Colleges of Education, in London, and subsequently the University of Tasmania. He is the author of *Education and the Value of Knowledge* (Routledge, 1982) and of a range of papers in the philosophy of education, with particular reference to ethics and teaching. Recently his attention has been turned towards a more historical examination of the roots of the ideas that he has explored in the course of his research and teaching.

Andrea English is Assistant Professor of Philosophy of Education at the Faculty of Education, Mount Saint Vincent University. Her research areas include theories of teaching and learning, John Dewey and pragmatism, continental philosophy of education, especially Herbart, the concept of negativity in education, listening and education. She recently published: with Barbara Stengel, 'Exploring Fear: Rousseau, Dewey and Freire on Fear and Learning', *Educational Theory* 60:5 (2010), pp. 521–542 and 'Listening as a Teacher: Educative Listening, Interruptions, and Reflective Practice', *Paideusis: International Journal of Philosophy of Education* 18:1 (2009), pp. 69–79.

Michael Hand is Reader of Philosophy of Education and Director of Postgraduate Research Programmes at the Institute of Education, University of London. He has research interests in the areas of moral, political, religious and philosophical education. His books include *Is Religious Education Possible?* (Continuum, 2006), *Philosophy in Schools* (Continuum, 2008) and, in the Impact policy-related pamphlet series *Patriotism in Schools* (PESGB, forthcoming).

Graham Haydon is Visiting Fellow at the Institute of Education, University of London, where until recently he was Reader in Philosophy of Education. His many publications on moral education include recently *Values for Educational Leadership* (Sage, 2007) and *Education, Philosophy and the Ethical Environment* (Routledge, 2006).

Michael S. Katz is Professor Emeritus of San Jose State University and past President of the North Amereican Philosophy of Education Society. Much of his recent research has focused on ethical issues in teacher-student relationships. Trained at Stanford in analytic philosophy, he has focused recent work on integrating film and literature within moral analyses of concepts such as caring, integrity, trustworthiness, fairness, and respect for persons. He is the lead editor of a volume entitled *Education, Democracy and the Moral Life* (Springer, 2009), which includes his own analysis of

viii   *Notes on Contributors*

'the right to education'. He previously was also the lead editor of a volume, along with Nel Noddings and Kenneth Strike, entitled *Justice and Caring: The Search for Common Ground in Education* (Teachers College Press, 1999).

Megan J. Laverty is Associate Professor in the Philosophy and Education Program at Teachers College, Columbia University. Her research interests include: philosophy of education, moral philosophy and its significance for education, philosophy of dialogue and dialogical pedagogy, and philosophy with children and adolescents in schools. She is the author of *Iris Murdoch's Ethics: A Consideration of her Romantic Vision* (Continuum, 2007) and recently published in *Educational Theory* and, with Maughn Gregory, in *Theory and Research in Education*.

Michael Luntley is Professor of Philosophy at the University of Warwick. Recent teaching responsibilities include Wittgenstein, the philosophy of thought and language. His research interests are Wittgenstein, philosophy of mind, and philosophy of education. He is the author of *Wittgenstein: meaning and judgement* (Blackwell, 2003) and recently published: 'Understanding expertise', *Journal for Applied Philosophy* 26:4 (2009), pp. 356–70, 'What's doing? Activity, naming and Wittgenstein's response to Augustine', in *Wittgenstein's Philosophical Investigations: A Critical Guide*, ed. A. Ahmed, Cambridge University Press, 2010, pp. 30–48, 'Expectations without content', *Mind & Language* 25:2 (2010), pp. 217–236, and 'What do nurses know?' *Nursing Philosophy* 12 (2011), pp. 22–33.

Christopher Martin is a researcher in the Faculty of Medicine, Memorial University of Newfoundland. He is also a lecturer in the Faculty of Education and the Department of English at Memorial University. A former school principal, he holds a PhD in philosophy of education from the Institute of Education, University of London. His research is focused on the ethical and political foundations of education. His most recent work deals with the relationship between the humanities and medical education. His publications include articles in the *Journal of Philosophy of Education* and *Educational Theory*, and his book *Education as Moral Concept* (Continuum) is forthcoming.

Krasimir Stojanov is Professor of Theory and Philosophy of Education at the Bundeswehr University of Munich, Germany. His topics of teaching and research include educational justice, education as a concept of social philosophy, ideology critique. His last monograph *Bildung und Anerkennung. Soziale Voraussetzungen von Selbst-Entwicklung und Welt-Erschließung* (Verlag für Sozialwissenschaften, Wiesbaden, 2006) deals with the relation between education and recognition. Currently he is writing a book on '*Bildung*' as a Social Phenomenon.

Bryan R. Warnick is an Associate Professor of Philosophy of Education in the School of Educational Policy and Leadership at The Ohio State University. His current research and teaching focus on questions related to the ethics of educational policy and practice, learning theory, philosophy of educational research, and educational technology. He is the author of *Imitation and Education* (SUNY, 2008) and has published articles in *Harvard Educational Review, Educational Researcher, Teachers College Record, Educational Theory*, and many other venues.

John White is Emeritus Professor of Philosophy of Education at the Institute of Education, University of London, where he has worked since 1965. His interests are in the aims of education and in educational applications of the philosophy of mind. His recent books include *The Child's Mind* (2002), *Intelligence, Destiny and Education* (2006), *What Schools are For and Why* (2007), *Exploring Well-being in Schools: A guide to making children's lives more fulfilling* (2011), and *The Invention of the Secondary Curriculum* (forthcoming).

Kevin Williams is Senior Lecturer in Mater Dei Institute of Education, Dublin City University and former President of the Educational Studies Association of Ireland. His books include *Education and the Voice of Michael Oakeshott* (2007) and *Faith and the Nation: Religion, Culture and Schooling in Ireland* (2005).

Preface

Writing in 1966, in the closing words of his now classic *Ethics and Education*, R. S. Peters ponders the possibility that we are suffering from a kind of malaise, accentuated by an overburdened economy. And he sees this malaise as manifested in a disillusionment with the institutions of democracy, including the institutions of education: this is a disillusionment that is experienced by traditionalists and progressives alike. Yet, although he acknowledges this reasonable disappointment, he concludes affirmatively with the recognition that the most worthwhile features of political life are in the institutions that we in fact have. For in the end it is the institutions of democracy that constitute the form of government that a rational person can accept.

Writing nearly half a century later, can we hold on to thoughts such as these? That was a time of prosperity, whereas now we face the varying deeps of a recession. That decade was heralded, so it now seems, with the much-quoted quip of the British Prime Minister Harold Macmillan that 'most of our people have never had it so good'. He was in fact speaking in 1957, but the remark was to become celebrated as an expression that supposedly epitomised the time. Hence, the general sense that the 1960s was a time of prosperity may make Peters' remarks about an overburdened economy now seem somewhat surprising. Compare that time with our current straitened circumstances, and you may wonder why disillusionment had set in. After all, you may be tempted further to think, don't we now face a situation, around the world, in which the financing of educational institutions is strained, where the institutions that finance them are stained, and where the possibilities of democratic access are progressively, surreptitiously curtailed?

There may be some truth in thoughts such as these, but to indulge such a view is conveniently to ignore the increases in real wealth that have been achieved in the intervening decades, as well as the extension of educational provision in so many ways. It was developments in the 1960s, in the economy and in ideas, surely, that provided the ground in which that expansion of education in many significant respects took root. In fact, Peters himself came into the field at a time when his own thinking about education could flourish, and the thoughts that he then disseminated in his writings and teaching had influence around the world. Moreover, apart from his influence through books and articles, Peters was himself a creator of institutions. Thus, in a very real sense, the pages you are now reading owe their existence to Peters' initiative, with the establishment of the Philosophy of Education Society of

Reading R. S. Peters Today, First Edition. Stefaan E. Cuypers and Christopher Martin.
Chapters © 2011 The Authors. Editorial organization © 2011 Philosophy of Education Society of Great Britain. Published 2011 by Blackwell Publishing Ltd.

Great Britain, and hence with the birth of the *Journal of Philosophy of Education*, of which he was the first Editor. The expansion of publication and conference activity in philosophy of education that has ensued in subsequent decades owes so much to what he did then. And in this light it is no exaggeration to say that his achievement remains unparalleled.

Can we then turn today to the institutions of education without cynicism, avoiding myths about the past as much as illusions about the future, in the way that Peters urged? In many respects his own writings prompt the kind of serious reflection on education that is the antidote to cynical and idealistic excess. In many respects what he has to say can be turned to the conditions we face today, however much the institutions of our democracies, not least our universities and schools, have changed. And this is precisely what is demonstrated in the chapters that follow. Stefaan Cuypers and Christopher Martin, coming from different academic backgrounds and different cultural contexts, independently developed ideas about the possibilities of a collection that might read Peters' work against a backdrop of contemporary change—in philosophy, educational policy and practice—but in the end it is their combined initiative that has brought together these assessments and responses from around the world. The journal is grateful to them for their efforts and insight in renewing our sense of the importance of reading R. S. Peters today.

Paul Standish

Introduction: Reading R. S. Peters on Education Today

STEFAAN E. CUYPERS AND CHRISTOPHER MARTIN

Paul Hirst ends his masterly 1986 outline of Richard Stanley Peters' contribution to the philosophy of education with these words:

> Whether or not one agrees with his [Peters'] substantive conclusions on any particular issue it cannot but be recognised that he has introduced new methods and wholly new considerations into the philosophical discussion of educational issues. The result has been a new level of philosophical rigour and with that a new sense of the importance of philosophical considerations for educational decisions. Richard Peters has revolutionised philosophy of education and as the work of all others now engaged in that area bears witness, there can be no going back on the transformation he has brought about (pp. 37–38).

As Hirst rightly notes, while his contribution is still a matter of discussion, all agree on Peters' status as one of the great founding fathers of contemporary philosophy of education. In the 1960s and 1970s he undertook a uniquely ambitious philosophical project by introducing and developing what might be called a singular *analytical paradigm* for puzzle-solving in the philosophy of education. This paradigm, whether something to be celebrated *or* resisted, continues to influence our work today. Peters, born in 1919 in India, who held the chair in the Philosophy of Education at the London University Institute of Education from 1962 until 1983, celebrated his 90th birthday in 2009. Therefore, we wish to take this occasion to critically engage with Peters' work with the aim of examining the ways in which and the extent to which his contribution has relevance for present day philosophy and educational theory.

The scene of (British) philosophy of education has transformed considerably since Peters' heyday in the 1960s and 1970s. David Carr's 1994 state of the art account can be read as an intermediate report on the fortunes of educational philosophy. With the advent of Thatcherism (1979–1990) and the rising influence of managerial conceptions of educational administration and bureaucratic control, the political and institutional circumstances drastically changed. Within the more utilitarian and instrumentalist climate of the 1980s, the philosophy of education took a more 'practical' turn and was more

Reading R. S. Peters Today, First Edition. Stefaan E. Cuypers and Christopher Martin.
Chapters © 2011 The Authors. Editorial organization © 2011 Philosophy of Education Society of Great Britain. Published 2011 by Blackwell Publishing Ltd.

concerned with 'political implications'. At the same time, many educational philosophers resisted an unquestioning acceptance of the market and consumer conceptions of narrowly neo-liberalistic education. Both for their critique and their alternatives, they drew not only on post-empiricist Anglo-American philosophy but also on Continental intellectual traditions such as Phenomenology, Existentialism, (Neo-)Marxism, Structuralism, Critical Theory and Post-Modernism. 'Thus', Carr observes, 'one is as likely to encounter such names as Habermas, Adorno, Horkheimer, Lyotard, Gadamer, Foucault, Derrida, Ricoeur, Althusser or Lacan in a contemporary article on philosophy of education as those of MacIntyre, Taylor or Rorty' (p. 6).

As of today, the situation has not altered much: at the end of the first decade of the 21st century, philosophy of education is still meritoriously eclectic and cross-cultural in character. True, to the list of names one would have to add Wittgenstein, Heidegger, Arendt, Levinas, Benjamin, Nietzsche, Cavell and McDowell. In addition, recent social changes have, of course, engendered new challenges to be dealt with in educational philosophy. The present-day scene features philosophical reflection (and empirical research) on the ways in which educational systems try to cope with, for example, multiculturalism and cosmopolitanism, globalisation, changing notions of citizenship, environmentalism, as well as with, for example, new conceptions of vocational education, the rise of information and communication technology (ICT) and the restructuring of higher education in both European and North American contexts. All these current issues are approached from different theoretical viewpoints and explored in diverse styles of reflection and research. The recent guidebooks to the field, such as *The Blackwell Companion to the Philosophy of Education* (Curren, 2003), *The Blackwell Guide to the Philosophy of Education* (Blake *et al.*, 2003) and *The Oxford Handbook of the Philosophy of Education* (Siegel, 2009), amply testify to the multi-paradigmatic condition of present day philosophy of education.

Far from considering Peters' analytical paradigm as somewhat out-dated, all the contributors to this book are of the opinion that it still has an important, if not essential role to play on the scene of philosophy of education today. They go back to Peters in an attempt to carry his thinking further into the future. For that purpose, they take up the main themes of his analytical project in order to seek a fresh look at the ways in which his writings reflect upon current concerns. This book is neither a *Festschrift* for R. S. Peters, nor a *Manifesto* for the analytical movement. Though, this being said, one cannot avoid engaging with the analytical claims and methods of an analytical philosopher such as Peters; nor should one avoid pointing out that analytical project's weaknesses in addition to its merits. The contributions of this book offer an inspirational rereading of Peters and a fruitful exploration of his analytical paradigm in the context of the heterogeneous and multifaceted present day scene of educational philosophy. We now locate the contributors against the backdrop of Peters' analytical project.

In the early 1960s Peters entered the field of philosophy of education as a first rate philosopher, well-versed in the Ordinary Language Philosophy of Ryle and Austin (for this post-war period in analytical philosophy, see Soames, 2003). Quite naturally for him, philosophy—and, of course, also philosophy of education—is concerned with questions about the analysis of concepts and with questions about the grounds of knowledge, belief, actions and activities. The point of doing conceptual analysis is that it is a necessary preliminary to answering other philosophical questions, especially questions of justification. Consequently, two basic questions delineate Peters' analytical paradigm in the philosophy of education: 1) What do you mean by 'education'?—a question of conceptual analysis; and 2) How do you know that 'education' is 'worthwhile'?—a question of justification. He studied not only philosophy but also psychology. This explains his strong interest in philosophical psychology—particularly in the analysis of the concepts of motivation and emotion—and, more pertinent to the field of educational philosophy, in the developmental psychology of Freud, Piaget and Kohlberg. He approached these empirical or quasi-empirical 'genetic' psychological theories from the standpoint of moral theory. Hence, another focal question demarcates Peters' project: 3) How do we adequately conceive of moral development and moral education? These three leading questions serve as a natural outline for the contributions of this book into three sections, with a fourth section serving to place Peters in context:

I. The Conceptual Analysis of Education and Teaching (Barrow, Laverty, Luntley, Warnick, English).
II. The Justification of Educational Aims and the Curriculum (Katz, Hand, White, Martin, Stojanov).
III. Aspects of Ethical Development and Moral Education (Haydon, Cuypers)
IV. Peters in Context (Degenhardt, Williams).

Peters' analytical project is, in a specific sense, *foundational*. The sense in which the term 'foundational' is used here should not be misunderstood. The project is not epistemologically foundational in the sense of trying to establish a set of infallible axioms for educational theory. As such, it is neutral as to the controversy between foundationalism and anti-foundationalism (coherentism, constructivism, contextualism, etc.) in contemporary epistemology and metaphysics. Peters' analytical paradigm is *conceptually* foundational in the sense that it deals with key concepts that are constitutive of the discipline—the philosophy of education—itself. It involves a conceptual inquiry into the very notions of education, learning, teaching, knowledge, curriculum, etc. (for a nearly complete list of these fundamental notions, see Winch and Gingell, 1999). Arguably, the treatment of all other educationally relevant concepts and issues asymmetrically depend upon the analysis of these key concepts. How can one adequately deal with the issue of multicultural education in the school if one has no clear view of *education*? How can one responsibly apply the concept of ICT in the classroom if one lacks an analysis of *knowledge*? Unless one has such key concepts in one's theoretical toolbox, talking philosophy of education quickly degenerates into 'edu-babble'. In their contributions to this book each author shows how some of the foundational concepts of Peters' analytical paradigm connect with and elucidate the current concerns mentioned above. While they may not all agree that the *particular* view of education developed by Peters is entirely cogent or sufficient, they do recognise the extent to which engaging with such key concepts is necessary.

Peters himself concludes his own 1983 state of the art—his philosophical testament in a way—with these words:

> Certainly this more low-level, down to earth, type of work [on practical issues] is as important to the future of philosophy of education as higher-level theorising. . . . I do not think [however] that down to earth problems . . . can be adequately or imaginatively dealt with unless the treatment springs from a coherent and explicit philosophical position. . . . But maybe there will be a 'paradigm shift' and something very different will take its [the analytical paradigm's] place. But I have simply no idea what this might be. I would hope, however, that the emphasis on clarity, the producing of arguments, and keeping closely in touch with practice remain (p. 55).

As indicated earlier, no paradigm shift has taken place in the meanwhile. What has come to the surface today is the multi-paradigmatic configuration of the philosophy of education. Yet Peters' rumination about the future reminds us of the foundational place of the analytical paradigm in this present day configuration. As such, it should play an essential role on the scene of philosophy of education today. Because Peters' paradigm is philosophical, analytical and foundational, it contributes not only to the clarity and argumentative structure but also to the seriousness of the discipline. It is Peters' reminder that we must reflect on what it is we are actually claiming when we talk about education. Only by way of such a reflexion can we ensure that an inclusive, multi-paradigmatic philosophy of education, in its attempts to be responsive to the concerns of the moment, does not lose sight of what makes it a valuable and distinctive contribution to the philosophical enterprise.

REFERENCES

Blake, N., Smeyers, P., Smith, R. and Standish, P. (eds) (2003) *The Blackwell Guide to the Philosophy of Education* (Oxford, Blackwell).

Carr, D. (1994) The Philosophy of Education, *Philosophical Books*, 35, pp. 1–9.

Curren, R. (ed) (2003) *A Companion to the Philosophy of Education* (Oxford, Blackwell), pp. 221–31.

Hirst, P. H. (1986) Richard Peters' Contribution to the Philosophy of Education, in: D. E. Cooper (ed.) *Education, Values and Mind. Essays for R. S. Peters* (London, Routledge & Kegan Paul), pp. 8–40.

Peters, R. S. (1983) Philosophy of Education, in: P. H. Hirst (ed.) *Educational Theory and its Foundation Disciplines* (London, Routledge & Kegan Paul), pp. 30–61.

Siegel, H. (ed) (2009) *The Oxford Handbook of the Philosophy of Education* (New York, Oxford University Press).

Soames, S. (2003) *Philosophical Analysis in the Twentieth Century, Volume 2. The Age of Meaning* (Princeton, NJ, Princeton University Press).

Winch, C. and Gingell, J. (eds) (1999) *Key Concepts in the Philosophy of Education* (London, Routledge).

1

Was Peters Nearly Right About Education?

ROBIN BARROW

I

Despite my title, my focus in this chapter is more on the question of Peters' philosophical methodology than on his substantive claims about education, although I shall suggest that broadly speaking he was right about education in his early work, and did not need to conclude subsequently that it was 'flawed by two major mistakes' (Peters, 1983, p. 37). Peters did not of course invent or develop a unique kind of philosophical method. But what he did do, very much a man of his time and philosophical background, was rigorously pioneer a form of philosophical analysis in relation to educational discourse. That form or type of philosophical analysis has from the beginning been subject to criticism and is today relatively out of fashion, particularly in the field of education. This is not to suggest that there are no philosophers of education who see themselves as engaged in analysis in the Peters' tradition, nor that the work of such philosophers is never published. There is no conspiracy theory here. But it is to suggest that much work in philosophy of education and, in particular, much teaching of philosophy of education is not focused upon the kind of sustained and close analysis that Peters advocated.

I shall argue that much of the objection to Peters' methodology is based on a misunderstanding of what it does and does not involve. Consequently, philosophical analysis is often wrongly seen as one of a number of comparable alternative traditions or approaches to philosophy of education, between which one may or needs to choose, and that, partly consequentially, there is a relative lack of philosophical expertise among today's nominal 'philosophers of education'. Furthermore, once his methodology is vindicated, it can perhaps be said that Peters was indeed 'nearly right about education', perhaps more so than he subsequently came to believe himself.

In 1975 Peters published a paper entitled 'Was Plato nearly right about education?' (Peters, 1975, pp. 3-16). His answer was that Plato was right apart from the fact that he was mistaken in his conception of reason. Few would dispute Peters' claim that Plato thought that all reasoning led to certainty on

Reading R. S. Peters Today, First Edition. Stefaan E. Cuypers and Christopher Martin.
Chapters © 2011 The Authors. Editorial organization © 2011 Philosophy of Education Society of Great Britain. Published 2011 by Blackwell Publishing Ltd.

the model of geometry, or his view that in this belief Plato was mistaken: we do not necessarily arrive at certain and indisputable truth in the moral sphere, for example, by reasoning. Implicit in recognising this point, of course, is that we can legitimately question the validity of Plato's or Peters' conception of education. Again, I doubt that many would be uncomfortable with this. John Wilson sometimes seemed to argue for a strong essentialist position such that education necessarily was what it was, but for the most part contemporary philosophers, no matter how they label themselves, would accept the view that, in W. B. Gallie's phrase, at least some concepts are 'essentially contested', and that it is part of the business of philosophy to argue, sometimes inconclusively, about the various merits of rival conceptions.[1] Furthermore, it is naive to imagine that philosophers, by and large, are unaware that particular viewpoints may be materially shaped by various social and psychological considerations. If Plato believed, for example, as some caricatures would have it, that there is one and only one form of relationship possible between human beings that is, always was and always will be, 'marriage', then few if any of us today are Platonists. But, to me, that would indeed be a caricature of Plato, and it certainly has no bearing on Peters' position.[2]

At this point, however, a crucial and fundamental distinction must be noted. A lack of certainty is not the same thing as arbitrariness. Similarly, to acknowledge room for argument and inconclusive conclusions is not the same thing as saying that the truth is entirely a matter of individual perception. In other words, we must be on our guard against moving from the received wisdom of our day that Plato wrongly thought objective truth was obtainable in all spheres of inquiry to the fashionable conclusion that there is no truth and that all opinions are entirely the product of time and place. Plato's conception of education may in various ways have been faulty or inadequate, as may Peters' or yours or mine, but this does not mean that one can have any conception of education one chooses (as indeed reference to 'faults' and 'inadequacy' in rival conceptions clearly implies).

These introductory remarks relate to my main purpose in this way: I shall argue that Peters' methodology does not deserve some of the criticism it has received and indeed that he may have recanted more than he should have at later points in his career. So, one part of my concern is to clarify and defend a certain type of philosophical analysis. The other part is to argue that analysis of this sort does not currently enjoy the favour it should. This will involve a brief consideration of what may sometimes be referred to as alternative or rival styles or traditions of philosophy, such as realism, Marxism or postmodernism. But I should note that I am not here primarily concerned to pursue arguments about the inadequacies or shortcomings of alternative approaches.[3] Rather, I wish merely to argue for the need for more sustained philosophical analysis such as Peters engaged in, and to establish that in various ways, regardless of their internal coherence, merits and demerits, so-called alternative philosophies (or types or styles of philosophy), are not alternatives at all, because they are not comparable in relevant respects.

Deciding, for example, whether to adopt realism or philosophical analysis is, I shall argue, quite evidently a case of apples and pears.

My practical concern is that educational discourse in general and perhaps debate in teacher-education in particular has to a considerable extent reverted to the 'mush' famously derided by Peters, albeit 'mush' of a far more complex and sophisticated texture than in the past. I want to suggest, therefore, that the teaching of philosophy of education would benefit from a more systematic analytic approach, as opposed to the widespread current tendency to offer isolated courses in such things as 'existentialism and education', 'a phenomenological inquiry into education' or 'postmodern perspectives'.

II

One of the earliest and more vituperative criticisms of Peters' methodology came from David Adelstein in 'The Philosophy of Education or the Wisdom and Wit of R. S. Peters' (Adelstein, 1971). Adelstein drew to some extent on Ernest Gellner's *Words and Things* (1959), and more broadly on the Marxist tradition then enjoying considerable favour, particularly in the so-called sociology of knowledge. Peters was depicted—as enemies generally seem to be treated in the Marxist-Leninist tradition—as being somehow both a dupe and a hypocritical time-server of the powers that be. But, if we pass beyond the rhetoric and party-posturing, there are some criticisms here that have been more widely held. Perhaps the most notorious of these relates to Peters' use of such phrases as 'we would not say ...' as in 'we do not call a person "educated" who has simply mastered a skill'.[4] Such phrasing, not surprisingly perhaps, evoked the response: 'Who are the "we" referred to?' And to many the answer to that is: '"We" are those who think and therefore speak like me', which in turn was commonly glossed either as those in power or authority or, alternatively, as those who are uncritically subservient to the dominant culture or thought. More widely there was the charge that so-called 'ordinary language philosophy' begged every important question by treating some language use as more normal, ordinary or acceptable than others, without warrant. Again there was commonly a class angle introduced, and philosophers were accused of validating certain types of speech such as the Oxford English spoken by most university dons at the expense of working-class speech. In short, linguistic philosophy was criticised as doing no more than giving preference to the thinking implicit in the particular talk of middle-class people and illegitimately claiming that such language was somehow more 'ordinary', and hence to be respected, than others. But this is all very confused, not least in the simplistic equation of Oxford philosophy, linguistic philosophy, and ordinary language philosophy with each other and, more importantly, with philosophical analysis in the sense of conceptual analysis.

Gellner, in a book that no analytic philosopher of Peters' persuasion need have anything but admiration for, made the entirely valid point that words are not things; and anybody who thought that explicating everything that can be said about how the word 'education' is used would lead to a definitive account of the phenomenon of education itself, would be sadly mistaken. But did anyone ever seriously think that? Even J. L. Austin, who was undoubtedly and unashamedly interested in *How To Do Things With Words* (1962), and who, for example, was intrigued by the various applications of a word such as 'real', explicitly said that 'ordinary language has no claim to be the last word, if there is such a thing' (Austin, 1961, p. 133), and clearly did not imagine for one moment that, by pondering over a question such as what we should call the 'real' colour of a deep sea fish, he was contributing in any direct way to a metaphysical question such as 'what is the nature of reality?' (if there is such a thing).

Gellner's thesis has more force against the Wittgensteinian belief that 'meaning is use', but even here we should recognise that the claim that the meaning of a word is to be found in its use is distinct from the claim that the meaning of a concept is to be found in the use of the word that denotes it. But note that in any case Austin's ordinary language philosophy is distinct from Wittgenstein's theory of meaning and both, I would maintain, are distinct from the kind of philosophical analysis that Peters practiced. Of course he drew eclectically on these and other contemporary ideas, as we all do. But it is crucial to understand that his style of analysis is not to be equated with any one specific school of thought, any one method, or any one procedural principle. And while Gellner was correct to distinguish words and things, it is perhaps unfortunate that he did not equally explicitly go on to distinguish concepts and things, for the fact is that we need to bear in mind the distinction between words *and* concepts *and* things. Concepts are not things, both in the sense that some concepts are of abstractions such as love, which are not generally regarded as 'things', and in the sense that the concept of a stone is not the same as a particular stone (which is a thing). Despite the fact that formally few would dispute it, many in taking a critical stance towards philosophical analysis of the type practiced by Peters seem to forget this basic point. (While various specific views about language and meaning need to be recognised as distinct, I shall treat 'philosophical analysis' of the type I am concerned with as synonymous with 'conceptual analysis'.)

Conceptual analysis is concerned with trying to explicate a concept: with trying to map out, define or describe the characteristics of an abstract idea such as love or justice or education. It seems certain that, since we are creatures who think in terms of language, any such analysis will begin with some consideration of words. Inevitably, we are going to begin by establishing that 'to educate' is not a synonym for 'to torture' or 'to eat'; more than that, we are in most cases going to take for granted some kind of dictionary definition as a starting point: in inquiring into education we are inquiring into what is and is not essential to our idea of bringing up the young. But the word is not the concept: the philosophical concern is not with what the word 'relevance', for example, means, which is in fact fairly clear and straightforward, but with what constitutes relevance in that sense.

The limits of the significance of language use are apparent from the beginning. We do not, for example, take account of etymology, save only as being potentially suggestive. That is to say, not only do we not accept a particular view of education simply because it derives from the Latin *educere*; we specifically repudiate this kind of linguistic argument. (The fact that 'happiness' derives from the word 'hap', meaning 'chance', is not an argument for concluding that people today believe that happiness is purely a matter of chance, still less that it is in fact so. And this is to ignore the point that many etymological claims are questionable. There is in fact no more reason to suppose that education derives from the Latin *educere* than that it derives from the Latin *educare*.)[5]

Not only is philosophical analysis not a species of etymology, it is also simply incorrect to claim that its method is to extrapolate uncritically from the current use of a select group. On the contrary, we explicitly acknowledge both varied contemporary use and, as often as not, historically located use. Thus Woods notes that as a matter of fact sports journalists do talk about the 'educated left foot' of the footballer, and Peters recognises that Spartans would have called a certain kind of person 'educated' whom the Athenians would not have so called.[6] In both cases they proceed to reason to their own conclusions about these varying uses and are in no way bound by them.

Again, it must be stressed that conceptual analysis is not to be defined in term of any particular procedures or methods. There are of course tricks of the trade or gambits that the seasoned philosopher can engage in. For example, sometimes it is helpful to consider the opposite concept, sometimes to consider border-line cases, sometimes indeed to take hints from usage (anybody's usage) or even etymology. What it is best to do is largely a function of the concept in question, but always the question of how to proceed is a matter of judgement. In the final analysis engaging in conceptual analysis is an imaginative exercise rather than a calculative one. Of course one must take account of various non-conceptual and non-evaluative facts, but fundamentally analyzing the concept of education is a matter of trying to produce reasons for regarding it as more plausible to see it this way than that.

This brings me back to Peters' use of phrases such as 'we would not say . . .'. Not only have philosophers such as MacIntyre confused the issue by wrongly equating philosophical analysis with linguistic analysis, they have also tended to interpret this kind of phrasing as evidence that the philosopher is engaged in an empirical survey of linguistic usage.[7] But this is clearly not what is going on in such cases. Phrasing such as this is the philosopher's way of inviting the audience (reader, interlocutor) to think for themselves, and challenging them to disagree. It is the only kind of argument, very often, that characterises what is often loosely called 'dialectic'. There is no way of 'proving' that the mere mastering of the skill of standing on your head is not sufficient to establish that you are educated, at least no way of 'proving' in the senses that we are familiar with from other disciplines such as science and mathematics. But while we cannot 'prove' it, we can get people to think about it and come to see what they had not hitherto perceived, as a result of which nobody of my acquaintance would accept such a conception. And that is essentially what is involved in Peters' style of analysis: the attempt to do some extensive and imaginative thinking and to encourage others to consider critically what one has to say. While it is true that we aim to define a term and to explicate the essential characteristics of a concept, it is important to recognise that philosophical analysis is equally concerned with fine discrimination and revealing the logical implications of our concepts.

A little more can be said. Though we cannot define analysis in terms of a specific set of procedures, we can suggest that there are at least four objectives that we should seek to meet. It is widely acknowledged that while we might in principle aim to provide a set of necessary and sufficient conditions for every concept, we cannot in practice succeed in doing so. Many concepts, as I have noted, simply are essentially contested. But we can always make some sort of progress in presenting an account of a concept that is a) clear, b) complete, c) coherent and d) compatible. Attempting to meet these four Cs is ultimately what I would call the business of conceptual analysis.

The value of clarity goes without saying, and it is surely one of the strongest arguments there is for the need for more analytic ability; so much argument in politics, the arts and the humanities in particular is conducted by means of concepts that whatever else they may be are simply unclear (for example, postmodern, bourgeois, embodied meaning, God). In order to explicate a concept, one needs not only to use clear terminology but also, very often, to unpack other concepts involved in the definition. Thus, if we say that education involves the imparting of worthwhile knowledge, that, though clear terminologically, obviously invites further questions about what is involved in worthwhile knowledge. What I mean by aiming for completeness is aiming to ensure explication of such further ideas as are significant in explicating the original. By this time one is likely to have a fairly lengthy, detailed and complex description of the concept in question. It is now important to consider whether it is entirely coherent, by which I refer to its internal consistency. An acceptable analysis obviously must not involve a complex idea that in some way or other is self-contradictory. Finally, if the concept is now clear, complete and coherent it needs to be checked against one's other knowledge including one's wider conceptual repertoire, but also including non-conceptual matters such as matters of fact or value—and of course against relevant publicly warranted knowledge. There is something wrong with your understanding of 'explosive' if what you define as 'explosive' doesn't explode; and there is something wrong with your definition of happiness if what you define as happiness has everybody weeping in misery.

It is incidentally my view that if we could more successfully analyse our concepts in this way, we might find an unexpected degree of commonality. Thus currently more or less every regime in the world claims to be democratic. Step one (considering usage) would tell us that some people are simply misusing the word in as much as their regime has nothing to do with rule either by or for the people in general. But we would then rapidly find that nonetheless there are a number of distinct regimes which might perhaps be termed democratic. By examining these actual regimes and describing them in terms that are clear, complete, coherent and compatible (in the senses described), we would in all likelihood reasonably conclude that some are not in fact democratic in any plausible sense, but that others though differentiated in detail, are nonetheless equally legitimate forms of democracy. (Not even Plato thought that because all beds partake of the one form of bedness they have to be identical in all respects.)

To recap the argument so far: Peters' style of philosophical analysis may be regarded as synonymous with conceptual analysis, but is emphatically not to be confused or identified with linguistic philosophy, ordinary language philosophy or the Wittgensteinian equation of meaning with use. It is ultimately concerned with concepts, which are distinct from words, although of course it is acknowledged that any conceptual analysis will have to begin with some basic linguistic clarification. There is no single or determinate set of methods for conducting this analysis; rather, it involves imaginative reflection leading to the setting out of as clear, as complete and as coherent a description of the characteristics of a given idea as may be, and ensuring that the concept thus described is compatible with wider understanding and beliefs. It is a truism that nobody's account of anything can avoid being influenced by the individual's particular situation. But it is simply false to assert that analysis of this type is necessarily or even particularly likely to be merely a reinforcement of convention or the status quo.

Indeed, it is something of a paradox that Peters, in arguing for what on the face of it is a minority view (and always has been) of education as a matter of developing understanding for its own sake, certainly at a variance with most governmental conceptions, should have been accused of being a lackey of the powers that be. But then, as noted, criticism of his position has overall been entirely contradictory. To some, what he has to say about education is too specific, to others it is too empty; to some it is too prescriptive, to others not prescriptive enough; to some it is too traditional and conservative, to others it is too idiosyncratic, even iconoclastic.

III

Peters was one of the first people to explicitly seek to analyse the concept of education. Of course others had implicitly or indirectly done so since the time of Plato, and of course others in the 20th century had busied themselves with analysis of various educational concepts. But it was Peters who most obviously made and acted upon the point that if education is the name of our game, then it is on the idea of education itself that we ought to focus. This point has not had the recognition it deserves. It is not a mere detail or a matter of program planning and organisation. There is a clear and great difference between examining certain educational ideas in isolation and doing so in the context of a preliminary inquiry into the very enterprise of education itself. (By analogy, contrast the merely shrewd and knowledgeable lawyer with the lawyer who has given thought also to the nature of law.) One might criticise Peters' work on the concept of education for being formal and not in itself very determinate, but to some extent, even if this criticism were valid, it misses the point. Even if analysis of the concept of education does not yield a great deal that is both specific and substantive, it will focus the mind on the nature of the activity in which we are engaged.

There are in fact two parts to his analysis of education. First there are the formal criteria. Peters suggests that an educated person is to be distinguished from a trained, a skilled, or a socialised person by four characteristics. All have some kind of knowledge or understanding but the educated person has not merely facts or information but also 'some understanding of principles for the organization of facts'; he is, secondly, not merely unthinkingly able to regurgitate facts such as historical dates, but is to some degree in some way affected or 'transformed' by this knowledge. He sees the world differently than he would otherwise have done as a result of this understanding. Thirdly, the educated man must care about the standards imminent in his field of interest: an educated person takes seriously the standards and procedures of science, for example, and is not merely cognisant of them. Finally, the educated person does not simply have a field of knowledge but what Peters calls 'cognitive perspective', meaning a wider framework such that, for example, his scientific knowledge co-exists with historical and cultural understanding.[8]

Much of the criticism of this part of Peters' work is not mistaken in its characterisation so much as in its judgement or evaluation. It is, for instance, correct to say that these criteria are formal. That is to say we are told that cognitive perspective is required and we are told what that means, but we are not told in precisely what it consists. But why should this be counted an objection? All concepts have certain formal characteristics and it is as well to start by outlining them. But then it may be said that these criteria are too vague. Here we encounter another common mistake, namely the confusing of breadth with vagueness. A concept may be broad and clear or broad and vague, conversely, it may be specific (narrow) and unclear or specific and precise. In this case, the concept of education is itself in fact a fairly broad one; it is also fairly obviously the case that it is polymorphous. That is to say, while all educated people must be supposed to meet some common criteria if they are indeed to be described equally as 'educated', nonetheless the precise form of their education may differ. Thus, we would expect them to have cognitive understanding of some sort, but it may be that different individuals have equal degrees of perspective displayed in different domains. There is, I would suggest, nothing vague or unclear about the four criteria Peters introduces, but they are both broad and formal. That, of course, means that this is both a flexible and generous conception of education: it clarifies our understanding without delimiting possibilities. In the circumstances, it is surprising that some saw Peters as being too prescriptive.

But, secondly, Peters went beyond these four criteria, for he also argued that education necessarily involved the transmission of worthwhile understanding. In view of the fact that Peters talked about certain specific types of knowledge, such as science and history, and particularly in view of his close association with Paul Hirst and the latter's influential work on forms of knowledge, there is an initial ambiguity here. It is at least arguable that it was never as clear as it might have been whether the claim was that educated people had certain kinds of knowledge (for example, science and history) and such knowledge was worthwhile, or that educated people necessarily had worthwhile knowledge and it could be separately argued that disciplines such as science and history had the requisite value. Nor does Peters' self-criticism, when writing in 1983 about the state of philosophy of education, help to clarify the matter, for he remarks that he feels his earlier work (particularly in the seminal *Ethics and Education*, 1966), 'was flawed by two major mistakes. Firstly, a too specific concept of 'education' was used which concentrated on its connection [with?] understanding',[9] (which perhaps suggests the first interpretation), while the second flaw was a failure to give 'a convincing transcendental justification of worthwhile activities', which suggests the second. He goes on to say that the concept of education is 'more indeterminate than I used to think. The end or ends towards which processes of learning are seen as developing, e.g. the development of reason which we stressed so much [,?] are aims of education, not part of the concept of "education" itself and will depend on acceptance or rejection of the values of the society in which it takes place' (Peters, 1983, p. 37).

Although we are now entering into consideration of Peters' substantive view of education, which is not my primary focus in this chapter, I have to say that I find this recantation very odd. And a recantation indeed it is, for part of Peters' wider argument had been the claim, surely correct, that the aims of education are intrinsic to it, as opposed to extrinsic, and as such, I should have thought, by definition part of the concept. Furthermore Peters' 'admission' that 'conceptual analysis has been too self-contained an exercise', the comment that 'criteria for a concept are sought in usage of a term without enough attention being paid to the historical or social background and view of human nature which it presupposes', and his subsequent illustrative observation that usage cannot determine whether 'teaching' is only properly used when learning actually occurs, seem to betray some of the confusion of which his critics are guilty (Peters, 1983, pp. 43, 44). As I have argued, the view that 'criteria for a concept are sought in the usage of a term' is true only of certain specific approaches to philosophy such as that of some Wittgensteinians, and as a matter of fact it is not true of Peters' own work in the round. And the obvious conclusion to be drawn from the fact that some people use the word teaching only when learning does take place while others do not, is indeed that linguistic usage is not sufficient to determine conceptual sense (or that we have two distinct concepts).

But Peters' actual work, both on the concept of education and more generally, is not open to these criticisms. With a wide cultural and historical awareness, and, of course, beginning with some common sense observations about the word in order to locate the argument (we are talking about 'education' not 'swimming', and, more to the point, about 'education' which we want to distinguish from such things as 'training' and 'socialization'), he invites us to recognise that different as our initial substantive views may be, we would not, when we think about it, classify a person with an esoteric set of skills, regardless of how much we admired them, as educated on that account alone. And no more would a classical Spartan or Athenian have done. And I would suggest, *à propos* Peters' recantation, that in fact the identification of education and worthwhile knowledge is entirely correct. Granted there is the separate and further question of what knowledge is worthwhile (although here the four formal characteristics have a bearing at least on the question of what is *educationally* worthwhile), it is surely something that any thoughtful person of any society and era would agree upon: educated people are those who have what is regarded as worthwhile knowledge.

This does mean, of course, that the next and in a sense more important task is to determine what knowledge we take to be worthwhile. But that task, contrary to many a prevailing viewpoint, is not simply a matter of exchanging entirely subjective opinions. It is a question of focusing on the nature of knowledge and on the quality of arguments surrounding particular value claims.

IV

There is a long tradition, in the United States in particular, of teaching philosophy of education by way of various schools of thought or '-isms' (as in 'realism', 'pragmatism', etc.). Thus, to take a prominent example, Ozmon and Craver's eighth edition of *Philosophical Foundations of Education* (2008) has chapters on Idealism, Realism, Eastern Philosophy and Religion, Pragmatism, Reconstructionism, Behaviorism, Existentialism and Phenomenology, Analytic Philosophy, and Marxism, with a final chapter entitled 'Philosophy, Education and the Challenge of Postmodernism'.

Now, if one's purpose is merely to become acquainted with a number of diverse 'philosophies', in the vulgar sense of 'theories of various kinds about various distinct kinds of thing', this is all fine and well. There is of course such a thing as a behaviourist view of human activity; there is the Marxist interpretation of history and a variety of other Marxist perspectives on this, that and the other; there are those who describe themselves or are classified by others as existentialists; and so on and so forth. But the emphasis here must fall on words such as 'diverse' and 'distinct kinds of thing' (not simply 'distinct things', please note), for the various '-isms' are not simply different—they are of many different sorts. And, on the one hand, these different schools of thought are not necessarily competing and incompatible alternatives (for example, some such as Sartre have claimed to be Marxist existentialists); on the other, one cannot coherently embrace absolutely any combination one chooses (it would be difficult to be an idealist and a behaviourist, for instance).

One's first concern with approaching the world of ideas and theory by means of such a classification system is that the labels are, generally speaking, very broad, which means that possibly similar but nevertheless decidedly different thinkers or theories are categorised alongside each other, as idealism may typically cover Plato, Hegel and certain Christian thinkers. Secondly, besides being broad, they are often very vague labels. I do not need to further alienate some of my readers by pointing out yet again that it is far from clear what 'postmodernism' or 'phenomenology' mean—what exactly the terms cover or refer to and what they don't.[10] Sufficient to point out that while Ozmon and Craver classify Rousseau, for example, as a 'pragmatist', others classify him as a 'naturalist' and in one instance he is seen as 'akin to an idealist'.[11] This could, of course, be explained by the complexity or even confusion of Rousseau's thought, but it seems clear to me that generally speaking these broad and vague labels serve to place ill-assorted bed fellows in Procrustean beds.

But much more important is the point that these various classifications are of quite different kinds. For example, idealism when it is applied to Plato refers to a specific epistemological theory about the nature and objects of knowledge. By contrast, behaviourism is a specific theory about how to conduct research into human conduct (and in some extreme cases about how to define human actions). Existentialism, being a quasi-metaphysical view on the human condition, is different yet again, as, in turn, is Marxism which is primarily an explanatory system of social dynamics. In most cases these '-isms' are partial or reductive: that is to say, they either focus only on one aspect of life or they see all of life through only one prism. A very real danger with this approach is thus that one will be tempted to choose between these various perspectives or traditions rather than, where possible, linking them and extrapolating from them. Nor has any convincing case been made for linking any of these schools of thought to a particular educational theory or viewpoint. (See, for example, Phillips, 1994, pp. 4451 ff.).

But the major concern is that in such a list one item sticks out like the proverbial sore thumb. Analytic philosophy, at least as understood here, is quite distinct from each and every one of the other schools of thought considered by Ozmon and Craver, because analytic philosophy is a type of inquiry and one that is appropriate to a limited set of questions only, parallel to but distinct from scientific inquiry. To be committed to philosophical analysis is unique among these 'schools of thought' in that it implies no commitment to any particular theory, particular methodology, particular explanatory theory or particular substantive beliefs. To be an analytic philosopher implies nothing necessarily about one's views on the reality of Platonic forms or the existentialist claim that existence precedes essence. It may happen to coincide or not with the belief that all or most of our understanding is shaped by the fundamental economic shape of our society, but it implies no necessary explanatory theory about how we come to believe what we believe. And, to repeat, while of course the analytic philosopher proceeds in certain ways, this is not the same thing as saying that analysis is to be defined in terms of a specific methodology.

There was a time when Marxists tried to argue that 'rationality' was just another form of ideology. This line of argument was often implicit in debate on indoctrination when the riposte to the claim that imposing unquestioning commitment to Marxism was indoctrination was that imposing commitment to reason was also. And today there are still those who would see a commitment to analytic philosophy as a commitment to an interpretive view of the world. But this won't do at all.

Philosophical or conceptual analysis of the type Peters advocated and practiced involves no set procedures, which is perhaps one of the reasons why it is quite hard to teach in the initial stages. One cannot begin by telling students what they need to do in the sense of what procedures they need to adopt. It is defined by its questions: it can only be characterised in terms of explicating or inquiring into concepts, the ways to do this, as said, being many and various, but generally imaginative and reflective rather than technical or calculative. In this respect it may perhaps be a little like hermeneutics. Not hermeneutics as originally conceived by 18th century German scholars, who used the term to connote a very specific set of techniques for pursuing understanding of religious texts, but more in line with contemporary usage as a broad term meaning little more than 'inquiry' in general. Prominent hermeneutical thinkers such as Gadamer seem to me to be eminently sensible, but I confess to being unable to see anything distinctive in his work that requires or justifies the use of the label 'hermeneutic'. Of course, one might point to certain broad approaches commonly associated with hermeneutics, such as repeatedly considering parts of a text in relation to the overall text, being especially attentive to interactions across the contexts of the writer and the reader, or attempting to understand what aspects of focal phenomena might be said to exist outside of inquiry. But no such list of putative strategies constitutes a 'method' or 'methodology' in the sense usually aspired to in the social sciences; nor is such a list distinctive of hermeneutics as distinct from various other forms of inquiry (including philosophical analysis). Perhaps all one can say on this specific matter is that if 'hermeneutic' refers to some specific theory or mode of inquiry, then, it will not be comparable to philosophical analysis, whereas if it simply refers to an open-minded critical approach to non-empirical issues then it is a largely redundant term (as I believe it generally is, particularly in the many graduate theses sub-titled 'a hermeneutical inquiry').

Something broadly similar may need to be said of phenomenology, though again it is sometimes unclear to those not on the inside of this school of thought what precisely it involves. It appears to be based upon the conviction that we cannot go beyond appearances and, therefore, cannot do more than focus on the perceived phenomenon, but there is, to me at any rate, a distinct lack of clarity as to how one is supposed to set about focusing on the phenomenon in question. It might, I suppose, be said that this is more true of some phenomenological writings (particularly in education) than others. And certainly it might be argued that a founding father such as Husserl had a relatively specific project in mind: he aimed to lay a basis for a natural scientific form of inquiry by attempting to pick out those categories of mind that enabled a perception of things as they are phenomenally, outside of social constructions and acquired learnings. But, first, it is far from agreed to what extent Husserl succeeded in this. Secondly, his thinking can itself be regarded as complex, possibly confused, and in need of greater conceptual clarity. Thirdly, if we were to take the view that his position were clear and correct, this would entail commitment to a specific methodology and a specific view of the way things are, such as would differentiate it entirely from philosophical analysis. For present purposes the relevant point to note is that different as Husserl's view and the broader contemporary notion of phenomenology may be, both are, in their different ways, somewhat opaque; but, either 'phenomenology' refers to a school of thought that involves specific beliefs, procedures, or explanatory theories, in which case it is to be sharply distinguished from philosophical analysis, or it does not, in which case it too appears to be a somewhat unnecessary label, since, unlike analysis, it does not even pick out a particular kind of object of inquiry.

Philosophical analysis is thus considerably clearer and more straightforward as a label than either hermeneutics or phenomenology and more open. It makes no *a priori* assumptions about reality, appearance or anything else.

When it comes to something like existentialism the situation is slightly different, but the overall point remains essentially the same: it cannot be directly compared with philosophical analysis. An existentialist believes that existence precedes essence; some sort of sense can perhaps be made of this and it may even have a certain plausibility. Existentialism is also associated very often with a certain attitude or mind-set towards the world, consequent on this basic conviction—the famous existentialist angst, supposedly (necessarily?) following a recognition of our predicament. This is clearly a view about the nature of human existence, and, as such, quite distinct from any form of inquiry. All too often people seem to confuse the incontrovertible truth that as inquirers we are bound to have various preconceptions and points of view, with the quite false assumption that we cannot in principle reason objectively and, more particularly, question our preconceptions. Thus as an existentialist one might either uncritically accept the doctrine and use it as an explanatory system or look at it critically, making use amongst other things of conceptual analysis.

Finally, by way of examples of various schools of thought, Marxism is essentially an explanatory theory, at its simplest the view that everything is determined by the economic organisation of a given society. Over-simplified though this may be, the fact remains that, however sophisticated or complex the theory may become, it involves a belief or set of beliefs about how the world operates and consequently, in principle, one can read off the Marxist interpretation of events as readily as one can a Catholic or Utilitarian interpretation.

My point here has been to briefly illustrate that conceptual analysis is not in any way another '-ism' or 'school of thought', and it should not be placed alongside them, whatever their respective merits and uses. Analysis is quite different in kind, and is one necessary kind of inquiry (along most obviously with mathematical and scientific inquiry) that we need to understand and appreciate if we are to make sense of our world. I suggest that the prevalence of the 'schools of thought' approach to studying philosophy of education may account partly for the relative decline of philosophical analysis as a formal part of educational study. When it is treated as merely one of many competing perspectives, traditions, or styles it obviously may fall into relative disfavour.

Certainly in my experience studying philosophy of education increasingly means reviewing an eclectic list of '-isms and education', so that one might at best come to study only, say, 'pragmatism and education' and never come to engage systematically and deliberately in raising conceptual questions (even about pragmatism, let alone education). And this style of studying philosophy of education has perhaps contributed in turn to a broadening of the concept of 'philosopher' when it comes to making appointments in education departments. In Canada, at any rate, there are very few 'philosophers of education' who have degrees in philosophy. The majority perhaps have only a doctorate in education which could be classified as philosophical, their undergraduate and even master's degrees being as often as not in quite different areas. But, for reasons I have given, it is apparent that, while of course they might have great philosophical ability, it is equally possible that their sole background for teaching philosophy of education is a thesis that they were pleased to label, for example, a hermeneutic or an existentialist study, without it being clear that it involved any philosophical reasoning in the sense of rigorous conceptual work (let alone the rigorous analytic study of the canonical texts in philosophy).

I fear that the 'mush' in educational discourse that Peters referred to is back with us. People talk of, pontificate about, and adopt practical policies relating to giftedness, multiculturalism and inclusion, for example, and prate of caring and happiness, without having any coherent and plausible account to give of those concepts.[12] But contemporary philosophers of education, broadly speaking, do not seem much inclined to tackle these fundamental conceptual questions. Conversely, a great deal of what they *do* do seems to involve the adoption of preconceived positions, be it of value, epistemology, or explanation.

Peters did not simply apply his preconceptions: his work is an attempt to review, refine, explicate and justify his preconceptions, if you like, as all our work should be, it being likely that if we approach the matter in this way many of our preconceptions will become transformed, if not jettisoned.

V

I have tried to suggest that one thing that Peters did was argue for the need for a certain kind of inquiry in educational discourse. This type of inquiry may be labelled either philosophical or conceptual inquiry. What he meant by this and what he practiced was neither ideological nor power-based. What he championed above all was clarity and cogency. Certainly his approach did not consist in saying either 'this is how I use the word . . .' or 'this is how others use the word', but in saying something like this: 'taking into account all we know about the use of the word, which is suggestive of how people tend to think and may provide useful hints, our task is to scrutinise our ideas and look out for lack of clarity, lack of coherence as in internal contradiction, lack of compatibility as in inconsistency with various other beliefs we hold, and above all to aim for completeness by amplifying a given concept and when necessary moving on to explicate some further aspects of the original concept'.

It is arguable that, partly because we have failed to do the conceptual work, educational theory and practice have ended up with a false view of what it is to be human, and hence a false view of education. We have a mechanistic view of humans, and see their flowering as merely a network of skills, their values in mere terms of utility, often economic, while the intricate imaginative possibilities of the mind are reduced to processes. One of the things educationalists seem least to understand is that awesome thing, human understanding.

But, finally, what are we to say about Peters' initial conviction that education was about developing the mind, human reasoning and understanding, as fully as possible, for its own sake (notwithstanding the fact that it might also have great utility)? Well, we can of course 'say' anything we like. And it has long since been conceded that we cannot 'prove' that he is right or wrong in the sense of that word familiar from other disciplines. But I should like to conclude by trenchantly asserting the plausibility of this conception for precisely the kinds of reason that Peters gave: When all is said and done people do not associate education with such things as health, wealth, fame, popularity, charm, happiness, esoteric skills, or particular proficiency. They do not have to be part of some power-conspiracy or even confined to 21st century Western society to see that 'she's obese, she must be uneducated' or 'how happy she is, she must be well-educated' are silly remarks. Everybody who thinks about it recognises that education is about developing the kind of mind or understanding one admires. What kind of understanding is to be admired will of course partly reflect our current understanding (of understanding amongst other things) and our values, but that does not invalidate the point that education is about developing worthwhile understanding. Yet while we all acknowledge this when we think about it, we live with policies and practices that are not formulated with this in mind, that by and large indeed actually militate against this ideal.

Some readers no doubt will respond in a manner beloved of academics by praising with faint damn: it will be said that this is of very little consequence because everybody agrees that analysis has its place and may be practiced alongside one's commitment to Marxism, phenomenology or whatever. But I am suggesting that while that is true in principle, in fact very little adequate analysis is taking place. The sort of 'analysis' that does take place is often more akin to the kind of analysis that theology involves: that is to say a restricted and restrictive mode of interpretation within a closed system: theologians can of course be very sophisticated when arguing about the meaning of the claim that God is three persons in one, but there discourse does not really touch on the conceptual question facing the proverbial person in the street, which is not 'what is the technical (i.e. religious) definition?', but what does it *mean* to say that someone is three persons in one (particularly when one of the 'persons' is the 'holy ghost')? Similarly Marxists have written reams on their definition of such terms as the 'bourgeoisie' and 'dialectic' but that does not mean that they have presented us with clear, complete, coherent and compatible conceptions. The concern is quite simply, but surely very worryingly, that so much of what is currently written in philosophy of education is more or less incomprehensible to those who are outside a given tradition, theory or school of thought.

A relative lack of emphasis on and ability pertaining to the kind of philosophical analysis that Peters espoused and exemplified leaves too many powerless to seriously critique the particular framework of explanation or interpretation of the world to which they adhere, and doomed to seek to explain everything through the lens of a single ideology or perspective. What is needed is the ability to take no such school of thought or -ism on trust. The first step is to recognise that embracing philosophical analysis is not itself to embrace any kind of ideology.

NOTES

1. For example, see Wilson, 1985 and Barrow, 1983 and 1985. A useful guide to the history of philosophical analysis since 1900 is provided by Soames, 2003.
2. On Plato's Theory of Forms, see further Barrow, 2007, esp. pp. 48–60.
3. In recent years it has become increasingly difficult to distinguish caricatures of postmodernism from the real thing. See, for example, Searle, 1995; Sokal and Bricmont, 1998; Crews, 2006; and Sokal, 2008.
4. Peters, 1966, p. 30. Cf., e.g., p. 33.
5. And, incidentally, the range of meanings of both words is considerable and overlapping. See Barrow and Woods, 2006, p. 115.
6. See Barrow and Woods, 2006, p. 31, and Peters, 1966, p. 30.
7. MacIntyre (1981) rejects philosophical analysis as something that 'will not help us' (p. 2). But he arrives at this conclusion by first identifying philosophical analysis with linguistic analysis, and then equating the latter with a particular version of ordinary language philosophy.
8. I am drawing primarily on Peters, 1966, Part 1, esp. pp. 30–35.

9. The text (Peters, 1983, p. 37) actually reads 'a too specific concept of "education" was used which concentrated on its connection and [sic] understanding'. I presume this is a misprint.
10. See, e.g. Barrow, 1999.
11. Gutek, 1988 and Neff, 1966 for example.
12. Noddings (2003, p. 2), for example, wonders 'why so few educational theorists have written about happiness'. She then cites three who have: A. S. Neill, Tsunesaburo Makiguchi and, flatteringly, myself (Barrow, 1980). But Makiguchi, she feels, has a focus that 'may seem a bit odd to Western readers' (p. 3). Nobody could accuse Neill of engaging in careful conceptual analysis on happiness or any other key educational concept. Sadly, Noddings acknowledges that I do 'present an analysis of happiness' which is 'well worth reading' but then adds, the crucial point, that 'some readers may find it too abstract' (p. 3). Well, yes, analysis is an abstract activity. That may partly *explain* why there is not much of it about, but it does not alter the fact that there isn't. Noddings herself fails to elucidate the concept in any meaningful way.

REFERENCES

Adelstein, D. (1971) The Philosophy of Education or the Wisdom and Wit of R.S. Peters. (London, Students Union of London University Institute of Education). Reprinted in T. Pateman (ed.) (1972) *Counter Course* (Harmondsworth, Penguin), pp. 115–139.
Austin, J. L. (1961) *Philosophical Papers* (Oxford, Clarendon Press).
Austin, J. L. (1962) *How to do Things with Words* (Oxford, Clarendon Press).
Barrow, R. (1980) *Happiness* (Oxford, Martin Robertson).
Barrow, R. (1983) Does the Question 'What is Education?' Make Sense?, *Educational Theory*, 33.3–4, pp. 191–195.
Barrow, R. (1985) Misdescribing a Cow: The Question of Conceptual Correctness, *Educational Theory*, 35.2, pp. 205–208.
Barrow, R. (1999) The Need for Philosophical Analysis in a Postmodern Era, *Interchange*, 30.4, pp. 415–432.
Barrow, R. 2007 *Plato* (London, Continuum).
Barrow, R. and Words, R. (2006) *Introduction to Philosophy of Education*, 4th edn. (London, Routledge).
Crews, F. (2006) *Postmodern Pooh* (Evansston, IL, Northwestern University Press).
Gellner, E. (1959) *Words and Things* (London, Gollancz).
Gutek, G. L. (1988) *Philosophical and Ideological Perspectives in Education* (Upper Saddle River, NJ, Prentice Hall).
MacIntyre, A. (1981) *After Virtue: A Study in Moral Theory* (London, Duckworth).
Neff, F. C. (1966) *Philosophy and American Education* (New York, Centre for Applied Research in Education).
Noddings, N. (2003) *Happiness and Education* (Cambridge, Cambridge University Press).
Ozmon, H. A. and Craver, S. M. (2008) *Philosophical Foundations of Education*, 8th edn. (Columbus, OH, Pearson).
Peters, R. S. (1966) *Ethics and Education* (London, Allen and Unwin).
Peters, R. S. (1975) Was Plato nearly Right about Education?. *Didaskalos*, 5.1, pp. 3–16.
Peters, R. S. (1983) Philosophy of Education, in: P. H. Hirst (ed.) *Educational Theory and its Foundation Disciplines* (London, Routledge and Kegan Paul).
Phillips, D. C. (1994) Philosophy of Education: Historical Overview, in: T. Husen and T. N. Postlethwaite (eds) *The International Encyclopedia of Education*, 2nd edn., vol. 8 (Oxford, Pergamon), pp. 4451 ff.

Searle, J. (1995) *The Construction of Social Reality* (Harmondsworth, Penguin).
Soames, S. (2003) *Philosophical Analysis in the Twentieth Century*, vols. 1 & 2 (Princeton, NJ, Princeton University Press).
Sokal, A. (2008) *Beyond the Hoax: Science, Philosophy and Culture* (New York, Oxford University Press).
Sokal, A. and Bricmont, J. (1998) *Intellectual Impostures* (London, Profile Books).
Wilson, J. (1985) The Inevitability of Certain Concepts (including Education): A Reply to Robin Barrow, *Educational Theory*, 35.2, pp. 203–204.

2
Learning Our Concepts

MEGAN J. LAVERTY

INTRODUCTION

It is difficult to say what concepts are, and yet everyone recognizes their centrality for human communication and life. They enable us to distinguish flowers from trees, have a preference for the colour blue, admire an individual as courageous, and to mature as a parent. Our concepts express the differentiations that matter most to us. They enable us to share experience and pave the way for a fuller participation in one another's lives. For example, a teacher who has a highly-nuanced understanding of disappointment is likely to respond to a student's dejected demeanour by engaging him tenderly and constructively in conversation about his failing. This, in turn, may lead the student to talk more openly about his aspirations, difficulties and challenges, making him more willing to strategize and collaborate with the teacher in the future. Given the supreme importance of concepts, it is ironic that they should escape our notice so much of the time. The more effectively our conceptual understanding enables us to speak and behave in the world, the more we are inclined to take it for granted. Our conceptual understanding remains operative even when we are least aware of it because concepts merge into a background that is taken as 'given' which allows them to covertly direct our ordinary unreflective sayings and doings.

Generally speaking, only the experience of conceptual dissonance brings concepts back into focus as subjects of renewed interest. Inspired by Elizabeth's Anscombe's pioneering article 'Modern Moral Philosophy' of 1958, contemporary philosophers concentrate on conceptual loss.[1] They mostly analyze communities that persist in using certain words even though these words lack their former meaningfulness due to the absence of certain background cultural conditions. Jonathan Lear, for example, imagines the struggle of the Crows (an American-Indian community) to live courageously after their warrior life-style had been decimated by the Anglo-Europeans. Lear's analysis reminds us that inter-cultural exchange provides dramatic occasions of conceptual dissonance; and most of us have experienced miscommunications engendered by cultural difference. On a lighter note, while I was at a conference in South Korea I chose to show my respect to my

Reading R. S. Peters Today, First Edition. Stefaan E. Cuypers and Christopher Martin.
Chapters © 2011 The Authors. Editorial organization © 2011 Philosophy of Education Society of Great Britain. Published 2011 by Blackwell Publishing Ltd.

hosts by dressing formally. I wore a skirt only to discover that when I was seated the display of my bare knees shocked my traditional-minded Korean colleagues—thankfully one colleague kindly offered me a handkerchief with which to cover my offending limbs. Even individuals who expect to disagree about concepts like honour and nobility can be surprised to discover culturally diverse standards for such things as comfort, hygiene and privacy.

The conceptual dissonance occasioned by inter-cultural exchange is so tangible that it can cause us to overlook the ubiquity of conceptual dissonance caused by intra-cultural exchange. Conceptual dissonance is an integral feature of our daily lives and often occasioned by frustrated expectations. For example, imagine two individuals (let's call them G and T) who talk about themselves as becoming friends. After G cancels dinner for the third time T feels resentful and begins to wonder if G is in fact treating her as a friend; she poses questions to herself about what it means to be a friend. As a result, T might decide to initiate a conversation with G about their potentially different understandings of friendship. They learn that for T friendship entails the fulfilment of certain duties, whereas for G friendship entails the relinquishment of duty. Thus, through this dialogue, friendship re-enters their lives as a contestable concept. Another form of conceptual dissonance occurs when an individual discovers that his or her concept is hopelessly inadequate. Imagine that as a result of her conversation with T, G finds her own concept of friendship superficial. She may attribute this to a lack of thought on her part or she may suddenly see it as the result of certain pervasive cultural influences (books, television, or other media) that do not challenge her to think more deeply about friendship.[2] It is likely to be the authority of T's example, combined with G's desire to enjoy a friendship with her that compels G to be more reflective about friendship. Finally, imagine that after her conversation with G, T sees a dog sitting in a window waiting patiently or perhaps stoically for the person(s) of the house to return. In that moment T might be struck by the impoverishment of her own sense of fidelity.

These examples highlight the quotidian nature of conceptual dissonance. We all recognize the experience of having our routine sense-making interrupted by the call to take greater responsibility for our conceptual understanding. Our complacent reliance on convention is disrupted by the summons to revise and refine our concepts to make them more meaningful. Manifestly, we do not always know whether our conceptual understanding is becoming more, rather than less, meaningful. It is extremely difficult, if not impossible, to distinguish the necessary and universal features of a concept from ones that are contingent and historical. Judgments about our concepts are inescapably circular: individuals have no choice but to trust the received meaning of concepts, while seeking opportunities to alter them. Sceptical worries aside, conceptual understanding is experienced as a task to be undertaken or, alternatively, as an obligation to be fulfilled—it is, if you like, our distinctly human vocation. It prohibits individuals from simply receiving their concepts as a straightforward birthright, inheritance or 'dowry', to use Friedrich Nietzsche's term. Rather, they must take up these concepts and make them fully and uniquely their own (Nietzsche, 1967, pp. 221).[3]

Not surprisingly, philosophers debate the nature of this conceptual labour and who is best qualified to conduct it. In the next section, I consider analytic philosophy of education as exemplified by Richard Stanley Peters' position in this debate. I begin with his distinction between concepts employed at the first-order (our ordinary language-use), and second-order conceptual clarification characterized as the 'spectatorial mapping' by philosophers 'of concepts employed at the first order' (Cato, 1987, p. 35). I explain why Peters thinks that professionally trained philosophers are uniquely. qualified to perform second-order conceptual clarification.[4] I consider the implications of Peters' philosophical methodology. I conclude that he has a profound appreciation for the critical importance of concepts in human practices. While his separation of second-order conceptual clarification from first-order conceptual use might be effective from a short-term professional point of view, unfortunately it limits the analytical approach. The isolation of conceptual clarification from conceptual use deprives each of an important element located in the other: conceptual use is no longer constituted as an inquiry into what our concepts mean; and conceptual clarification is no longer motivated by what matters. Both are bound to stagnate as a result.

R. S. PETERS AND ANALYTIC PHILOSOPHY OF EDUCATION

Peters held the Chair of Philosophy of Education at the University of London from 1962 until 1983. During that time he reinvigorated philo-sophy of education 'as a major intellectual enterprise of practical significance' (Hirst, 1986, p. 8). He redefined the field by founding it upon the analytic premises that he brought with him from philosophy. The twenty-year tenure of Peters' leadership marks a high point in the field's history. First, it was a time of tremendous scholarly productivity which advanced our understanding of teaching and learning (particularly in relation to epistemology and ethics). Second, philosophers of education became very influential in educational policy and teacher education; and third, the field was characterized by a sense of vibrancy, vitality and collegiality. According to David E. Cooper, Peters' influence on philosophy of education remains unparalleled; no other single figure has exercised such an influence over a branch of philosophy in such a short time (Cooper, 1986, p. 2). The significance of this period owes something to Peters' passionate, energetic and visionary leadership; but it also owes something to the appeal of the analytic approach that he ushered in.

With the exception of his inaugural presentation as Chair of Philosophy of Education at the University of London, Peters rarely theorized his analytic approach to philosophy of education.[5] His collaborator, Paul H. Hirst, attributes this to a variety of influences, from his studies in classical and modern philosophy to the 'different contemporary influences on him during his formative years, influences ranging from the work of Moore, Ryle and Wittgenstein to the personal impact of study and collaboration with Popper, A. C. Mace, Oakshott, Hamlyn and Phillips Griffiths' (Hirst, 1986, p. 11). Peters' embrace of the 20th century revolution in philosophy is demonstrated in his use of such phrases as: '*aristocratic* pronouncements', 'the *garden* of knowledge' and 'the analytic *guillotine*' (Peters, 1966a, p. 15). He excitedly declared that in the 20th century, philosophers would no longer presume to formulate 'high-level directives' on how to live (*ibid.*). Rather, they would cast themselves in the mundane role of 'underlabourers in the garden of knowledge' (*ibid.*). For Peters, there was nothing new in this idea. 'Socrates, Kant, and Aristotle did much the same. What is new is an increased awareness of the nature of the enterprise' (*ibid.*).

Ironically, Peters' vision of the philosophical enterprise reinstates the privileged epistemic status of philosophy crediting philosophers with possessing a highly sophisticated and technical expertise that provides them with knowledge that is both invaluable and secret.[6] Philosophers no longer presume to fix anything at the first order precisely because to do so would jeopardize their unique form of expertise, namely, that of neutrally describing our thinking. They take responsibility for identifying the logically necessary (and sufficient) conditions of our ordinary language-use. They clarify the distinctions that our words were developed to designate by seeing '*through* the words' to the structure or rules 'underlying how we speak' (Peters and Hirst, 1970, p.10). This places philosophers in a unique and privileged position of being able to *answer* questions about the relative truth of competing worldviews by uncovering their conceptual assumptions.

In Peters' view, philosophy should involve a particular mode of thinking directed to 'the disciplined demarcation of concepts, the patient explication of the grounds of knowledge and of the presuppositions of different forms of discourse' (Peters, 1966a, p. 15). Philosophy examines how meaning is determined and knowledge established through language usage, a process Peters identifies as its 'high-level or second-order character' best represented by the image of the spectator (*ibid.*). He writes: 'just as a spectator, to a certain extent, detaches himself from the activities of which he is a spectator in order to watch and comment on them, so also does the philosopher detachedly ponder upon and probe into activities and forms of discourse in which he and others engage' (*ibid.*). Unlike other spectatorial labours—journalism and sociology for example—the philosopher's study of language-use is informed by questions about the demarcation of meaning and the grounds of knowledge. To quote Dennis Cato, the philosopher's role is 'that of patient and detached recorder of those forms of thought through which reality is cognized at the first order' (Cato, 1987, p. 26). Philosophers are required to 'analyze concepts like "justice" in an effort to understand our normative commitments, and "time" in an effort to understand our status in reality' with a view to making us wiser about 'about how things are in the world and of the possible stances that we can adopt towards our predicament in it' (Peters and Hirst, 1970, p. 12).

Peters advocates analyzing concepts without adhering to an essentialist theory of meaning. The analytic approach, in his view, does not assume *a priori* linguistic necessities.[7] Hirst quotes Peters as saying that 'the point of examining ordinary usage is not to spot some linguistic essence but to take one route to explore distinctions which may prove important in the context of a thesis' (Hirst, 1986, p.13). Peters derives his inductive method from Socrates. In the *Republic*, Socrates illuminates what justice means by experimenting with different denotations to determine whether they will stand in place of the concept. He considers whether 'justice consists in giving every man his due' or whether 'justice is in the interest of the stronger', and so on (Peters and Hirst, 1970, p. 7). By means of this process of trial and error, Socrates clarifies the conceptual structure of justice. This is a painstaking and difficult process that defines the concept in a weak sense. A concept is defined in a weak sense when 'another word can be found which picks out a characteristic which is a logically necessary condition for the applicability of the original word' (p. 5). Peters illustrates his point with the example of punishment arguing that we have a weak definition of punishment if we can substitute 'inflicting something unpleasant on the guilty' for all cases in which the word 'punishment' is used in ordinary language (pp. 5–6).

Philosophers must resort to defining concepts in a weak sense because their inquiry is confined to the publicly observable substitution of words. Peters thinks Wittgenstein was right to claim that the class of activities called 'games'—tennis, chess, hopscotch, poker and tag, for example—is not held together by a single unifying characteristic but by a set of overlapping family resemblances. Peters also held that Wittgenstein was wrong to overlook the possibility of a 'general principle' that distinguishes all games (as unified by a set of family resemblances) from activities like marriage and gardening, for example. The fact that a game is not an activity which is undertaken seriously allows us to produce a weak definition of the concept of game.

Peters stresses that identifying a concept (i.e. defining it in a weak sense) is not the same as having it (i.e. defining it in a strong sense). Here 'having' denotes a sense of 'inhabiting' or 'living with' a concept. He states that 'the public criterion is necessary to identify having a concept, but having a concept is not identical with it' (p. 28). Understanding a concept involves more than identifying what it designates because individuals use words purposefully to fulfil a range of non-linguistic goals and aspirations. Individuals use words as 'tools' to perform 'specific jobs in social life' (p. 7). To use concepts in combination with other concepts, individuals must be able to use them in new and unforeseen ways. Peters concludes that in order for an individual to have a concept (i.e. definition in a strong sense), he or she must grasp the general principle informing its use. He can see no other explanation for how individuals can combine concepts with one another. For Peters, understanding a concept in a strong sense involves 'both the experience of grasping a principle *and* the ability to discriminate and use words correctly' (p. 28).

The character of a concept's general principle remains imprecise. According to Peters, a concept's general principle necessarily presides over all real and possible uses of a concept—for how else, as he suggests, is an individual going to combine concepts in new and original ways. Peters makes it seem as if these general principles are indeed rules that govern ordinary language-use: to grasp a concept's general principle is to follow a rule that dictates how that concept is to be used in all cases. In turn, this implies that when an individual uses a concept in combination with other concepts, he or she will look to other people for confirmation that the concept is being used correctly, that is, whether he or she has grasped the general principle that guides its use. Other individuals fulfil the role of verifying my own language use. Such a thesis would seem to prohibit the imaginative use of concepts and the view that linguistic regularities are emergent, i.e. they arise from the creative use of language in our daily interactions. Peters does not say enough about these general principles or the necessity that we grasp them. Since the experience of grasping a principle is so subjective he feels justified in not giving it any sustained serious attention. Unfortunately, this is a slippery slope: something we cannot speak about becomes something we need not speak about which becomes something that maybe does not exist. As Iris Murdoch pithily states: 'If something is no use it does not matter much whether it's there or not' (Murdoch, 1970, p. 11).

Generally speaking, analytic philosophers of education embraced the task of analyzing central concepts like education, teaching and knowing, confident that their findings would resolve educational problems and improve educational practice and policy. Like the mythic god, Atlas, they shouldered the burden of conceptual analysis, heeding Peters' warning that 'we may not always be successful in our search for logically necessary conditions for the use of a word. But sometimes we may be' (Peters and Hirst, 1970, p. 6). Assuming the responsibility for second-order conceptual clarification gave philosophers of education both a clear sense of purpose (to identify the logically necessary conditions of our language-use), and a definite set of procedures (the inductive approach) (Peters, 1966b, pp. 60–61). Peters summarizes his methodology as follows: 'As the concept in question is usually one the possession of which goes with the ability to use words appropriately, what we [philosophers] do is examine the use of words in order to see what principle or principles govern their use. If we can make these explicit we have uncovered the concept (Peters and Hirst, 1970, p. 4). The approach is complicated by the fact that ordinary language-use is constantly changing. As Peters' says, 'If we think that we have got a concept pinned down, we are apt to come across a case where we would naturally use the word but where the condition which we have made explicit is not established' (p. 6). He gives the example of punishment: a philosopher might define punishment as 'inflicting something unpleasant on the guilty' only to come across talk of boxers 'taking a lot of punishment' (p. 12).

In summary, Peters was clearly influenced by the revolution of post-war philosophy, particularly Wittgenstein's original contribution; but he also strove to establish the revolution's continuity with 'the historic roots of philosophy' (Hirst, 1986, p. 11). Peters sought a course of reconciliation and to that end he attached 'considerable importance to the *mapping of conceptual relations* through the *examination of linguistic usage*' (*ibid.*). In his early work, he sought to define concepts in their relationship to, and distinction from, other concepts assuming that to uncover a concept is to reveal its location within a set of conceptual relations. For example, he endeavoured to see the relationship of education to personhood, value and knowledge, as he distinguished education from indoctrination. Peters later criticized the narrowness of his earlier approach, arguing that it was 'too self-contained' and that philosophical research must incorporate findings from psychological and sociological research (Kleinig, 1982, p. 20, n. 2) as his later work on understanding moral motivation, development and education did.[8] He urged philosophers to draw upon other disciplines and to examine technical and ordinary language-use. Scholars continue to disagree about whether Peters' commitment to conceptual analysis waxed or waned in his later research (p. 16). Regardless of whether it was due to his diminishing interest or the emergence of alternative Marxist and post-modern perspectives, the analytic approach became less influential during the early nineties.

Contemporary devaluing of the analytic approach is a regrettable development in the history of philosophy of education. I do not think, however, that we need to return to conceptual analysis as it was practiced by Peters, Hirst, Israel Scheffler and others. Rather, we need to recover their faith in concepts and the spirit of their commitment to conceptual analysis. Proponents of the analytic approach appreciated the centrality of concepts to human experience, activity and communication. They understood that to improve anything—whether it is a craft, community, marriage or school— requires overturning old conceptual understandings. They saw the value in attending to our concepts and to engaging in conceptual labour. Today, many consider defining concepts somewhat *passé*. Persuaded by the scholarship of Nietzsche, Michel Foucault and others, some contemporary philosophers of education incline towards a hermeneutics of suspicion. They assume that our conventional discursive practices harbour traces of structural and historical power inequities and, as such, lack an agentive, creative quality. To understand a concept, according to this outlook, is to understand how it works within the context of these structural and historical inequities. These thinkers are sceptical about the possibility of our ever being able to arrive at an exercise of reason that is free and independent. As a result, they often turn their attention to those 'experiences' that transcend human conceptual understanding: the sublime, death, and apprehension of the Other.[9]

Critiques of injustice are critical and I hope will always remain a part of our field's work. And yet, it is in the very spirit of human justice—or justice toward the human—that I have examined here what it means to learn our concepts. I have come to believe that concepts are capable of disclosing reality and have, to use Stephen Mulhall's phrase, 'genuine substance' (Mulhall,

2007, p. 35). They are *not* mere epiphenomena. Concepts have the potential to be deep because they are concerned with something real and valuable that individuals seek to understand. My reasons for this view are empirical and ethical.

Empirically speaking, our life using language is not entirely determined (as adherents to the hermeneutics of suspicion assert), but neither is it entirely free (as the Enlightenment thinkers proposed); rather, it is both free and determined which has implications for our understanding of each of these terms. Ethically speaking, individuals have an obligation to speak their words, and listen to those of others, as if they have meaning. Language is the principal means by which individuals address and recognize one another as having something to say. To assume that words have meaning does not entail the assumption that their meaning is either unchanging or impersonal. On the contrary, a highly personalized conceptual understanding can only deepen within the context of conceptual meaningfulness.

In the next section I argue that conceptual understanding has an inescapable pedagogical dimension. By this I mean that our relationship to concepts is characterized by learning and teaching.[10] Ordinary language-use is not a matter of successfully using words in different combinations, having correctly analyzed 'the rules' governing our linguistic conventions. For if it was like this then conceptual understanding would be a matter of mere competency or skill: language proficiency would be demonstrated by the consistent use of words across different contexts. Our relationship to language is just not like this, except perhaps on a very rudimentary level. Ordinary language is a medium of understanding and communication through which we seek to say things to one another.

For this reason, to understand a concept is to be able to participate in life with it; to have a sense of the shape that it gives to one's interactions and activities (Diamond, 1988, p. 265).[11] When an individual uses a concept, he or she is not looking to others to verify its correct usage, i.e. that the individual has grasped the general principle of its use. Rather, the individual is looking to the difference that this new understanding makes to his or her involvement in the lives of others. As Peter Winch writes, 'The child learns the language from people who are living it, and that is not a matter of training' (in Rhees, 2006, p. xxv). Individuals do not aspire to use language correctly—if there can be such a thing—so much as they want to speak and live *well*. Occasionally, an individual does get it right, not in the sense of having securely understood a rule, but in the sense of discovering a way of speaking and living that is authoritative because it enables others to share and learn from the experience.

REVISITING FIRST-ORDER ORDINARY LANGUAGE-USE

Peters' distinction between concepts employed at the first-order and second-order conceptual clarification does not reveal what our concepts could, or possibly *should*, mean. His characterization of language-use implies that an individual *has* or that an individual *does not have* a concept. This assumes that to have a concept is to have it absolutely—we rarely think of ourselves as almost-having, or almost-not-having, a concept—and that a concept has a fixed identity which must be the criterion by which we distinguish between having and not having it. A concept's fixed identity consists in the rule or general principle that guides its use. Peters is not alone in this view and was no doubt influenced by Ludwig Wittgenstein's *Philosophical Investigations* (1958). As Cora Diamond explains, it is common to 'think of language in terms of rules fixing what can and cannot be done' (Diamond, 1988, p. 268). It should come as no surprise, therefore, that we think of learning a language in terms of learning how to follow its rules or principles. The difficulty, however, to quote Diamond again, is that language is definitely '*not* fixed in that way' because individuals are constantly 'coming into life' with its terms, using them 'in ways, perhaps no one else would, expecting others will follow what one has said' (*ibid.*).

Murdoch provides a realistic description of coming into life with a concept. She illustrates that understanding a concept involves engaging in an inquiry about what it means. In Peters' terms, it requires that second-order concern be internal to first-order use. Murdoch gives the example of a man trying to determine whether he can legitimately identify himself as repentant. In order to ask himself this question, the man needs to be familiar with the term 'repentance' and have a sense of what it means in ordinary discourse. This knowledge, however, does not advance the man's inquiry into his own state of mind. The man can only access his feelings through the concepts that he uses to express them. The question is not 'Is what I am feeling, repentance?' which implies the presence of a feeling and a term that either does or does not designate that feeling. Rather, the question is 'What is the most truthful way to understand what I feel?' which implies that the man must select a concept that does justice to the feeling by eliminating other possible concepts such as regret, contrition, penitent, shame and remorse. To do this he must think about what he means by these concepts, how he has used them in the past and what, if anything, has changed in his understanding of them. The possibilities are endless: perhaps he once associated repentance with religion but no longer does (he describes himself as repentant rather than ashamed); perhaps he is developing greater humility with age and so is more prepared to acknowledge his mistakes (he describes himself as repentant rather than simply regretful); perhaps he read Ian McEwan's *Atonement* and then saw the film; and the list is endless.

Irrespective of the specifics, this man is engaged in what Murdoch describes as 'the active "reassessing" and "redefining"' of his concepts (Murdoch, 1970, p. 25). His 'specialized personal *use*' of them is largely a function of his situation and history; it forms part of his 'continuous fabric of being' (p. 23). Repentance is going to mean something different to the man at different points in his life, as his understanding alters in light of the new insights and disappointments occasioned by the interaction of his previous understanding with experience. It is within the complex interplay of meaning and life that concepts come to be understood in greater depth. Conceptual understanding is progressive. Although it is not necessarily private, we each remain uniquely responsible for it. In this regard, language-use is like dieting, exercising or learning a foreign language (p. 22).[12] What I have been saying makes sense intuitively if we have in mind concepts such as repentance, honour or grief, as most of us would accept that a mature adult is more likely to have a nuanced understanding of what they mean than a young child. The point about the progressive nature of our understanding applies to all concepts, however, including such seemingly mundane ones as red, bird and sweet. We might think of artists in their relationship to colour; bird watchers in their relationship to birds; and lovers of dessert in their relationship to sweetness. There is no end to their learning.

Murdoch and John Dewey both invoke art and artfulness to convey what our life with language is like (Murdoch, 1970, p. 41; Dewey, 1954, p. 184). The purpose of the comparison is, as I interpret it, to highlight that language must be lived as a creative task: *we* must make something of our concepts in the context of our lives. As with good art, language lived well is educative. It allows us to see things differently, heightening our appreciation of the commonplace. A conversation with the teacher who responded appropriately to her under-achieving student might have helped a novice teacher to understand a range of concepts related to schooling: student communication; the role of teacher; as well as the difficulties and value of failing. The novice teacher would not be able to replicate the response, or the thinking behind it, but he or she could allow it to touch his or her own conceptual understanding and living. Finally, language used well, like good art, establishes communion through the creation of shared meaning. We understand one another, and the world around us, better, saving us from the despair of a solipsistic universe.

That said, individuals need to get on with living their lives; the man of Murdoch's example must determine whether or not what he feels is repentance. Once he determines this he will expect others to follow him, in both a weak and a strong sense. He will expect others to understand what he says and does, even if they do not share his point of view—this is the weak sense. He will expect others to find what he says and does pedagogical—this is the strong sense. The strong sense reinforces that any personalized use of a concept has the potential to be exemplary and definitive because conceptual understanding is inherently normative: another's life with concepts serves as a potential corrective to my own, and vice versa. If the man in Murdoch's example decides that what he feels is repentance, then he expects that others will understand him *and* come to a fuller understanding of what it means to be repentant. In other words, the man thinks of himself as having grasped the truth about the concept of repentance. This connects with Peters' grasping a concept's 'general principle of use' if we assume that: first, concepts do not possess general principles but that general principles get realized, and re-realized, each time a term is used; and second, that the principle works retrospectively to describe past experience, but nothing follows from this for how the individual may view future experiences.

If individuals are to reach a common understanding, then they must be responsive to others' personalized use of terms, that is, their conceptual worlds. This is particularly the case in education. So, for example, fine art students will seek to deepen or 'thicken' their understanding of colour by observing their art teacher and listening to him or her speak about painting, and the art teacher will seek to revisit her 'thin' concept of colour in order to awaken and refine her students' awareness of its role in painting. Clearly, no two conceptual worlds are identical, nor are they entirely different; rather, moving points of connection, overlap and differentiation exist between them. Responsiveness, then, entails that individuals exercise the concepts that belong to others' lives and inform their 'doings and thinkings and understandings' (Diamond, 1988, p. 276). The exercise of one another's concepts is critical for building community and creating the recognition of a shared world.

CONCLUSION

The strength of the analytic approach is that it provides a clear role for professional philosophers, particularly within the context of education, for they alone fulfil the vitally important function of second-order conceptual clarification capable of guiding teachers, school administrators and policy-makers. However, the fact that we learn our concepts as we use them raises a question about the nature of philosophy and its role in education. If I am right about the progressive nature of conceptual understanding, then the role of philosophy in education should be to provide educators with an occasion to reflect on what they mean by teaching and learning, and where they find teaching and learning in their lives. Prospective teachers must be able to participate in their own conceptual analysis with the assistance of philosophers of education as models, guides and conversational partners. It is likely that the impersonal and personal dimensions of understanding will interweave and overlap as students discover the unnaturalness of thinking about concepts without talking about those experiences in which the concepts became most fully realized. Sometimes thinking philosophically about a concept will help an individual to understand a particularly powerful memory; at other times, a person's memorable experience gives him or her access to a key educational concept. By this means, educators will revitalize their participation in life with their concepts as they seek to cultivate greater conceptual curiosity, sensitivity and continuity— qualities that R. S. Peters would appreciate and indeed ones that he exemplified.[13]

NOTES

1. See Anscombe, 1997 [1958]; MacIntyre, 1985; Diamond, 1988; and Lear, 2006.
2. G may go so far as to conclude that she is suffering from the cultural condition which Stanley Cavell refers to as 'a form of mindlessness' or 'amentia' and colorfully describes as 'the degree to which you talk of things, and talk in ways that hold no interest for you, or listen to what you cannot imagine the talker's caring about' (Cavell, 1979, p. 95).
3. Quoted in Miller, 1993. See also Michel Foucault's essay 'What is enlightenment?' (Foucault, 1994). This essay refers to an essay by the same title in which Kant identifies being enlightened with the public, as opposed to private, use of reason. An individual makes a private use of reason when he or she exercises reason according to his or her circumscribed profession or social role. An individual makes a public use of reason when he or she is reasoning as a free human being (i.e. reasoning from conscience alone). Foucault agrees with Kant, in principle at least, that Enlightenment comprises the individual's independent exercise of reason, which we must seek to ensure. For this reason, Foucault is inclined to see enlightenment and humanism 'in a state of tension rather than identity' (p. 314).
4. I use 'philosopher' as shorthand for the phrase 'academically trained philosopher'. I use the phrase 'academically trained philosopher' to highlight the fact that Peters considers philo-
   sophical facility for second-order conceptual clarification to derive from a rigorous education in the discipline of philosophy.
5. According to Hirst, Peters engaged in major philosophical works so that his method might speak for itself. Peters' clearest articulation of his method appears in his first article, 'The Philosophy of Education' [Peters, 1966b], and in the introduction to his major work, *Ethics and Education* (Hirst, 1986, p. 10).
6. Peters acknowledges that non-philosophers might be tempted to engage in second-order clarification; however, he predicts that without the requisite philosophical training their analysis would be recreational and trivial (Peters and Hirst, 1970, p. 10).
7. According to Hirst, Peters 'espoused no particular theory of meaning either explicitly or implicitly. He has certainly sought to map conceptual usage often hunting for necessary and sufficient conditions to set out the relations between concepts' (Hirst, 1986, p.12).
8. Peters' later works include: *Moral Development and Moral Education* (1981); *Psychology and Ethical Development* (1974); and *Reason and Compassion* (1973). See the following articles on Peters' mature scholarship: Ericson, 1984; Gardner, 1985; Tobin, 1989; and Winch, 2004.
9. I am thinking of our field's engagement with scholarly and literary works by Maurice Blanchot, Georges Bataille, Martin Heidegger, Jean-François Lyotard, and Jean-Luc Nancy.
10. John Dewey's philosophy of language is consonant with the position represented in this chapter. He argues that language does not represent experience so much as *create* it by converting the senseless 'push and pull' of qualitative immediacies into things with meaning or, alternatively, objects of thought (Dewey, 1929, p. 166). He states in *Experience and Nature* that 'when something can be said of qualities they are purveyors of instruction. Learning and teaching come into being, and there is no event which may not yield information' (p. 167). I interpret Dewey to be doing more than making a claim about the ability of language to facilitate instruction (teaching and learning) as one form of cooperative activity. Although he is right to highlight that language is instrumental for community, this view is not the focus in this instance. Rather, he is saying that our relationship to language and experience is inherently pedagogical; meanings present themselves as questions and there is no limit to our learning. Our relationship to language is a necessary and not contingent fact about us. Understanding is an

endless task and we only move closer to the mystery of the world by engaging more fully in it.

11. Diamond illustrates this point with reference to the concept of a human being. She explains that 'to have the concept of a human being is to know how thought and deeds and happenings, and how happenings are met, give shape to a human story; it is a knowledge of possibilities, their weight and their mysteriousness' (Diamond, 1988, p. 265). The intimate relationship between how an individual lives and his or her concept of a human being leads Diamond to conclude that 'the work of imaginative writers like Tolstoy and Levi illuminates for us the concept of a human being and at the same time can elaborate and deepen it' (*ibid.*).

12. Murdoch writes: 'Its details are the details of *this* personality; and partly for this reason it may well be an activity which can only be performed privately' (Murdoch, 1970, p. 23). However, she seems to contradict this elsewhere (pp. 32–3). See Diamond's article, 'Losing Your Concepts', for an excellent discussion of Murdoch on this issue.

13. I would like to thank Ms Givanni Ildefonso for her invaluable research assistance as well as Professor David Hansen and Dr Diana Barnes for their valuable comments on an earlier draft. I am grateful to the editors of this volume for their thoughtful remarks.

REFERENCES

Anscombe, G. E. M. (1997) [1958] Modern Moral Philosophy, in: R. Crisp and M. Slote (eds) *Virtue Ethics* (Oxford, Oxford University Press), pp. 26–44.

Cato, D. (1987) Getting Clearer about 'Getting Clearer': R. S. Peters and Second-order Conceptual Analysis, *Journal of Philosophy of Education*, 21.1, pp. 25–36.

Cavell, S. (1979) *The Claim of Reason: Wittgenstein, Skepticism, Morality, and Tragedy* (Oxford, Oxford University Press).

Cooper, D. E. (ed.) (1986) *Education, Values and Mind: Essays for R. S. Peters* (London and Boston, MA, Routledge and Kegan Paul).

Dewey, J. (1929) *Experience and Nature* (London, Allen & Unwin).

Dewey, J. (1954) *The Public and its Problems* (Athens, OH, Ohio University Press).

Diamond, C. (1988) Losing Your Concepts, *Ethics*, 98.2, pp. 255–277.

Ericson, D. P. (1984) Emotion and Action in Cognitive Psychology: Breaching a Fashionable Philosophical Fence, *Philosophy of Education: Proceedings of the Annual Meeting of the Philosophy of Education Society*, 40, pp. 151–162.

Foucault, M. (1994) What is Enlightenment?, in: P. Rabinow (ed.) *Ethics: Subjectivity and Truth* (New York, The New Press), pp. 303–320.

Gardner, P. (1985) The Paradox of Moral Education: A Reassessment, *Journal of Philosophy of Education*, 19.1, pp. 39–48.

Hirst, P. H. (1986) Richard Peters' Contribution to the Philosophy of Education, in: D. E. Cooper (ed.) *Education, Values and Mind: Essays for R.S. Peters* (London and Boston, Routledge and Kegan Paul).

Kleinig, J. (1982) *Philosophical Issues in Education* (New York, St. Martin's Press).

Lear, J. (2006) *Radical Hope: Ethics in the Face of Cultural Devastation* (Cambridge, MA, Harvard University Press).

MacIntyre, A. (1985) *After Virtue*, 2nd edn. (London, Duckworth).

Miller, J. (1993) *The Passion of Michel Foucault* (New York and London, Simon Schuster).

Mulhall, S. (2007) *The Conversation of Humanity* (Charlottesville, VA, University of Virginia Press).

Murdoch, I. (1970) *The Sovereignty of Good* (New York and London, Routledge).

Nietzsche, F. (1967) *The Will to Power*, W. Kaufmann and R. J. Hollingdale, trans. (New York, Vintage).

Peters, R. S. (1966a) *Ethics and Education* (London, Allen and Unwin).

Peters, R. S. (1966b) The Philosophy of Education, in: J. W. Tibble (ed.) *The Study of Education* (London and New York, Routledge and Kegan Paul), pp. 59–90.

Peters, R. S. (1973) *Reason and Compassion* (London and New York, Routledge and Kegan Paul).

Peters, R. S. (1974) *Psychology and Ethical Development* (London, Allen & Unwin).

Peters, R. S. (1981) *Moral Development and Moral Education* (London, Allen & Unwin).

Peters, R. S. and Hirst, P. H. (1970) *The Logic of Education* (London and New York, Routledge and Kegan Paul).

Rhees, R. (2006) *Wittgenstein and the Possibility of Discourse* (Phillips, D. Z. ed. (Oxford, Blackwell).

Tobin, B. (1989) R. S. Peters' Theory of Moral Development, *Journal of Philosophy of Education*, 23.1, pp. 17–27.

Winch, C. (2004) Work, the Aims of Life and the Aims of Education: A Reply to Clarke and Mearman, *Journal of Philosophy of Education*, 38.4, pp. 634–638.

Wittgenstein, L. (1958) *Philosophical Investigations*, G. E. M. Anscombe, trans. (Oxford, Blackwell).

3

On Education and Initiation

MICHAEL LUNTLEY

In 'Education as Initiation' Peters carved out his conception of education in a way that was designed to do justice to both traditional and liberal agenda. The traditional agenda is concerned with the transmission of values and beliefs. The liberal agenda concerns education as the development of capacities for the critical scrutiny of this inheritance. The traditionalist concern focuses on the content of the inheritance transmitted in education; the liberal concern focuses on the mode of transmission and the requirement that pupils be brought to have a critical care for their inheritance. The notion of 'critical care' might sound awkward, but it signals an important point. One of the things that Peters stresses is that the capacity for critical scrutiny is not just a capacity for logic chopping. It is a capacity to come 'to care about the valuable things involved ... [to] want to achieve the relevant standards' (Peters, 1978, p. 91). It is important not to lose sight of this element of the idea of critical scrutiny. I return to it below. At one point Peters parodies Kant to summarise this marriage of the traditional and the liberal: '[C]ontent without criticism is blind, but criticism without content is empty' (p. 100).

In this chapter I shall not take issue with this marriage. I want to concentrate on the adequacy of the concept of initiation in giving an account of how education serves both partners. I shall argue that, at best, the concept of initiation provides a provisional label for something deserving of much closer scrutiny and analysis. At worst, it provides a badge that can be mistaken for a substantive claim about the nature of education. A careful reading of Peters' inaugural lecture finds both kinds of usage, but I prefer to think of the present endeavour as a critical continuation of something that Peters started, rather than a corrective.

1. INITIATION

If one were content with a traditionalist concept of education, the concept of initiation might appear to have no more than a marginal role in one's reflections on education. On the traditionalist conception, in which the

Reading R. S. Peters Today, First Edition. Stefaan E. Cuypers and Christopher Martin.
Chapters © 2011 The Authors. Editorial organization © 2011 Philosophy of Education Society of Great Britain. Published 2011 by Blackwell Publishing Ltd.

emphasis is on the transmission of values and beliefs, initiation seems little more than a surrogate for 'absorption'.[1] The role of the pupil is largely passive. Initiation comes into its own with the liberal concern that the content transmitted in education be passed on in a way that brings about various active capacities in the pupil—centrally the capacity to critically challenge the inheritance and the capacity to care about both the inheritance and its management, including the critical scrutiny of it. Although the word can be misleading, for short I will refer to these capacities as capacities for *managing* the content of inheritance. From now on, when I speak of managing content, managing inheritance, I mean the complex mix of capacities that include centrally a capacity to care about the content of beliefs and values, to critically scrutinise content and to care about the processes of critical scrutiny.

Initiation seems exactly the right word to describe a process in which the pupil has to acquire capacities for managing content, in addition to simply acquiring content. It is the right word because it emphasises that what is going on here is a 'joining-in'. The pupil's education involves a gradual joining-in in the enterprise of managing our shared inheritance, not just an absorption of it. Although initiation seems the right concept, it is deeply problematic to get right precisely what is meant by initiation and how it can serve a useful role in our understanding of an educational process that honours the Kantian marriage between tradition and the liberal.

In the abstract, here is the central conceptual problem with the concept of education as initiation. 'Initiation' is a label for a process that transforms an initiate; one who lacks the capacities that characterise experienced practitioners in managing content. The initiate has not yet taken part in what Peters calls such 'worthwhile states of mind ... characterized by breadth of understanding' (p. 98). The point of initiation is to bring it about that the pupil acquires the capacities that make them a participant in the practices that exploit capacities for managing content. That must mean that, prior to the initiation, they are, in some interesting sense, outwith the practices of those who exhibit such capacities. It must then mean that the initiate lacks the capacities for management. They lack the capacity to care about and to critique the content of inheritance. That is why initiation is transformative. There must be some sense in which this is the right thing to say, but the devil lies in working out what sense this is. For once you say that the initiate lacks the capacities to care and to critique, then what is the hook, the lure if you like, that gets them to participate in such practices and acquire these capacities? If you leave the initiate outwith the practices of those who possess these capacities, then you leave them with no capacities to care and critique, so what reason do they have to step inside? And it is no good to say that they do not need reasons to step inside, for if mere stimuli-response temptation were enough, then we would have no need of the liberal agenda in the first place. We want them to join-in, not just be pushed in! And if the idea of joining-in is to do any work here, it must work because we are able to offer the initiate something that looks like a reason for stepping inside. And we cannot do that unless we first equip them with some rudimentary capacities to care about and critique what is on offer. It cannot be the case that they acquire those capacities by being initiated; they must already have them in some measure in order for them to be able to respond to the invitation to join in and be initiated.

You might protest that I am overstating an abstract point, but once it is in focus, it becomes apparent that there is a problem here that runs to the very heart of what we mean by 'learning'. Suppose you are tempted to express the point in the previous paragraph by considering those that are indifferent to all that civilisation has to offer, those who lack the capacities for managing content. You might then say, as Peters does, that children are like this. You might then say that 'They start off in the position of the barbarians outside the gates. The problem is to get them inside the citadel of civilization so that they will understand and love what they see when they get there' (p. 104).

And if you are so tempted, you have then rendered education as initiation impossible. For if the task is to bring the barbarian inside the gates, but the point of the metaphor is that it is only the insiders who have the capacities for management, then what you offer to bring the barbarian in must be quite different in kind to what you will say to them (and what you hope they'll say to themselves) once they're on the inside. It seems then that in getting them to come inside, you will have to trick them with some lesser account of what's on offer, for it is only once inside and acculturated, that they will have the capacities to respond to your own caring critical trusteeship of the inheritance. It suggests a 'deceptive strategy' to the initial phase of education.

There are two problems here. One is the ethical concern that it seems we might have to trick the outsider to come on in, for until they are in they lack the capacities to critically care. That issue is, I think, a real one. But the one I want to concentrate on is the deeper constitutive issue: assuming education is transformative, how is it so much as possible that this is so? And the version of this that I am pressing now is: Does the concept of initiation contribute to how we answer this question?

There is no recourse to say that the problem is a function of the liberal agenda, for the problem that I am getting at also infects the traditional concept of education. At its most general, the problem is this: It seems truistic to say that the central relation between teacher and pupil is one in which the teacher seeks to engage the pupil in something that they, the pupil, does not understand. Education is transformative. The pupil moves from a position of not understanding something to understanding it. But the move they undertake is one that the teacher engages them in. That formulation provides a clear central challenge:

(1) How can the pupil engage in X if they do not understand X?

Clearly, their engagement cannot be a conceptual one, for if that were so they would already understand X. Perhaps you might say that (1) is too simple and bold a question, for the answer lies not in saying how they engage in X prior to understanding X, but in how they partially engage in X prior to acquiring full understanding of X. But that answer leaves the central issue untouched. Suppose 'partial engagement with X' means that the pupil has some concepts that enable them to engage with parts of X, but not the whole. That means that there are still elements of X for which they have no conceptual purchase. So, the question comes back: How does the pupil engage in those elements of X that they do not understand prior to acquiring a concept that picks out those elements? And that, of course, is just another version of (1). The appeal to partial engagement is not an answer, but just an insistence that engagement takes place prior to understanding. I agree with that. I think it is a condition on there being a substantive account of learning that one accept that there is such a thing as engaging with X prior to understanding X.[2] The issue is how to characterise this so as to enable a genuine developmental trajectory from a basic form of engagement which does not require the target concept or any concept(s) that picks out X. If such a basic form of engagement is acknowledged, then this engagement is available as a condition for making the target concept a possible acquisition for the pupil. It provides the basis for a genuinely transformative developmental trajectory of learning. This way of formulating the issues affects the traditional agenda just as much as the liberal.

Consider a crude traditionalist agenda in which all that matters is that the pupil absorbs the values and beliefs of the tradition. Absorption still means acquiring the concepts necessary for formulating the values and beliefs to be absorbed. So the version of (1) that troubles the traditionalist agenda is:

(2) How can the pupil absorb new concepts C_1–C_n without already having the conceptual structure into which these concepts fit?

That question is, of course, the question that Fodor famously presses in his account of the paradox of learning.[3] The point is that absorption of a new concept requires a prior ability to experience the relevant saliences that the new concept picks out. First the pupil must, in some sense, experience so-and-sos before they learn that they are to call so-and-sos 'such-and-such'. But if they can already experience so-and-sos as a kind, then they already possess something that looks suspiciously like a concept for so-and-sos. If so, all that they really learn is the label 'such-and-such' that is used for that concept in language; they do not learn a new concept. They had it all along! Such, in outline, is Fodor's challenge to an account of learning. It is the challenge to give an account of the developmental trajectory of concept acquisition that shows that real transformations take place. Pupils really do move from a position in which they lack concepts to concept possession. The real worry with the concept of initiation is: Is 'initiation' any more than a label for the claim that this happens, rather than an account of the developmental trajectory at stake?

2. PHILOSOPHY, PEDAGOGY AND METHODOLOGY

Here is the issue as it arises from a conception of education as initiation. If there is such a thing as engaging a pupil in something that will provide them with the resources to acquire a new concept, the specific question that makes (1) seem intractable is:

> (3) How is engagement achieved without concepts?

If there is an answer to this question, then we have in outline a substantive account of concept acquisition and a real developmental trajectory for learning. If there is no answer to this question, then, in the absence of any alternative, the appeal to initiation as a concept for understanding education does no real work. The appeal to initiation will be no more than a descriptive tag for a process that includes no real sense of transformation. As such, it is a description for something that barely warrants being called learning.

I think we can and should attempt to provide an answer to the above question. We need, however, to distinguish at least two different kinds of answer that we might want to pursue. One answer concerns an abstract philosophical question; the other is an answer within the theory of pedagogy. I want to start by distinguishing these questions, the sorts of methodology appropriate to each and to make a suggestion about how they can usefully inform one another.

The philosophical question raised by (3) is a 'How possible' question. It is:

> (4) How is it so much as possible that a subject can have the resources to engage in X prior to acquiring a concept for X, on the understanding that the engagement provides the basis for concept acquisition?

The idea that the engagement provides the basis for education means that it is an engagement with X that makes it appropriate to then classify X with the concept being learnt. The thought here is that whatever else we say about engagement it is more than merely a causal encounter. The idea of an engagement with X is the idea of *experiencing* X. It is the idea that the subject be provided with an awareness of X, not merely that X be something that they are causally exposed to. A subject might be exposed to the virus for the common cold, but that sort of engagement is not the basis for acquiring the concept for the common cold. Acquiring the concept requires a form of engagement that makes it appropriate to use the word 'cold'. Simply catching a cold does not given the subject reason to call their medical state a cold.

There are two aspects to the idea of engagement. One is the point that for an engagement with X to provide a basis for concept acquisition it needs to be a form of engagement that makes use of the relevant word appropriate; the other is that the engagement is an engagement that operates at the level of personal experience. The two points are related.

The first is the requirement that the basis of concept acquisition is an engagement with the things that make up the extension of the concept where that engagement makes sense/gives reason for/makes appropriate the use of the word. In short, the engagement is one that provides the subject with the concept's extension in a way that is ordered, or patterned suitable for labelling with the word for the target concept. The idea of order or pattern is the idea of an order that supports the notion of the correct/incorrect application of words. The target in concept acquisition is the use of the word for the concept where that use is one that is subject to standards of correctness and incorrectness. The first point is that if such a pattern of correct usage is to result from learning, then the engagement with the concept's extension must already be an engagement of such sorts of order delivered by the experience of the extension. The second point is simply the idea that such engagements are the engagement of the subject, not of modules of their cognitive machinery. It is the idea that if the subject is to find application of the word for the target concept appropriate, then appropriateness of use is something that applies to the subject, not to their brain. It is the pupil who finds the use of the word for X appropriate, otherwise they are not learning. Put very simply, what we are interested in here is the learning of the subject, not the training of sub-personal responses.

Once these two aspects to the idea of engagement are in view, it can then seem that questions (3) and (4) are impossible to answer. If engagement with X is to make it appropriate ('right') to use the word for the target concept, then it gives reasons for using the word. But the only sorts of thing that can give reason for applying a concept are themselves conceptually structured. Only conceptually organised events—experiences and such like—can give reasons for applying concepts. But then the engagement with X must already be a conceptually structured experience. If that were so, then in order to learn the target concept the subject would already need the capacity to engage with its extension conceptually in experience. But that is to say they already have a concept for the extension, even if they do not apply the commonly accepted linguistic symbol for it. So, all they can be learning is the correct symbol, not the concept. This was the point we reached at the end of the previous section.

The difficulty of making sense of genuine transformations in learning risks re-introducing the 'deceptive strategy' that was lurking behind Peters' metaphor of the barbarians outside the gates of civilisation. And it takes away the very part of the liberal education agenda that Peters insightfully picks out by invoking the concept of initiation; namely, that our attitude to the pupil is one of inviting them to join-in, not just causally badgering them through the gates! Initiates are invited, not tricked or propelled. So how do we frame the invitation?

In tackling the philosophical 'How possible?' question, we seem boxed into a corner. On one side we have the nativist strategy that entails there is no real conceptual development under way in learning: there is no real learning. On the other side, we start with a conception of the pupil's abilities that puts them 'outside the gates' of educated practices with no clear conception of the point and method of access. I want to suggest that the way out of this philosophical impasse is to embrace the idea of the pupil as a non-barbarian. That is to say, we should accept that the starting point of the initiate is not one of someone who stands outside the practices of care and critique that education is supposed to deliver to the pupil. That means, of course, that whatever transformation is effected by learning, it is not as dramatic as the entry of the barbarian into the citadel of civilisation. That model simply overstates the transformation. But then the philosophical point that flows from this corrective is substantive. It is to acknowledge that the pupil does not start outside the capacities of the practice they are being invited to join in. They start with an already sophisticated set of capacities. It is a substantive issue to demarcate this set accurately, but that they are, in some useful sense, already 'within the gates' is not an option. Reflection on the 'How possible' question demands that we drop the barbarian metaphor.[4]

In outline, the answer to the philosophical 'How possible?' question is to credit the pupil, even at the earliest stages, with a much more actively inquisitive role. It is to accept that the real point of the leitmotif of education as 'joining-in' is that pupils have much to contribute to the activities of learning. You only get to be an initiate into the practices of caring critical enquiry by starting out as a subject with a basic orientation of one who cares critically about enquiry. It's not that we do not let barbarians in our schools; the very idea is misplaced. There are no barbarians.

This is a very abstract answer to the philosophical question. It has, I believe, direct consequences for pedagogy, but before turning to those I want to say a bit more about the outline shape of the answer to the philosophical question. Understanding the sort of methodology required to make sense of this answer will also bear on how the philosophy can inform the pedagogy.

It is one thing to affirm that the initiate never starts with less than sufficient capacities to care critically about how their life is going. It is another thing to fill out that claim in a way that is both persuasive and offers some sort of real answer to question (4). The real challenge in (4) is to provide an account of how a subject can experience the extension of a concept prior to acquiring the concept and for this experience to be the sort of thing that makes using the relevant word appropriate. Here are two different methodologies for tackling this issue that I'll call the descriptive and theoretical approaches.

On the theoretical approach, the task is to provide an account of the mechanism by which experience can render the extension of a concept salient to the subject where this means that the experience has some content that represents the extension but in which the content of the experience is not conceptual. Howsoever that works, this is an approach that provides a theoretical model of the detail of how a pupil's engagement with that which they do not understand is accomplished. Having done that, such a model will then need to show how engagements structured in this manner can be the sort of things that can make it appropriate to collect together conceptually. The theoretical approach provides a detailed mechanism, if you like, for negotiating what otherwise seems an impossible divide between things that fall outside concepts and things that fall under concepts. It tries to fill the space between encounters in the realm of causes and engagements in the realm of reason by identifying an in-between level comprising engagements with a content that is not conceptual. Whether such a strategy can possibly work, rather than merely duplicate the initial gateway between the barbarian causes and the rational insiders in a regress of more discriminative gateways is far from clear. Furthermore, it is not clear to me that this theoretical approach has obvious bearings on pedagogy.

The theoretical approach looks for further theoretical resources to characterise the engagements that form the basis of understanding. In contrast, the descriptive approach does not offer novel theoretical categories with which to fill the gap between encounters and engagements. Rather, the descriptive approach aims to see if there are resources already within our engagements with things that contribute to an account of how it is possible to engage with things we do not understand.[5] And there is an obvious resource here that has been under-employed.

Suppose we ask:

(5) What is the contribution of consciousness to our engagement with things?

That can seem like an odd question, for you might think that 'consciousness' is not the sort of thing that contributes to our engagement with things, but is merely another name for our awareness of things. It is, if you like, the window through which we engage, not a contributor to the engagement. But that is, in effect, to endorse a passive role for the conscious subject. It is to suggest an image of them as a passive recipient of the contents of engagement through the window of consciousness. It is that image that invites the theoretical approach of trying to construct new models and mechanisms for the contents of consciousness so that the incoming stream can supply an engagement that is not conceptual. But that view is not compulsory.

We can make sense of the idea that consciousness itself has an explanatory role in our project.[6] Rather than concentrating on the contents of consciousness howsoever you try to characterise them, we can think of consciousness relationally as an openness to things. When we are conscious of our surroundings, it is not compulsory to think of this as the receipt of a stream of content that then needs to be synthesised and arranged in order that it might bear on belief, concept formation, etc. Rather, we can think of our consciousness of our surroundings as the simple bare relation of awareness to things. Consciousness is what puts us in touch with things. It is not the empty window through which content streams, it is a relation of awareness to things.

This idea comes into focus best if you think of the relation of awareness in terms of the searchlight of attention. This is an active conception of consciousness. Consciousness is the active attending to the environment. It is the basic first form of awareness that makes conceptual engagement possible, but it is, first and foremost, a form of engagement. It is not merely the window through which we encounter things.

There is then an answer to (4) that comes from recognising that (5) is not an odd question. What makes it possible for a subject to have an engagement with something prior to understanding it and having a concept for it is the availability of a conception of consciousness as that by which we relate to things. For sure, to get this conception of the explanatory role of consciousness into focus, it helps to acknowledge that this is an active role for consciousness. It is a conception in which the conscious mind does not wait to be given content to get it interested in things; rather, the conscious mind is an attentive aware subject finding the environment as the relata of its awareness. There might be all sorts of explanations of how various bits of the environment get to be things that consciousness finds, but such explanations do not need to appeal to personal modes of awareness that provide a content to consciousness, let alone a conceptual content. The explanations of how bits of the environment get to be the things that consciousness alights on need only appeal to the complex variety of mechanisms by which things become salient just so long as those mechanisms do not introduce a content to consciousness. Such accounts do not provide a conception of consciousness as directed by content, but rather fill out the description that shows that consciousness as such can have a striking role to play in our conception of how we relate to things. Such a role is then available to account for how a subject can be engaged in X prior to having a content that represents X and therefore, have an engagement with X without understanding X.[7]

Much more could and should be said about the explanatory role of consciousness. It sits best with a conception of the subject as an active presence in the world looking for and usually finding order and pattern. The awareness that explains concept acquisition is an awareness that is actively trying to put things in order.[8] This is not the place to pursue the deep and abstract issues in the philosophy of mind that need to be treated to put the explanatory conception of consciousness in full view. But the idea that such a conception is an option is enough for present purposes, for it signals a key change in the metaphors with which we think about initiation.

Peters was tempted by the metaphor of the uninitiated as the barbarians outside the gates of the citadel of civilisation, waiting to acquire the capacities that would enable them to care for and critically take on custody of civilisation's inheritance. It is only a metaphor, but it makes vivid the real philosophical problems in understanding the idea that education can be transformative. I can think of no better metaphor to offer in its place than the following.

First, we must tear down the citadel. Do not think of the inheritance as an edifice or monument. Think of it as an ongoing achievement. Think of it as a dance. The initiate is invited to join-in and the invitation makes sense to them because they got rhythm. They are looking for, latching their awareness onto, patterns and orders to which they will contribute simply in virtue of standing in a relational awareness to these patterns. Once joined in, these patterns and rhythms grow and become more complex. They get names and concepts are created. But no one starts outside and nothing gets the permanence of the monument.

Changing the metaphor and giving the sort of answer to the philosophical version of (3) that I have indicated depends on taking a stand on a range of substantive core issues in the philosophy of mind. There is no short-cut to understanding the key concepts in the philosophy of education. There is no detour to understanding the concept of education as initiation that avoids hard problems in mainstream philosophy. The account that I have outlined bears upon how we answer (3) in our pedagogy. The answer to the philosophical 'How possible?' question suggests a pedagogy that holds that the engagement of pupils without concepts is achieved by teachers who take seriously the voluntary pattern making and urge to join-in that is found in even the youngest learners. And there are clear examples of such pedagogy to be found in recent sustained detailed descriptions of the daily life of teaching environments.

3. DETAILS OF A PEDAGOGY

If you accept the methodology of a descriptive metaphysics that looks not for detailed theories of engagements without understanding but simply detailed descriptions of the modes by which such engagements are achieved, then there is no reason why the philosophical project so undertaken should not and could not segue effortlessly into the descriptive ethnography of classroom life. Peters brought the professional skills of analytic philosophy to bear on the conceptual analysis of key educational concepts. On the conception of that methodology that I have been pursuing, there need be no distance between the abstract descriptions of initiation that can change our self-conception and the detailed descriptions found by attending to the histories of how classrooms work. I want to elaborate on the answer to the 'how possible' question that I have suggested by appealing to the empirical detail of classroom life as reported in Julie Diamond's startling testimony to the richness of teaching (Diamond, 2008). Diamond is, in effect, providing a detailed answer to the pedagogical version of question (3). But the relation between the philosophical and pedagogical answers to (3) does not represent projects that are different in kind. The difference is one of focus and detail. Philosophy provides a broad and revealing answer that puts a number of abstract concepts in their proper relation to one another. The empirical history provided by Diamond, fills in the fine brushwork to the initial outline philosophical sketch.

There is much that is valuable and to admire in Diamond's book. She presents a history of a year in the life of a New York kindergarten class. There are, naturally, limitations to the lessons one can draw from one such history, but I want to select just a few examples that show how her account exemplifies the sort of philosophical picture I have sketched. You might think that the account of the initiate that I have provided asks too much of them. But Diamond shows that it is not too much, even with kindergarten pupils.

The barbarian image of the initiate effectively treats them as a blank slate, waiting to be brought within the fold of an educated culture. Diamond strikingly inverts this metaphor. It is the teacher who is the blank slate. Her book is a combination of reflections on a school year and diary entries of observations. In one of the latter entries she reports on a conversation with a colleague:

> *On the way to school, Linda and I talk about this period of time before school starts. She says, right now we know nothing; she's 'a blank slate'—because of not knowing these particular children. It's all anticipation, all getting ready. Like the line in Hamlet, 'Readiness is all'* (Diamond, 2008, p. 11).

The prompt for this thought lies in Diamond's preparation of the physical space ready to receive the new kindergarten class. She says that she wants the room to have 'a spare appearance, because the children's work will fill it up .... I want them to feel—in their bones—this is their room' (p. 8). But the space she wants to create for the children to occupy and make their own is not just the physical space of the room. She continues:

> *I have to make a space, I have to not be my summer self—active, occupied with my own interests. Emptying myself, in a way.*
>
> Being a blank state is work, takes effort. I'm struck by Linda's analogy. Traditional education pictures children as the slates, teachers doing the writing. If *we're* receptive—to children, to what they bring to school—the relationship is reversed. We're the slates, they do the writing. Just as I create a space in the room for the work children will do, I have to find it in myself (p. 12).

The recognition that what children bring to school is as much a driver to what happens in the classroom as to how the teacher shapes the physical, cognitive and emotional space that receives them is key to thinking through the pedagogic consequences of the approach I have been promoting. The idea runs deep in Diamond's reflections. She is committed to the idea of the classroom as a 'laboratory, workshop'; she says the room should function as the setting to 'stimulate the active inquiry of the children themselves' (p. 10). This is a serious and thought through description of the educational enterprise that gives centre stage to the concept of joining-in. Diamond is treating her kindergarten pupils as initiates but is totally alive to the idea that initiates join-in by bringing much to the dance. She needs to create space for them so that their contribution can be added to hers. She is not there to guide them round the citadel.

The active role expected of her pupils is a role for thinking, for interrogating. The management of time is just as important as the management of space. She says she wants to 'give the children time to think, time to make decisions; to give them the same luxury that I took for myself in setting up the room . . . time to figure out what questions to ask' (p. 14). There are powerful ideas here for a pedagogy that takes seriously the demands of understanding education as initiation. As Diamond notes,

> For teachers to protect children's right to time—to *empty time*—requires courage, especially at this moment in history. Our lives . . . are over-programmed, without occasions for something unplanned. There's a benefit when teachers don't pack each moment. Time allows children to develop as people with broad interests and capacities; it allows them to gain a sense of conviction about their choices (p. 15).

From the point of view of much educational policy that focuses on top-down strategies for one part of the curriculum after another, this may sound like the most radical kind of child-centred liberalism. It is not. Like Peters, Diamond sees learning as a complex blend of tradition and critique. She describes in great detail how the educational activity is the joint upshot of her best sense of the inheritance that provides the broad structures to time and space plus the contribution of the young initiates whose inquisitiveness and raw natural capacity to join-in fills out the time and space of learning. The pupil already cares and is already critical in their caring: '. . . children's efforts—their art, their thinking, their building and construction, their investigations—are *human* activities. They are versions of what adults do' (p. 16).

Diamond is not advocating a radical child-centred approach to teaching; it is human-centred. It comes from a clear acknowledgment that learning is jointly achieved and that acquiring the capacities for caring and critiquing our common inheritance is not a late and mysterious extra that comes late in the process. It is there in the beginning. The initiate is not the barbarian, no matter how rough and clumsy their capacities for a caring critique may be.

The joint construction of learning is explicit in Diamond's distinction between routines and rituals, 'routines are imposed by the teacher . . . rituals are generated by children as they respond to this new physical and social environment (p. 17). She spends a whole chapter on routines and rituals (pp. 17-42). Her detailed descriptions of how her pupils come to occupy, own and celebrate the very physical fabric of the classroom in its signage, decoration, organisation and policing is a striking testimony of the pedagogic consequences of taking initiation in the manner I have sketched. Diamond is explicit: 'Much of what I plan is intended to help children make sense of their world . . . I assume agency—that individuals can be active, can think, conclude' (p. 28). That's the key insight. Diamond's pupils are sense-makers; they are actively looking for, finding and owning patterns to their thinking, behaviour, social environment and the emotional contours to their common lives.

Her chapter on artwork in the class illustrates the point well. At its most extreme, child-centred education encourages the idea that the aim of education concerns the mere development or self-realisation of the individual and it encourages an emphasis on self-expression over the discipline of subject matter.[9] Diamond can agree with Peters' critique of such approaches. She is clear that art 'engages children's capacity for understanding' (p. 43). It is not merely a matter of self-expression; it is a contribution to understanding, furthermore, by valuing children's art as belonging to them 'children can see themselves as insiders in the world of art' (p. 44). Again, they are joining-in. Their art is, like adult art, a contribution to the business of making sense of ourselves and that is not mere child-centred expressivism. It's a contribution to a common activity.

Diamond describes a balance that exemplifies in the daily life of her class just the sort of marriage of the traditional and liberal that Peters aimed for. She thinks curriculum 'emerges', for it is 'inherent *in* the relationship among children, teacher and content' (p. 70). This is neither a child-centred curriculum nor a teacher-directed curriculum. Here we have the simple admission that the curriculum is the joint product of the inheritance (content), the teacher's aims and aspirations and the children's capacities for joining-in the common activity of making sense of things in all the many and varied dimensions in which that can be achieved. The key word here is 'relationship' and the key lesson is that to take this seriously you need to credit the pupil as initiate with a prior capacity to engage and join-in.[10]

The point is emphasised in Diamond's description of 'authentic work'. This is work that 'respects the child's style of learning and developmental stage; it respects children's intelligence and thinking' (p. 82). Importantly, work that respects the child's capacity to join-in does not deploy the sort of deceptive and coercive strategies that seem inevitable with the image of the barbarian outside the gates of civilisation. As Diamond objects, much kindergarten work is not authentic when 'teachers and programs use cute pictures and artificial tasks to manipulate children, ignoring intrinsic motivations, as if children must be tricked into participation and education must be coercive' (ibid.). It is the idea of 'intrinsic motivations' that identifies Diamond's endorsement of the concept of the initiate that I have been promoting.

4. PETERS AND BEYOND

Peters used the word 'initiation', for it is a term that is general enough to cover the different types of transactions involved in teaching, training, instruction, etc. He also emphasised that 'initiation must be into worth-while states of mind that are characterised by breadth of understanding' (Peters, 1973, p. 98). I have argued that although initiation is the right concept to use when seeking an account of education as a marriage between the traditionalist and liberal agendas, the concept exposes a deep philosophical problem about how to make sense of the transformative nature of education. It is this problem that, I suggest, Peters does not tackle. Indeed, he misses it altogether. It is not just the metaphor of the barbarian outside the citadel that causes the problem. Peters leaves the initiate at the beginning of education bereft of the resources required to join-in shared inquiry. He says, 'No man is born with a mind' (ibid.). If we are to make proper sense of the idea of initiation, that cannot be true. Although I have followed Peters in working to clarify how the concept of initiation can be put to use in forging the sort of mixed agenda that he sought, on this point I think he simply had it wrong.

Of course, when Peters says that no man is born with a mind, he goes on to say that a 'child is born with an awareness not as yet differentiated into beliefs, wants and feelings' (ibid.). That might sound compatible with the idea, canvassed above, that consciousness itself can figure in an explanation of how a pupil can be engaged in something they do not understand. But that would depend on precisely what Peters meant by such an undifferentiated form of awareness. The evidence suggests that it is not rich enough to carry the weight I was indicating for consciousness. The brief developmental picture that Peters paints speaks of an 'embryonic mind' that creates pools of predictability. But it also presents that mind very clearly as 'the product of initiation into public traditions enshrined in a public language' (ibid). And that idea goes to the heart of the philosophical problem that Peters leaves us and to which I have tried to respond. If the skills and capacities of caring critique are the product of initiation, with what does the initiate enter the process without being deceived, cajoled and tricked into something that they do not yet understand? If the mind with the capacity to engage a caring critique is the product of initiation rather the initial resource, then there is no answer in sight to how we engage pupils with things they do not understand. We lose grip on the idea that education is transformative.

I think education is transformative. I think Peters thought so too. He was right to put the concept of initiation central to how we understand the transformative capacity, but he under-equips the initiate. In order to progress the sort of understanding of education that Peters gave us we must disagree on the initiate. Humans are born with a mind. It is that which equips them with the care, spirit and need to join-in the common critical dance of the trustees of our inheritance.[11]

NOTES

1. See Haldane, 1995 for a clear statement of such a traditionalist conception.
2. It is this condition that is denied by nativists about concepts. Fodor is the best example, for he explicitly denies the transformative character of learning with respect to language acquisition. He denies that you can learn a language with an expressive power greater than a language you already know (Fodor, 1975, p. 86).
3. See Luntley, 2008 for more discussion of Fodor's paradox.
4. Another way to think of the dilemma of nativism versus the barbarian conception of the initiate is to see it as a choice between conceiving of the learner either as starting already

within the space of reasons or starting as an object conceived within the space of causes. See McDowell, 1994 for his appropriation of Sellars' distinction between the space of reasons and the space of causes. Although my point that there are no barbarians amounts to placing the initiate within the space of reasons, it should not be assumed that I am thereby endorsing McDowell's quietism about how thought gets to be about things. As I go on to argue, there is still scope for an explanatory account of how concepts are acquired, as opposed to a mere description of the history of their acquisition. McDowell's invocation of the Sellars' distinction does not permit scope for tackling the sort of 'how possible' questions that I am placing centre stage. See Huemer, 2006 for an assimilation of Wittgenstein's discussion of training into a McDowellian framework and see Luntley (2008b, 2009) for a contrasting reading of Wittgenstein on this.

5. Recall Strawson's distinction between descriptive and revisionary metaphysics (Strawson, 1959). The idea of descriptive metaphysics is of a piece with Peters' methodology of conceptual analysis. We do not seek a revisionary model of the mechanisms of education, just an illuminating description that will throw into relief the aspects of our engagements with things that we are prone to miss on first reflection. Once pointed out, they resonate as familiar, for what we have done is to remind ourselves of things whose salience we had overlooked but which, when properly acknowledged, can come to have striking impact on both our self-conception and the accounts we provide of the things we do, e.g. teach people by engaging them in things they do not at first understand.

6. I draw upon Campbell, 2002 at this point, see also Campbell, 2008; 2010, for more details on the explanatory conception of consciousness. This move is not to be taken lightly. The move to endorse a relational account of consciousness opposes the current orthodoxy in favour of representationalist accounts of experience in which a key debate concerns the nature of the representational content of experience—e.g. is it conceptual or nonconceptual? In developing Peters' account of education as initiation there is no short cut or detour around a number of substantive issues in contemporary philosophy. The move I make here is heavily laden with substantive theoretical baggage from mainstream philosophy of mind.

7. The range of things covered by 'mechanisms' might include accounts of the cognitive machinery by which items in the environment are made salient for consciousness, e.g. see Campbell, 2002, but it could also include accounts of the role affective states play in making things salient. For the latter see Luntley, 2008a; 2010.

8. This introduces a voluntarism into the account of the sense-making of the initiate, but that is perhaps no bad thing. See Pears, 2007 on Wittgenstein's voluntarism regarding linguistic regularity.

9. See Peters, 1978, pp. 88–91 for his critique of the progressive child-centred ideology.

10. See Osberg and Biesta, 2008 for a recent discussion of the idea of an 'emergent curriculum' which draws upon different philosophical resources but arrives at a similar conception. Once you take seriously the idea of a relational account of consciousness, the idea of an emergent curriculum that gives proper weight to the pupil's engagement with both the environment and with others makes the move towards an emergent concept of curriculum almost inevitable.

11. Thanks to Stefaan Cuypers for comments on a previous draft.

REFERENCES

Campbell, J. (2002) *Reference and Consciousness* (Oxford, Clarendon Press).
Campbell, J. (2008) Consciousness and Reference, in B. McLaughlin and A. Beckermann (ed.) *Oxford Handbook of Philosophy of Mind* (Oxford, Oxford University Press).

Campbell, J. (2010) Demonstrative Reference, The Relational View of Experience and the Proximality Principle, in: R. Jeshion (ed.) *Essays on Singular Reference* (Oxford, Oxford University Press), pp. 193–212.

Diamond, J. (2008) *Welcome to the Aquarium* (New York, The New Press)).

Fodor, J. (1975) *The Language of Thought* (Cambridge, MA, Harvard University Press).

Haldane, J. (1995) Education: Conserving Tradition, in: B. Almond (ed.) *Introducing Applied Ethics* (Oxford, Blackwell), pp. 73–88.

Huemer, W. (2006) The Transition from Causes to Norms: Wittgenstein on Training, *Grazer Philosophische Studien*, 71, pp. 205–25.

Luntley, M. (2008a) Conceptual Development and the Paradox of Learning, *Journal of Philosophy of Education*, 42, pp. 1–14.

Luntley, M. (2008b) Training and learning, *Educational Philosophy and Theory*, 40.5, pp. 695–711.

Luntley, M. (2009) The Teaching and Learning of Words, in: D. Levy and E. Zamuner (eds) *Wittgenstein's Enduring Argument* (Boston, MA & London, Routledge), pp. 135–55.

Luntley, M. (2010) Expectations Without Content, *Mind & Language*, 25.2, pp. 217–236.

McDowell, J. (1994) *Mind and World* (Cambridge, MA, Harvard University Press).

Osberg, D. and Biesta, G. (2008) The Emergent Curriculum: Navigating a Complex Course between Unguided Learning and Planned Enculturation, *Journal of Curriculum Studies*, 40.3, pp. 313–28.

Pears, D. (2007) *Paradox and Platitude in Wittgenstein's Philosophy* (Oxford, Clarendon Press).

Peters, R. S. (1978) Education as Initiation in *Authority, Responsibility and Education*, 3rd edn. (London, George Allen & Unwin), pp. 81–107.

Strawson, P. F. (1959) *Individuals* (London, Methuen).

4

Ritual, Imitation and Education in R. S. Peters

BRYAN R. WARNICK

INTRODUCTION

Over the past four decades, the concept of ritual has been increasingly used to study schools and the process of education. Ritual has been recognised as something that permeates everyday life rather than, say, existing only in esoteric religious ceremonies. Recently, the concept has been invoked to examine a host of educational issues: parental involvement in schools (Bushnell, 1997), homework (Van Voorhis, 2004), campus tours (Magolda, 2000), education reform movements (Cornbleth, 1986), the practice of teaching (Ensign, 1997), internships (McAllister, 2008), kindergartens (McCadden, 1997), medical white-coat ceremonies (Huber, 2003) and educational leadership (Deal and Peterson, 1999), among many other topics. The concept has also made an appearance in philosophy of education journals (Losito, 1996; Quantz, 1999), with some of the primary questions being: What is ritual? What sorts of rituals are present in education and what is their social meaning? What place should ritual have in education?

R. S. Peters was something of a pioneer in thinking about ritual in school contexts. Ensign and Quantz (1997) write about the initial wave of interest in everyday ritual begun by sociologist Erving Goffman's groundbreaking book, *Interaction Ritual: Essays on Face-to-Face Behavior* (1967). Goffmann, they argue, succeeded in 'switching our focus from the study of tribal societies to the mundane use of ritual in the everyday life of modern industrial societies' (1997, p. 218). Peters' major statements about ritual appeared in 1966—roughly the same time that Goffmann's book was published—thus placing him, it seems, within that particular pioneering zeitgeist. Peters' discussions of ritual investigate the use and function of everyday ritual in schools. Discussions of ritual are present not only in Peters' well-known text, *Ethics and Education* (Peters, 1966), but also in an essay on the topic that Peters published with Basil Bernstein and Lionel Elvin, 'Ritual in Education' (Bernstein, Elvin and Peters, 1966). After the late-1960s, Peters appears to

Reading R. S. Peters Today, First Edition. Stefaan E. Cuypers and Christopher Martin.
Chapters © 2011 The Authors. Editorial organization © 2011 Philosophy of Education Society of Great Britain. Published 2011 by Blackwell Publishing Ltd.

have lost interest in the topic of ritual and does not, as far as I have been able to tell, write much about it. He does, however, maintain a continuing interest in an area that he initially links to ritual, namely, the imitation of teachers by their students.

In this chapter, I reconstruct Peters' underlying theory of ritual in education, highlighting the link between ritual and the imitation of teachers that Peters proposes. I will then discuss the tension that arises in Peters' work between his affinity for ritual and imitation in education, on the one hand, and his views of liberal education and the 'criteria of an educational process,' on the other. The question I ask is this: If ritual and imitation are supposed to work outside of the realm of a teacher giving reasons for knowledge, how can it be part of a liberal education or part of an acceptable educational process? In the end, I attempt to show how these seemingly incompatible concepts can be reconciled, and I suggest future directions of work in this area, especially as it relates to school violence.

I PETERS ON RITUAL IN EDUCATION

A major question in ritual studies asks about the different roles that ritual might play in social groups. In answer to this question, the function of ritual (to oversimplify) has been stipulated to either preserve or transform cultures. Emile Durkheim, the grandfather of ritual studies, viewed ritual as a way to form social solidarity and to pass along conventional norms. His views arose to prominence with the publication of his book, *The Elementary Forms of the Religious Life: A Study in Religious Sociology* (1915). Cultural anthropologist Victor Turner, in contrast, in books such as *The Ritual Process: Structure and Anti-Structure* (1969), argued that rituals were to be understood in terms of how they transformed societies rather than preserved them.

Peters' most extensive statement of ritual is the article that he co-authored with Bernstein and Elvin in 1966, 'Ritual in Education'. In this article, the voice of sociologist and linguist Basil Bernstein seems to dominate. In fact, in a later reprinting of Bernstein's essays, Peters and Elvin are not even listed as co-authors, and Bernstein claims in the preface that Peters simply 'encouraged' him to write the paper (Bernstein, 1975, p. 4). While Peters may not have been the driving intellectual force behind the article, though, we can at least surmise from his listing as a co-author that he agreed with the article's thesis and was influenced by it.

In this article, Peters and his co-authors identify ritual as 'a relatively rigid pattern of acts specific to a situation which construct a framework of meaning over and beyond the specific situation meanings' (Bernstein, Elvin and Peters, 1966, p. 429). Through the use of symbol, ritual is said to connect the individual to the social order. The article goes on to distinguish between 'consensual' and 'differentiating' ritual. Consensual rituals, for their part, are repetitive actions that are intended to unify a social group. Such rituals highlight the conventions and norms of the community, and they instil a sense of common purpose and enterprise. In contrast, differentiating rituals mark off different social groups within the schools and are usually based on differences in age, sex, and 'house membership' (p. 432). Of course, consensual ritual and differentiating rituals work together in some sense; each solidifies an 'in-group' and differentiates it from an 'out-group'. Differential rituals make distinctions within the school community, but at the same time serve to unify the subgroups through making a distinctive identity.

At the end of 'Ritual in Education', Peters and his co-authors place ritual in context within a larger economic order. In a society with increasingly high levels of economic specialisation, schools become more *instrumentally* focused (e.g. focused more on preparing students for adult roles) and less focused on the expressive order (e.g. focused on social relationships, and the conduct and character of student). The diversity brought about by instrumentalisation and economic specialisation reduces the level of social consensus. 'Educating for diversity of economic and social function in pluralistic societies often involves a strengthening of the instrumental and a weakening of the expressive culture of schools', the authors write (p. 435). In the face of diversity, with less cultural homogeneity, schools rely less on ritual as school-wide ritual depends on some degree of social consensus and uniformity among the students. Because students come from different backgrounds and are being prepared for different social roles, there is less of a fixed and shared social order to pass on and to celebrate. Thus, the use of school rituals becomes less pronounced. In response to specialisation and instrumentality, though, students begin to initiate their own rituals: 'Pupils are then likely to generate their own consensual and differentiating rituals in order to assist in the development of a transitional identity' (ibid.). As the school's use of ritual declines, students initiate and regulate their own rites, ceremonies, and traditions. The authors may have been thinking of the emergence of the early counter-culture movements of 1960s, the rise of a youth culture centred on popular music, and so forth.

In the Bernstein article, Peters agrees with the notion that ritual fundamentally involves creating solidarity, transmitting values, and perpetuating social control. In so doing, Peters and his co-authors largely side with Durkheim's analysis of ritual as conserving and perpetuating social meanings. School rituals, for Peters and his co-authors, serve to 'facilitate the transmission and internalisation of the expressive culture of the school, create consensus, revivify the social order within the individual, deepen respect for and impersonalize authority relations' (p. 436). The job of ritual is to maintain and pass on a community's value system and to 'prevent questioning of the values the expressive culture transmits' (ibid.). The influence of this view of ritual is also seen in Peters' individual writings, such as in *Ethics and Education*, where he states that rituals 'link the past with the present and mark the value of what is being passed on without anything being explicitly stated' (Peters, 1966, p. 260).

What counts as a school ritual for Peters? Peters understands ritual in a very broad sense. In *Ethics and Education*, Peters not only identifies ritualistic aspects of educational ceremonies, where markers such as academic gowns and diplomas unify the school community and differentiate the initiated from those on the outside. He also sees ritual as present in everyday settings such as 'committees, councils, and perfect systems' (p. 318). The spirit of ritual is even embodied in physical artefacts such as books, whose very binding can symbolise importance: 'Books were produced,' Peters wistfully laments, 'in such a way that they could be thought of as possessions forever' (p. 259). In the Bernstein article, the authors observe that rituals often make use of 'liniments of dress, the imagery of signs, totems, scrolls and plaques for the revivifying of *special* historical contexts and other symbolic features' (Bernstein, Elvin and Peters, 1966, p. 430).

In *Ethics and Education*, ritual plays a role in shaping the social climate in a way that makes teaching more effective and learning more deeply felt. Rituals are said to 'convey atmosphere' (Peters, 1966, p. 260). They symbolically highlight the importance of certain people and topics for students who cannot yet understand the reasons a teacher might give for their significance. Rituals work very much under the radar of human attention and reason: he says that rituals work 'insensibly', they 'intimate' their messages and they work 'without anything be explicitly stated' (pp. 259–60). The underlying message of most school rituals, Peters believes, is to designate the 'special importance of the development of the mind' (p. 259).

More specifically, ritual for Peters plays two central roles in the education of students. First, Peters draws a link between the performance of ritual and the identification with, and imitation of, legitimate and rational authority figures. Second, ritual serves as an invitation to enter a practice or, as Wittgenstein would say, to enter a language game. After the ritual summons the student to enter a practice by marking it out as important, the student can come to see the value of practice. Rituals invite the student to experience a practice and, later, this experience becomes central to the task of properly evaluating that practice. I will discuss each of these aspects of ritual— imitation and invitation—in turn.

Ritual and Imitation

At least in *Ethics and Education*, Peters stipulates a close connection between ritual and the imitation of teachers. It is not immediately obvious why the two concepts of ritual and imitation should be brought together, and Peters himself does not emphasise this connection in later work. But the reasons that Peters offers in *Ethics and Education* for linking these two phenomena are worth noting. First, Peters makes an argument related to the 'tone' of the educational environment. In the proper environment, ritual sets the atmosphere for further learning. As the ritual atmosphere connects past and present, one comes to identify with teachers, the values of the school, and the educational project the teacher wishes to accomplish. In *Ethics and Education*, Peters' first discussion of ritual occurs in his discussion of teacher authority. He writes:

> The importance of such rituals is that they convey atmosphere; they link the past with the present and mark the value of what is being passed on without anything being explicitly stated.
>
>   What is being argued is that, psychologically speaking, some kind of identification has to take place between teacher and pupils so that the pupil takes into himself the values of the teacher. He must come to feel that what is being studied is important and that it matters whether the appropriate standards are attained. This is enormously helped by the tradition and 'tone' of the school; for then the process of identification is strengthened and legitimized by peer-group pressure. Ritualistic devices aid this process by intimating symbolically the significance of what is being transmitted, and hence by influencing sentiments. Lessons are obviously not quite the same as initiation ceremonies, but they are certainly most effective when they share some of their atmosphere (p. 260).

Ritual, it seems, reinforces the role of the teacher in several different ways. First, ritual creates an atmosphere that points to the work of teachers as something valuable. By invoking certain emotions, it legitimises school traditions, and thus connects the school to its history. In an atmosphere where there is importance and value attached to the ongoing work of the school, students begin to pressure one another to conform to those values. With the tone set and the peer environment attuned to the proper frequencies, students come to identify with the values of their teachers. Ritual thus harnesses emotional responses and peer pressure in support of student identification with, and imitation of, teachers.

It makes sense that Peters would want to discuss the process of imitation at this point since imitation plays a central and consistent role in Peters' educational thought. As Peters sees it, imitation is the principle mechanism by which culture has been transmitted in world history. He takes educational writers, especially John Dewey, to task for what he sees as their neglect of imitation: '[I]t is rather cavalier for a thinker with an evolutionary orientation like Dewey to disregard one of the main mechanisms which the human race has evolved for the transmission of culture' (Peters, 1981a, p. 84). Elsewhere, Peters maintains that the critics of imitation:

> ... overlook the main mechanism by means of which the human race has survived, which is that of imitation of and identification with, others who are more experienced. It is mainly through these mechanisms that cultural transmission takes place ... [M]ost beliefs and forms of conduct have been learnt by the human race ... by picking them up from example and instruction of more experienced people who rank as authorities or experts in a community (Peters, 1977, pp. 82–83).

In *Ethics and Education*, imitation and identification with teachers is called in as an essential part of initiation. He repeatedly emphasises that traits like good judgment and a rational respect for authority are 'caught rather than taught' (Peters, 1966, pp. 60 and 166). '[T]hose in authority', he also writes, 'can contribute much if they provide paradigm examples of reasonable behaviour, and if they can help adolescents to accomplish one of the most difficult things of all—the development of a rational attitude towards authority' (p. 315). In *Moral Development and Moral Education*, Peters highlights imitation as one of the key processes of learning. Imitation is a process of 'assimilation' by which a learner makes academic content knowledge 'his own' (Peters, 1981b, p. 123).

Rituals and Invitation to Traditions

In addition to serving as a stage for imitative learning, ritual also serves as an invitation. That is to say, ritual points students to social practices rather than just to individual examples. A ritual, for Peters, hints at something that cannot be fully explained to the student, something that cannot be defended with reasons that the student will understand. Often, we cannot grasp the value of a practice until we have experience with that practice—sometimes a good deal of experience. Rituals are useful when a student has to be internal to the practice to appreciate what it has to offer. Rituals offer a flavour of the practice to the uninitiated.

There are two instances in *Ethics and Education* where Peters lays out this invitational role for rituals. First, in his description of teacher authority, he writes: '[Rituals] intimate, at second hand, as it were, that something of interest and value is at stake; they may thus provide an atmosphere which may permit the teacher to get his pupils to enjoy first-hand experience of what is so marked out. If all goes well, intrinsic motivations will develop' (Peters, 1966, p. 260). Ritual is thus a second-hand experience; it provides a feeling for the atmosphere that animates the practice or, again, simply a feeling that something important is going on. The second-hand experience propels the students into a first-hand experience. Once the students are able to 'taste' the practice in this way, they will enter more deeply into that practice and ('if all goes well') will see its intrinsic worth.

The next textual link between educational ritual, authority, and the invitational function arises in his discussion of democracy. For Peters, school climate is essential in crafting the democratic personality, particularly in the education of public officials. If teachers, for example, are treated in an authoritarian manner, teachers are more likely to treat students in an authoritarian manner, and, hence, the students will not develop a 'rational attitude towards the exercise of authority' (p. 318). Rituals become part of proper authority because they invite students inside a worthwhile way of life, without forcing them inside.

> Rituals, as well as the use of authority, are a method by means of which the importance of a practice can be marked out and children made to feel that it is something in which they should participate. It is surely better than

bribing them or goading them. Rationalists often attack rituals because they lack instrumental value; they do little to promote any palpable purpose. This, of course, is just the point about them. If a practice had an obvious instrumental value, e.g., taking a train to work, there is no need for it to be ritualized. If, however, the point of the practice is difficult to discern because, perhaps, it is largely internal to it, then ritual both serves as a lure for those who are outside and also helps to revive and sustain the belief in it by those who are inside. There are many whose cynicism about the actual workings of Parliament has been tempered by participating in some of the majesty of its rituals, most of which are steeped in historical significance. Such rituals help to unite the past with the future and to convey the sense of participation in a shared form of life. They do something to mitigate the feeling any rational being must have about the triviality and transience of his life upon earth. They do much, too, to develop that feeling of fraternity which is the life-blood of any effective institution (pp. 318–9).

Here again, ritual gives a feeling for the historical significance of the educational endeavour. The sense of history seems to be related to the sense of worth: as one participates in the rituals of Parliament, one sees the institution in historical context, and therefore comes to feel that it is worthwhile. Thus, Peters seems to agree that rituals have no obvious instrumental value (this, he agrees, 'is just the point about them'), but he also argues that they are useful in 'luring' us to experience practices where the instrumental value of the practices themselves is somewhat hidden.

There is a bit of confusion, at this point, in Peters' discussion of ritual. The rational instrumentalist, in this quote, is complaining about the value of ritual, saying that rituals do not have a clear purpose. Peters pivots from the criticism that rituals lack purpose to talking about the internal values of the practices often associated with rituals. At this point, he argues that rituals are often used when the value of the practice itself is difficult to discern. These two issues— the hidden value of the ritual and the hidden value of the practice—are clearly separable. For instance, one could have a ritual associated with a practice that *does* have an obvious instrumental purpose (a white-coat ceremony, for example, is associated with the practice of medicine, which has an obvious instrumental purpose). It is true that Peters talks about 'ritualised' practices, but the formal ritual elements of a practice can, at least to some degree, be separated from the practical dimensions of the practice (in the United States, the President's inauguration ritual can be separate from the day-to-day tasks of governing).

Peters' response seems confused because the rational instrumentalist is not questioning the point of Parliament, just the ritual features of Parliament.

Peters, it seems to me, responds to what would be the most problematic situation from an instrumentalist perspective, namely, when an apparently useless ritual is associated with a seemingly useless practice. Consider an academic ceremony, for example, celebrating 'the life of mind' or 'liberal education'. Peters responds to this most problematic case by pointing to a set of practices in which the value of the practice is 'internal' or 'difficult to discern'. Taking a train to work does not need to be associated with ritual because of its clear instrumental purpose, but a liberal education might be different. The messy workings of Parliament may cause some to question its value, but the rituals associated with Parliament serve the very instrumental purpose of reminding us of the institution's historical role and significance. There are a set of practices whose import is easy to miss or to forget, and it is this sort of practice that most needs ritual. The internal value of the practice, once it is recognised, gives instrumental value to the ritual. Peters, then, responds to the instrumentalist by an instrumental justification for some rituals—the rituals of Parliament are valuable because they reveal something of value that is hidden about Parliament. This means, though, that Peters should not agree that the lack of instrumental value is 'the point' of ritual; from his perspective, ritual does have clear instrumental value.

II R. S. PETERS ON RITUAL AND IMITATION: AN ASSESSMENT

Imitation and Background Context

Given the importance of ritual, we might ask if Peters was right to link imitation and ritual in the ways that he does in *Ethics and Education*. This line of inquiry leads to more general questions: How do human beings become examples to imitate? How do human beings come to 'speak' in way that inspires others to act as they do? If a teacher is enthusiastic about a subject, how is it that students come to identify and imitate that excitement? (For a more detailed engagement with these issues, see Warnick, 2008.)

Of course, these questions at first seem as if they have an easy answer. If a teacher merely possesses a trait, then that is a sufficient condition to exemplify that trait. If a teacher can be categorised as a person who is 'enthusiastic about mathematics', then they are also an *example* of such a person simply by virtue of that categorisation. The question of exemplarity, it may seem at first, goes no deeper than that. But clearly things are not so simple as this purely logical understanding of exemplarity would imply. We, as human beings, can be said to possess an almost infinite variety of traits. For example, I was born in 1974, I have brown hair, I ate cereal for breakfast, I have very poor eyesight, and so forth. Do I also therefore exemplify someone born in 1974? Or someone with brown hair and poor eyesight that eats cereal for breakfast? A sample in a fabric store possesses a number of different attributes: shape, colour, texture, date of production, pattern, spatiotemporal location, molecular structure, and so on. However, as we look at a particular fabric sample, we clearly do not take it to *exemplify* all of these different features. While in the store, we take the fabric as an example of, say, colour and texture, but not size, spatiotemporal location, or molecular structure. As Nelson Goodman (1968) argues, exemplification must involve possession plus reference—an example must not only possess a trait but also communicate that trait. It must somehow make us aware of the trait, or highlight the trait. Not every feature is exemplified because not every feature exists in a *communicative* relationship between an exemplar and an observer.

If this is true, the key question becomes: How do things come to communicate the features they possess? Catherine Elgin has argued that examples gain a communicative function by highlighting 'obscure or elusive features'. She writes, '[An example] presents those features in a context contrived to render them salient. This may involve unravelling common concomitants, filtering out impurities, clearing away unwanted clutter, presenting in unusual settings.' She goes on to say, 'Stage setting can also involve introduction of additional factors. Thus a biologist stains a slide to bring out a contrast, and a composer elaborates a theme to disclose hidden harmonies' (Elgin, 1991, p. 199). For Elgin, then, a teacher would become an example of someone who is 'enthusiastic about mathematics' only when he or she is placed in a context or on a stage that renders this feature salient and that makes it stand out in a certain way. A thing, taken by itself, is never an example. An example is made an example only when a normative context highlights it as such.

In formulating the link between imitation and ritual, Peters seems to recognise the need for stage setting in order for exemplification and imitation to occur. Ritual sets the tone and focuses the attention of some individuals, and some traits of those individuals, over others. While stage setting does not need to occur through ritual (something of a stage always surrounds individual examples, whether we intended it that way or not), it is surely one thing that can contribute to the stage. Peters' sensitivity to the need for a stage-setting context for human examples to function, at least in *Ethics and Education*, is one of the books more interesting and least-recognised achievements.

Ritual and Liberal Education

The question of what constitutes a liberal education continues to be a source of considerable discussion (Evans, 2009; Levinson, 1999; Miller, 2007; Mulcahy, 2008). While the celebration of imitation and ritual may be fully compatible with some forms of liberal education, it does not seem to fit well with Peters' own view. In a discussion of imitation, Peters writes:

> Most of the things we learn we pick up from other people in various ways. We do not discover them. Nevertheless, we learn them. This only becomes an illiberal procedure if other people convey these things in such a way that we are discouraged from questioning them and if the method of instruction is such that it has a general tendency to discourage us to be curious or critical. There is no evidence that learning by example ... necessarily has an indoctrinatory effect (Peters, 1977, p. 82).

Peters here constructs one criterion for 'liberal' education, namely, that it consists of procedures that encourage open questioning and the evaluation of positions through critical reason. Recall, however, in his article on ritual, Peters and his co-authors had explicitly stipulated that rituals 'serve to prevent questioning of the values the expressive culture transmits'. This gives rise to the following dilemma:

(a) The discouragement of questioning is what makes an educational procedure illiberal.
(b) Rituals discourage questioning the values of expressive culture.
(c) Therefore, rituals are an illiberal educational procedure.

In this way, the use of ritual seems to violate a key criterion for liberal education. It thus may be more associated with inculcation or indoctrination than education.

Moreover, by arguing that there is no persuasive evidence that learning by example (which Peters has connected to ritual) has an indoctrinatory effect, Peters minimises valid concerns about imitative learning. One only has to look at footage of massive Hitler Youth marches, or the dead bodies surrounding Jim Jones's compound, to become suspicious of ritual, imitation, and identification with charismatic authority figures. Such tragic affairs involved ritual, the imitation of powerful people, and probably a good deal of indoctrination. Surely, Peters is wrong to dismiss so easily worries about the role that ritual and imitation *can* play in indoctrination. The question is whether such processes *necessarily* play a role in indoctrination. Can such processes be used in a liberal way, even if they do not open themselves up to critical inspection?

This issue is even more problematic when we consider Peters' criteria for educational processes, which he discusses in the first chapter of *Ethics and Education*. In his discussion of the nature of teaching, Peters argues that teaching 'requires us to reveal our reasons to the student and, by so doing, to submit them to his evaluation and criticism' (p. 39). The use of ritual, it seems, which does not involve giving reasons, would not be part of any process of true teaching. Ritual is invoked precisely because reasons are not (yet) operative. The same seems to hold true for identification and imitation.

If ritual cannot be a part of 'teaching', as Peters conceives of it, may it be part of an 'educational process' more broadly conceived? Peters points out that 'education' is used both to describe an outcome (it is an 'achievement word') and a process (it is a 'task word'). For a learning process to be 'educational' in the task sense, Peters first argues that it must involve a conscious awareness of goals:

A child might be conditioned, in a strict sense, to avoid dogs or induced to do something by hypnotic suggestion. But we would not describe this as 'education' if he was not conscious of something to be learned or understood. The central cases of 'education' are tasks in which the individual who is being educated is being led or induced to come up to some standard, to achieve something. This must be presented to him as something which he has to grasp (Peters, 1966, p. 41).

For a process to be educational, a student must be consciously aware of what they are supposed to be learning, along with 'the standards which they are expected to attain' (p. 42). Furthermore, the students must undertake the process more or less voluntarily, and with explicit consent. If they do not know what they are doing, a process cannot be voluntary. The criteria of 'wittingness' and 'voluntariness' are the twin criteria Peters suggests for picking out an educational process.

Neither of these two criteria applies easily to what goes on with ritual and imitation. Ritual, for Peters, operates under the radar of reasons and explanations. In rituals, students are often not conscious of what is to be learned; there is no explicit lesson being presented. Take the example of the school assembly. According to ritual theorists, an assembly might work to instil a sense of school unity, community, or tradition. But this goal, even if it is an explicit goal even for school administration, is not usually presented to students in that form. Even if reasons were given, the explanation would be meaningless—rituals convey what cannot be simply explained. An administrator might try to explain to a student that assemblies are important because they 'build a sense of school community', of course, but a sense of community at least partly must be experienced in order to be evaluated. Thus, there is no 'wittingness' about a belief being transmitted and in this sense it appears to be more like conditioning than educating or teaching. Since the purpose of the ritual is not consciously introduced, it is doubtful that students could 'consent' to the process in any sort of informed way.

And yet, Peters is surely right about the power of ritual and imitation in culture and individual human development. These are forces to be reckoned with and it seems like they cannot be simply dismissed or ignored in any educational endeavour. So, again, how are ritual and imitation to be used in liberal education?

Although there are several reasons to worry about ritual and imitation, there are also significant ways in which such processes are compatible with liberal education. These points do not suggest that all forms ritual and imitation are compatible with liberal values, but only that some forms *might* be compatible with liberal values. It all depends on the type of tradition that is being introduced through ritual, the sort of models that are being endorsed, the temporal trajectory of the larger project, and the forms of community that are created through ritual and imitation.

First of all, the nature of the tradition into which the student is being initiated makes a difference. For Peters, students are being initiated into a certain form of community life—most prominently, the life of the academic disciplines. Peters says that some traditions, like the 'life of reason', can be understood as the 'tradition of criticising traditions' (p. 303). In the case of, say, the Hitler youth, the rituals did not end up in a critical or transformative stance toward the practices of Nazism. In contrast, it seems an individual who is initiated in the academic disciplines (into, say, history or biology), would not be fully initiated into the disciplines if some interrogating of the tradition itself did not occur. That is to say, part of what makes one a member of an academic discipline is learning to criticise the tradition.

In one sense, learning to criticise a tradition is simply having a reasoned and justifiable account of the value of the discipline. So, a student of history comes to have a justifiable account of the value of history (as a discipline) in human life. As part of this, the student must also come to see the limitations of the traditions, the abuses of the tradition, and so forth. But a critical understanding of a discipline is even more than this; students also must have the ability to revise the judgment of the tradition as new facts and understandings come to light. It is this openness to fundamentally revising the tradition that distinguishes traditions of reason from other traditions. The value of the tradition is not held up as a conclusion, in other words, but as an ongoing question.

Of course, in actual practice, intellectual traditions can be open to criticism to a greater or lesser degree. Thomas Kuhn (1970) pointed out that young scientists are not taught to question the overriding paradigms that govern their disciplines, while young scholars in the humanities might be encouraged to question their 'paradigms' more forcefully and more directly. To the extent this is true, the humanistic disciplines might sometimes be more liberal than the scientific disciplines in their educational practices. But even the practitioners in the most open and self-questioning academic disciplines can fail to live up to the critical ideals of their disciplines. Whether ritual and imitation can be seen as liberal or not partially depends on the nature of the tradition that lies at the end of the process of initiation, and it also depends on how well the community is living up to its standards of openness. In the end, though, one cannot coherently be indoctrinated to accept the values of a tradition or community that itself values openness and criticality. If one is uncritical of a tradition that values criticality, one has simply not been properly initiated into the ideals of the tradition. If rituals and imitation initiate students into critical traditions, then they may be partially vindicated in liberal education.

Second, we need to recognise that the models that are imitated in this process of ritual identification might themselves model rationality and critical inquiry. Of course, it is possible to argue that imitation is doing something 'because somebody else is doing it' and that this reason can *never* constitute an acceptable reason for acting in the long run. Indeed, such a 'reason' seems to cede over one's own practical reason to somebody else (hence, Ralph Waldo Emerson's worry in his essay, 'Self-Reliance', that 'imitation is suicide'). It seems, however, that even if somebody acts on the reason 'because somebody else is doing it', there are still avenues of creativity and criticality that remain open. To see how this is possible, for example, we might differentiate between process-oriented and product-oriented imitation.

Product-oriented imitation attempts to reproduce the products of somebody else's activities, whereas process-oriented imitation attempts to reproduce a process by which one creates or criticises. A writer might imitate another by reproducing the actual product of another, namely, reproducing the writing itself. This can be considered a form of mannerism or even plagiarism, and is not generally considered a creative or critical achievement. Alternatively, a writer might imitate a process of creation; for example, one could take a walk before writing, directly imitating the writing process of another, and still come up with something new and transformative.

Processes of critical inquiry can be imitated and performed 'because someone else is doing it'. One might imitate Socrates by engaging in dialogue with others, and even though the value of dialogue may not be questioned, the imitator may end up with conclusions that are quite different from Socrates. In short, there are certain processes of critical inquiry that can be modelled—openness to testing ideas, to new evidence, to changing one's mind, and so forth. Plato seems to have had exactly such a model in mind as he wrote about Socrates; Plato was, in effect, trying to replace the Homeric heroes (whose values were questionable) with his own sort of hero—the champion of reason, wisdom, and dialogue. For all practical purposes, then, the blanket condemnation of imitation as unintelligent or illiberal seems to focus on the 'product' type imitation. An examination of 'process' imitation, however, reveals different possibilities.

Third, an examination of ritual and imitation would need to pay attention to the temporal trajectory of the educational process. If Peters were to construct a response to question of the legitimacy of imitation and ritual, this is probably what he would point to. Peters seems concerned about the construction of *future reasons*—reasons that will be made possible precisely because of ritual and imitation. It is true that ritual sometimes cannot be defended in terms that the student, being outside the practice, will be able to understand. It would be incorrect, however, to say that ritual and imitation are processes of education that are completely unhooked from the ideal of a teacher giving reasons for belief. For Peters, the formation of reasons is, after all, the point of the ritual activity. Students are participating in the activity *for the sake of formulating reasons*, even though they cannot grasp the reasons at the moment. The experience with ritual and imitation is supposed to give students a 'taste' of a particular practice that will draw them into that practice. After they have been drawn in, then they will have access to the particular sorts of reasons that are internal to the practice. Ritual and imitation are making certain sorts of reasons possible and meaningful.

Peters discusses this sort of process at greater length in his work on habit and moral education. He emphasises that children might need to be habituated to moral action without a full understanding of what they are doing. Over time, though, such reasons can be formulated. '[T]hrough instruction, praise and blame, reward and punishment by men who are already courageous and just, they can acquire action patterns which gradually become informed by a growing understanding of what they are doing and why' (Peters, 1981b, p. 96). The process by which this happens is that moral rules, initially learned through processes of habituation, are gradually connected to other rules and to larger moral principles. As Peters writes, habituation can be made intelligent 'by linking rules with other rules and with consequences which will eventually come to be seen as providing some point for them' (p. 106). Unthinking habitual action, even action promoted through imitation or ritual, can eventually be made more intelligent over time.

Given the temporal character of reason formation, what would differentiate a liberal use of ritual and imitation from an indoctrinatory use? One important difference would be the availability of a post-ritual or post-imitation reflection period. It may be the case that, after initiating an individual into a practice through ritual, there is no moment to reflect on the worth and value of the 'taste' one has received of the practice. This would be an illiberal use of ritual. Rituals may invite a student to a party, but once the festivities have begun, the student needs to be able to reflect on the party and decide whether the invitation is still to be considered valuable. A liberal use of imitation and ritual would encourage these moments—moments to look backward to see if practices have been validated.

Finally, a liberal approach to ritual and imitation would need to insure that the student has a wide range of experience with ritual and imitation. One problem with what has been said so far is that a liberal approach to ritual and imitation still leaves the models and traditions above critical scrutiny. If you imitate a model by doing critical inquiry in the way that a model does it, one of the most important things that will elude critical inquiry is the model him- or herself. One may imitate Socrates and be critical in a certain way, but the example of Socrates itself is not brought under critical scrutiny. One may engage in the sort of criticism attached to the discipline of history, but that particular type of criticality remains above examination of critical reason. Is there any way of bringing these models and disciplines themselves under critical scrutiny, while still recognising a role for imitation and ritual in human life? Can we evaluate our fundamental models, without assuming we can step outside of our models for a God's-eye view?

The metaphor of 'tasting' is useful here. Rituals and imitation invite the students to 'taste' a particular form of life. Once we have experienced a practice through ritual and imitation, how is it that we can come to critically discern the value of one practice from another? It could be that the answer to this question lies in the idea of connoisseurship and in the processes by which one develops 'good taste'. The route by which one cultivates good taste is itself something of a mysterious process, but one thing seems indisputable: to be a connoisseur, one needs a wide range of 'tastes' to develop the skills of critical discrimination. Connoisseurs of fine wines, it can surely be said, have experienced a lot of wine. And it is not just a good deal of experience with one kind of wine; rather, they would have had experience across a wide range of different possibilities. We often do not know what we enjoy and what we consider to be superior until we have been able to taste from a range of available options. Thus, a liberal approach to imitation and ritual would connect to a variety of practices and models that would allow for the development of connoisseurship. So, students would experience a wide range of examples of critical reason, not just that of Socrates. In the plurality of different models of critical thinking, space for critical engagement with the models themselves becomes possible. It is evaluating examples, while remaining within exemplarity.

In sum, there are several suggestions I would offer for reconciling the dilemma that is presented in Peters' work on imitation and ritual. If these things are to be justifiable on liberal educational grounds, then several features must be in place. First, the processes of imitation and ritual are justifiable when linked to an initiation into traditions that are themselves more self-critical, creative, and open-minded. Second, the processes ought to be focused on processes of creation, activity, and intellectual work, rather than end products or final results. Third, these processes must be viewed as part of an activity that aims at the development of future reasons and that provide spaces to use these reasons to evaluate one's involvement with a practice. Fourth, these processes are best when they are linked to a multiplicity of traditions and models that allow for the development of good taste. Again, these features do not ensure that all uses of ritual and imitation will be acceptable, only that they might be acceptable if they meet these normative conditions.

FUTURE DIRECTIONS

Peters does not explain fully how ritual and imitation can be part of a legitimate educational process. Part of the problem, perhaps, was Peters' early Durkheimian emphasis on ritual as preserving existing cultural values, rather than Victor Turner's emphasis on the transformative potential of ritual. Turner argued that rituals create a liminal space, where society can be creatively transformed. In ritual, a person stands at a threshold with others in a new community—a *communitas*—where society is reduced to its basic elements. With these basic, multivocal elements of society exposed, they can then be recombined in creative ways. 'Liminality ... breaks', he writes, 'the cake of custom and enfranchises speculation' (Turner, 1967, p. 106). What this means is, in effect, that educational ritual may not simply be about passing on the existing culture. Rituals exist within a continuous process of cultural reconstruction. Greater attention to this alternative form of understanding ritual would have benefited Peters' work.

Nonetheless, there is much on ritual that Peters got right as well as much that remains provocative. He successfully points to the link between imitation and ritual stage setting, perhaps in a way that has not fully been grasped even in contemporary discussions of imitative learning. This is an important avenue in which Peters' thoughts on ritual could be developed in the future. Another avenue of future development is the idea of student-initiated ritual under conditions of economic specialisation. Peters and his co-authors predicted in their 1966 essay that a highly diverse and specialised society would find less room for communal school rituals. Rituals, if they were to exist, would be more and more student-initiated.

Perhaps the most important area in which this idea could be developed is the area of student shootings. Jonathan Fast has recently described how school rampage shootings become 'ceremonial' and ritualised as public performance. Fast closely examines five prominent school shootings and draws together commonalities: A student, finding him- or herself placed in a 'community of excluded' through student-initiated differentiating rituals (through, for example, bullying and harassment), contemplates suicide. As the student is egged on by others in the disenfranchised group, a collective fantasy of violence emerges among them, and the excluded student 'gets the idea of turning his suicide into a public ceremony' (Fast, 2008, p. 19). Once these factors are in place, the shooting ritual proceeds fairly predictably:

> Once the candidate gets the idea of turning his suicide into a public ceremony, he becomes absorbed in the planning of it, often documenting his thoughts in journals and other media. He may 'publicize' the event by telling certain friends about it, warning them to stay home that day, or suggesting a safe place from which to view the mayhem. Seung-Hui Cho . . . paused during the Virginia Tech Shootings in order to FedEx a press kit with photos, a DVD, and a document explaining his motives, to NBC news. The candidate may choose special clothing for the event. He may even choose background music. This kind of ceremony seems to be a throwback to something very ancient and primitive, where the supplicant plays the part of a god, and indulges in a forbidden or privileged activity prior to his own execution or banishment from the tribe (p. 19).

The school shooting becomes an expressive ritual—a way of speaking to the school and larger community, of connecting with other 'disenfranchised' students, and of garnering attention for the subsequent suicide. These plans culminate in a disaster as the ritual is actualised, and lives are lost.

Thinking of student violence as a form of student-initiated ritual caused by the fracturing of society and school communities, is an intriguing way of looking at the problem of school violence. Since Peters' article on ritual was first published, ritualistic school shootings have increased over the decades, even as the overall safety of schools has also increased (Dinkes *et al.*, 2006). According to my informal count of school shootings in the United States, there was one high-profile shooting in the 1960s, two each in the 1970s and 1980s, sixteen in the 1990s and, so far, twenty-five in the 2000s. The reasons for the apparent increase are, of course, many, including easier access to firearms and extensive media coverage of shooting incidents. According to Peters' work, we could also hypothesise that the increase in school shootings may be a form of student-initiated ritual, brought about by splintered communities that lack their own expressive rituals. In the face of the unrelenting instrumental focus on education, students look vainly to schools to give them a sense of community identity. Finding nothing, they are forced to construct their own identities through rituals of differentiation. They work to create elaborate student hierarchies that involve the popular students at the top and the abused and despised students on the bottom. When this differentiated structure is combined with severe bullying, psychological problems, family turmoil, a media that glorifies violence and easy access to firearms, student rituals involving violence—rituals initiated by the community of excluded—may sometimes result.

Of course, this explanation of student violence would not explain everything, but, to be fair, no one theory of student violence does that. Nor does it suggest any easy solutions to the problem to school violence. How can communities fractured around lines of economic specialisation and culture somehow be unified, or pretend to be unified, for the sake of students' developing identity? Can community rituals be reconstructed, somehow, to undercut the meanings of school shootings? There are no easy answers to these questions. In the face of such tragic circumstance, however, the more we are aware of the dimensions of our social life that contribute to the problem, the better off we are. For this reason, Peters' call to examine ritual and imitation remains highly relevant to pressing educational problems.

REFERENCES

Bernstein, B. (1975) *Class, Codes and Control: Toward a Theory of Educational Transmissions* (London, Routledge and Kegan Paul).

Bernstein, B., Elvin, H. L. and Peters, R. S. (1966) Ritual in Education, *Philosophical Transactions of the Royal Society of London*, 251.772, pp. 429–36.

Bushnell, M. (1997) Small School Ritual and Parent Involvement, *Urban Review*, 29.4, pp. 283–95.

Cornbleth, C. (1986) Ritual and Rationality in Teacher Education Reform, *Educational Researcher*, 15.4, pp. 5–14.

Deal, T. E. and Peterson, K. D. (1999) *Shaping School Culture* (San Francisco, Jossey-Bass).

Dinkes, R., Cataldi, E. F., Kena, G. and Baum, K. (2006) *Indicators of School Crime and Safety: 2006* (Washington, DC, US Government Printing Office).

Durkheim, E. (1915) *The Elementary Forms of the Religious Life: A Study in Religious Sociology* (London, George Allen & Unwin).

Elgin, C. Z. (1991) Understanding: Art and Science, in: P. French, T. Uehling and H. Wettstein (eds) *Midwest Studies in Philosophy, XVI* (Notre Dame, IN, University of Notre Dame Press), pp. 196–208.

Ensign, J. (1997) Ritualizing Sacredness in Math: Profaneness in Language Arts and Social Studies, *Urban Review*, 29.4, pp. 253–61.

Ensign, J and Quantz, R. A. (1997) Introduction: Ritual and Education, *Urban Review*, 29.4, pp. 217–9.

Evans, W. (2009) Iris Murdoch, Liberal Education and Human Flourishing, *Journal of Philosophy of Education*, 43.1, pp. 75–84.

Fast, J. (2008) *Ceremonial Violence: A Psychological Explanation of School Shootings* (Woodstock, NY and New York, Overlook Press).

Goffman, E. (1967) *Interaction Ritual: Essays on Face-to-Face Behavior* (Garden City, NJ, Doubleday).

Goodman, N. (1968) *Languages of Art: An Approach to a Theory of Symbols* (Indianapolis, IN, Bobbs-Merrill).

Huber, S. J. (2003) The White Coat Ceremony: a Contemporary Medical Ritual, *Journal of Medical Ethics*, 29.6, pp. 364–6.

Kuhn, T. S. (1970) *The Structure of Scientific Revolutions* (Chicago, University of Chicago Press).

Levinson, M. (1999) *The Demands of Liberal Education* (Oxford, Oxford University Press).

Losito, W. F. (1996) Philosophizing About Education in a Post-Modem Society: The Role of Sacred Myth and Ritual in Education, *Studies in Philosophy and Education*, 15.1/2, pp. 69–76.

Magolda, P. M. (2000) The Campus Tour: Ritual and Community in Higher Education, *Anthropology and Education Quarterly*, 31, pp. 24–46.

McAllister, M. (2008) Thank-You Cards: Reclaiming a Nursing Student Ritual and Releasing Its Transformative Potential, *Nurse Education in Practice*, 8.3, pp. 170–6.

McCadden, B. M. (1997) Let's Get Our Houses in Order: The Role of Transitional Rituals in Constructing Moral Kindergartners, *Urban Review*, 29.4, pp. 239–52.

Miller, A. (2007) Rhetoric, Paideia and the Old Idea of a Liberal Education, *Journal of Philosophy of Education*, 41.2, pp. 183–206.

Mulcahy, D. G. (2008) Newman's Theory of a Liberal Education: A Reassessment and its Implications, *Journal of Philosophy of Education*, 42.2, pp. 219–31.

Peters, R. S. (1966) *Ethics and Education* (London, George Allen & Unwin).

Peters, R. S. (1977) *Education and the Education of Teachers* (London, Routledge & Kegan Paul).

Peters, R. S. (1981a) *Essays on Educators* (London, Allen & Unwin).

Peters, R. S. (1981b) *Moral Development and Moral Education* (London, George Allen & Unwin).

Quantz, R. A. (1999) School Ritual As Performance: A Reconstruction of Durkheim's and Turner's Uses of Ritual, *Educational Theory*, 49, pp. 493–514.

Turner, V. W. (1969) *The Ritual Process: Structure and Anti-Structure* (Chicago, Aldine).

Van Voorhis, F. L. (2004) Reflecting on the Homework Ritual: Assignments and Designs, *Theory Into Practice*, 43.3, pp. 205–12.

Warnick, B. R. (2008) *Imitation and Education: A Philosophical Inquiry into Learning by Example* (Albany, NY, SUNY Press).

5

Transformation and Education: The Voice of the Learner in Peters' Concept of Teaching

ANDREA ENGLISH

While discussions of learning and the learner can leave out questions of teaching, discussions of teaching are nearly impossible without reference to learning. Richard Peters' discussion of teaching is no exception to this. His account of teaching takes into consideration that teachers are necessarily implicated in an intersubjective, often intergenerational, relationship with learners. On several occasions in his work, Peters identifies a difficulty inherent in teaching that underscores the complexity of this relationship: the teacher has the task of passing on knowledge while at the same time allowing knowledge that is passed on to be criticised and revised by the learner.

In his emphasis on these two aspects of teaching, Peters is implicitly addressing two particular models of teaching he strongly opposes—namely, the 'moulding' and the 'growth' models of education. He criticises the traditional 'moulding' model of education for its view of the teacher as one who imprints a fixed body of knowledge onto the learner's mind and leaves no room for the learner's individuality and critical thought. Yet he viewed the 'growth' model associated with progressive education as moving too far in the other direction. On this model, as Peters points out, teachers naively emphasise the learner's self-realisation without acknowledging their own role in aiding the learner's acquisition of knowledge and understanding of the world.

Underlying Peters' critique is the view that neither of these models understands the teacher's role in the learner's transformation through education. In this chapter, I examine Peters' critical perspective on teaching as it relates to the learner's transformation through education. Peters is correct in his judgement that education involving transformation does not amount to mere self-realisation, nor involve conforming to the existing view of the teacher. As I develop the matter here, for Peters, teaching that recognises the transformational aspect of learning involves a teacher who recognises *both* the otherness of the learner and the need to pass on the

Reading R. S. Peters Today, First Edition. Stefaan E. Cuypers and Christopher Martin.
Chapters © 2011 The Authors. Editorial organization © 2011 Philosophy of Education Society of Great Britain. Published 2011 by Blackwell Publishing Ltd.

heritage of humankind. I ask, first, how does he envision these two tasks coming together in teaching? And, second, does he go far enough in developing what it means for the teacher to recognise the difference and otherness of the learner?

At the heart of the matter in answering these questions is how to conceive of the connection between transformation and learning. Thus, before turning to Peters' work to answer these questions, I provide a context to my discussion by examining connections between transformation and learning within classical and contemporary education philosophical discourse. Following this, I will take up Peters' work in three central ways, by analysing his notion of teaching, by examining the ideas of learning and transformation embedded in his concept of teaching, and by inquiring into how these issues relate to his idea of philosophy of education as a central part of teacher education.

TRANSFORMATION AND THE NEGATIVITY AND DISCONTINUITY IN LEARNING

Learning as a transformational process is a process that takes place between right and wrong and changes how we conceive of right and wrong. Inquiring into the process of learning involves uncovering the discontinuity, disruptions and interruptions constitutive of learning, and the perplexity, frustration and irritation that characterise the learner's experiences, as well as those of teachers. These aspects of learning relate to the negativity of learning, which I can only touch upon here, and have consequences for how we understand teaching and how we understand what it means for a teacher to recognise and give voice to the difference and otherness of the learner.

The term 'negativity of experience' points to an interruption in experience, which occurs when we encounter something unfamiliar, strange, different or unexpected in our experiences. The interruption in experience identifies the moment when the world in some ways defies our expectations. These moments are often coupled with disillusionment, perplexity, frustration, doubt or discomfort due to the fact that we do not know how we got in to or how to get out of the situation in which we find ourselves. These moments occur in everyday life—for example, when the car breaks down on the way to work—and we often associate them with something bad and unwanted, something to be avoided. In educational contexts, however, the experience of the unexpected has productive meaning, such that the concept of 'negativity' is not meant in a pejorative sense; nor does it necessarily refer to something unpleasant. In learning, one moves towards something unfamiliar, be it an ability, an idea, a feeling, that one did not have before. It is in this precarious situation of dealing with the unfamiliar that negativity of experience arises. Thus, negativity plays a constitutive role in all experiences of learning, ranging from those of a child first learning object permanence to those of the scientist learning of new evidence that falsifies an entire scientific theory.

The term 'negativity' allows us to describe philosophically the human being's experience of the limits of his own knowledge and experience. Käte Meyer-Drawe calls this experience of one's limits a 'confrontation with one's own experiential history' (Meyer-Drawe, 1982, pp. 520f.).[1] Thematisations of this type of experience in learning can be traced back through the traditions of educational philosophy. For example, in Plato's *Meno*, Plato describes the learning slave boy who attempts to answer Socrates' questions as disillusioned and perplexed about his own knowledge. Through this process the boy eventually is lead to proclaim: 'I do not know' (Plato, 1961a).[2] This admission of ignorance is a pre-condition for the boy's search for knowledge. Hans-Georg Gadamer—developing an idea he finds in the philosophical thinking of Aristotle, Bacon and Hegel—speaks of experiences as 'negative' when they do not conform to our expectations and, therefore, cannot confirm previous experiences (Gadamer, 1960/1997, p. 353). For Gadamer, the 'negativity of experience' is productive in that it not only corrects how we view the newly experienced object, but at the same time also thoroughly transforms our knowledge. He refers to this transformative correction of past experiences as a 'determinate negation' (ibid.). Modern educational theory has also emphasised various forms of negativity in aesthetic, cognitive and moral learning and experience. In *Emile*, Rousseau emphasises that negativity of experience is part of the child's processes of sensory-formation from the earliest stages of the child's life. This can be seen, for example, in a child's perplexity and disillusionment when he thinks he can grasp an object that is within his field of vision, but beyond the reach of his outstretched arm (Rousseau, 1762/1979, p. 64). Herbart placed particular significance on negativity in the realm of moral learning. In his discussion, Herbart demonstrates that the learner's experience of difficulty and internal 'struggle' (*Kampf*) is indispensable when he is learning the difference between what he subjectively desires and what is good or right in the situation (Herbart, 1806/1902).[3]

Dewey's theory of reflective learning productively extends previous philosophical and education theoretical ideas. Dewey draws out the moment of suspense between the interruption in experience and the location of the difficulty in thought or action that may have lead to the interruption. This part of the experience of learning is an opening, a space for learning between known and unknown, a space where we dwell between old and new experiences, and where new and unforeseen opportunities arise. This space is located between pre-reflective and reflective forms of negativity. These two forms of negativity can be clarified with reference to Dewey's *Logic: A Theory of Inquiry*. In Dewey's terms, when we encounter the unexpected, we become perplexed, frustrated or confused because we are stuck in an 'indeterminate situation' and unsure how to get out (Dewey, 1938/1991, pp. 109f; see also Dewey 1916/1995). On this account, pre-reflective negativity can be defined as the interruption that occurs when something unforeseen and unexpected happens in an individual's experience, but she is not yet sure what has happened.[4] Once we begin to ask ourselves, 'What happened?', 'What went wrong?', we begin to reflect on the interruption in experience and inquire into it, such that the situation changes from an 'indeterminate' to a 'problematic' situation (Dewey, 1938/1991, pp. 109f.; see also Dewey, 1933/1989; see also English, 2005, 2008). Reflective inquiry transforms pre-reflective interruptions in experience into reflective forms of negativity of experience, which we can define then as 'problems' for examining and exploring.

Reflective inquiry into the interruption is just as necessary for learning to take place, as is the interruption that it pre-supposes. It is only on account of the pre-reflective interrupted experience that we can recognise the limits of our previously acquired knowledge and experience. In other words, we recognise that our previous experiences and accrued knowledge and ability do not suffice—they require expansion, correction or both. What this expansion or correction consists in, however, has yet to be found (Benner and English, 2004). When our experiences are interrupted, this space opens up, and opportunities arise for reflectively exploring and experimenting with new ideas and new modes of practice.

Examining connections between negativity and learning opens up the possibility of grasping meaningful differences between learning as mere correction of error and learning as transformation of self and world. Drawing on traditions of hermeneutics and phenomenology, contemporary theorists have analysed the connections between negativity of experience in learning and the transformation of the individual. With reference to Gadamer and Husserl, Günther Buck argues that the productive meaning of negative experience lies in the fact that it allows us to become conscious of ourselves (Buck 1969, p. 71; see also Gadamer, 1960/1997).[5] In other words, in the moment an individual is interrupted by the unexpected and unanticipated, he becomes conscious of the 'unquestioned motives that were guiding his experience up to that point' (Buck, 1969, p. 71). Deborah Kerdeman emphasises similarly that in our encounters with the unexpected, we become aware of our otherwise hidden 'attitudes, qualities, and behaviours' embedded in our pre-reflective understandings, such that our 'blind spots' are exposed (Kerdeman, 2003, p. 296). When learning brings about true change in the sense of a transformation, as Meyer-Drawe points out, it is experienced as a 'painful turn-around' (*schmerzhaften Umkehr*), in which one breaks with one's prior knowledge, but also with oneself as a person (Meyer-Drawe, 2003, p. 511; see also 1996, pp. 89f.). When our experience breaks with itself, then we can learn in a way that is not just a matter of adding on or correcting the content of our thought, or exchanging one aspect of knowledge for another. Rather, this negativity and discontinuity makes a different type of learning possible: learning becomes *Umlernen*, a transformative restructuring of one's entire horizon of foregoing and possible experience (Meyer-Drawe, 2003, p. 522; see also 1984).[6]

These types of experiences of learning are difficult to conceptualise. Part of the reason for this difficulty is that after one has learned something, one forgets the difficulties encountered along the path of learning (Benner/English, 2004). Once one learns to read, one forgets the fear and difficulty involved in the process. Once one understands the principle of multiplication, one forgets the frustration involved in arriving at this understanding.

Throughout my discussion, I will be explicating the connections between negativity, learning and transformation addressed here, but I will initially illustrate some of these connections with reference to Plato's allegory of the Cave. To conceptualise the path of learning as transformation, one might recall the experience of the liberated prisoner in the Cave. On his path out of the cave, the prisoner experiences the 'pain' of being blinded by the light on the outside of the cave. Then, when he is asked to the differentiate the objects he sees, he becomes perplexed since he had previously only seen the objects as shadows on the cave wall and thought they were truer than the objects now before his eyes. This image reveals the negativity of experience that arises for the prisoner in his confrontation with the new and unfamiliar, but it also gives insight into the problem of the forgotten negativity of experience. In the allegory, the reader is asked to imagine what it would be like for the prisoner, who is now accustomed to the light, to suddenly be taken out of the light and returned to the darkness of the cave. Upon his return, the prisoner can no longer see the shadows on the wall, because his eyesight is weakened by the darkness, and therefore he can no longer relate to the other prisoners, who have never left the cave. Whereas the other prisoners still believe the shadows on the wall are truth, the liberated prisoner now sees these shadows differently. The liberated prisoner's return to the cave demonstrates that in learning, what was once so familiar and taken for granted becomes strange, and what was once strange becomes familiar.[7]

RECOGNISING THE OTHER AS LEARNER: ON PETERS' CONCEPT OF THE TEACHER AS EDUCATOR

The problem for Peters and what he seeks to illuminate in his description and definition of teaching is that not all teaching is *educative*. In other words, it is not a general concept of teaching that interests him, but a notion of teaching that is characterised by how it is connected to the learner's process of education. For this reason it is necessary to distinguish teaching generally from teaching as it is part of educational processes. Each of these notions of teaching implies different types of relationships between the teacher and the learner. Peters' distinction underscores the fact that the teacher's orientation is not just towards another person, but towards the other *as a learner*.

Peters' analysis of the notion of teaching demonstrates his concern for the fact that when we talk about teaching as a concept, it brings with it certain implications of the underlying relationship between people—namely, between a teacher and a learner. Given this, Peters problematises the notion of teaching first by showing how the concept of teaching is tied to the notion of learning. As Peters points out, teaching is a term that can be understood both as emphasising a particular 'task' or activity that the teacher is engaged in when teaching and as emphasising a certain 'achievement' or result that the teacher is seeking out. If we focus on the task aspect of teaching, we are speaking of teaching as an on-going process, as something one is trying to do, independent of the result (Peters, 1967, p. 2). For example, one might say, 'I am teaching him French', implying that I am still teaching whether or not I am successful. However, as Peters points out, there is a sense to the concept of teaching someone something that 'implies success' (ibid.; see also 1966, p. 38). This idea is particularly important to understanding teaching for Peters, because the success that is implied is not just the success of the teacher, but also that of the learner. For this reason, Peters explains that 'the teacher's success ... can only be defined in terms of that of the learner' (Peters, 1967, p. 3; see also 1966, p. 38).

What does it mean to define the teacher's success in terms of the learner's success? Peters' conceptual analysis makes clear that the achievements of the learner are significant for the teacher's success. However, this aspect of the concept of teaching is insufficient for understanding teaching on his model. Beyond this, there is a distinctive normative component to his conception that further delimits how we are to understand the interconnection between teaching and learning that the concept of teaching implies. Peters gives two examples of teaching that indirectly identify the normative aspect of his concept by indicating what types of teaching he wants to rule out. The first case to be ruled out is the case of teaching someone something that is 'morally neutral or pernicious', such as astrology, forgery or the art of torture (Peters, 1966, p. 40; see also, 1967, p. 4); the second is the case of teaching someone one subject, for example, mathematics, to the exclusion of all other subjects, a form of limiting the perspective of the learner (Peters, 1966, p. 40).

If we are only concerned with the fact that the learner learned forgery or mathematics in each of the above cases, we could conclude that the teacher was successful. However, the fact alone that someone is learning fails to address teaching in the way Peters seeks to define it. On Peters' view, the teacher in the above example may be teaching, but he or she is not an 'educator' (ibid.). The question for Peters then is not just a question of what teaching is; it is rather a question of how we define teaching as part of an educational process. Educational processes connect processes of teaching and learning and thus connect the teacher and the learner in a particular way. On Peters' terms, to speak of the teacher as an educator is to consider the process of teaching part of a wider set of educational processes. This characterisation has certain implications for how the teacher's success is defined. The success of the educator cannot be determined simply on the basis of the learner's particular instances of learning, irrespective of *what* is learned and *how* it is learned. Rather, the teacher's success *qua* educator becomes more difficult to define; it is thoroughly intertwined with the ability to look beyond particular instances of learning towards a view of the *education* of another person.

Peters' distinction between 'the teacher' and the 'teacher as educator' hinges upon the fact that only the latter takes conscious account of the connection between teaching and the education of the learner. In the first chapter of *Ethics and Education* (1966) and in his article 'What is an Educational Process?' (1967), Peters identifies three criteria of educational processes that help clarify what it means for the teacher to have the education of the learner in view. According to these criteria, the teacher is concerned with the education of the learner when he is passing on something that is 'worthwhile', ensuring the learner gains 'cognitive perspective' in regards to the differentiated forms of human knowledge and awareness, and ensuring the learner is acquiring 'knowledge' and gaining an 'understanding' of the underlying principles of what he is learning (Peters, 1966, pp. 25f. and 1967, pp. 3f.). Whether or not one agrees that these criteria are necessary or sufficient for understanding education, I suggest that within Peters' discussion of these criteria there is something important to be said about what makes the teaching educational: namely, that for teaching to be educational it must lead to a certain type of transformation of the learner's perspective. Here, I would like to focus on two particular ways Peters makes explicit a necessary connection between education and transformation.

The first connection between education and transformation arises as part of Peters' discussion of the criteria of the 'worthwhileness' of the content of education. Peters' criteria of worthwhileness sheds light upon the responsibility and moral obligation attached to the relationship between teacher and learner (Peters, 1966, p. 25; 1967, p. 4). It suggests that as an 'educator', the teacher is looking not only narrowly to determine particular instances of a child's learning, but also broadly to get a sense of how what the child is learning at any given moment connects to the child's possible future. The criteria of worthwhileness underscores the teacher's obligation to determine the content of education on the basis of both the present *and* the future needs, concerns, abilities and questions of the child.

How do we determine what is worthwhile for the learner? Although Peters does not seek to resolve this question definitively,[8] he does place emphasis on intellectual pursuits such as history, philosophy and literary appreciation as particularly desirable aspects of the curriculum. While he has been criticised for this, the basis for his emphasis remains important. He places particular significance on these types of pursuits associated with liberal education, because of the potential of these studies to have transformational, rather than simply instrumental value. He explains that these types of studies open up new ways of thinking about the world and 'transform how [learners] see the world', such that life outside the classroom 'develops different dimensions' for them (Peters, 1967, p. 8). As Paul Standish (2007) explains of Peters' account, studies such as literature, history or sociology have a transformational quality because they can expand how we see what the world is dependent upon and can thereby understand the world and ourselves within it more fully. So, for example, through history the child sees connections between past and present that he otherwise may not have seen, or through literature he can begin to grasp what is possible in the world rather than just what is actual.

The second connection between transformation and education that we find in Peters' work has implications beyond questions of content and aims that extend to questions of the process of learning that the teacher is to cultivate, although Peters does not fully draw out these implications, as I discuss below. In his discussion of the criteria of 'knowledge and understanding' Peters indirectly implies that a teacher's consideration of the education of the individual involves considering more than learners' mere positive acquisition of knowledge and skills. He explains that the learner's ability to give correct answers in each of the differentiated realms of knowledge that were deemed 'worthwhile' does not suffice to qualify him as educated:

> It is possible for a man to know a lot of history, in the sense that he can give correct answers to questions in classrooms and in examinations, without ever developing a historical sense. For instance he might fail to connect his knowledge of the Industrial Revolution with what he sees when visiting Manchester or the Welsh Valleys. We might describe such a man as knowledgeable but we would never describe him as 'educated'; for 'education' implies that a man's outlook is *transformed* by what he knows (Peters, 1967, p. 7, emphasis added).

Peters' explanation implies that the individual who has memorised information in the form of facts, or has learned by rote and merely acquired 'inert' knowledge, lacks the type of understanding of what he has learned that affects how he sees the world. As Robert Dearden explains of Peters' model, the knowledge and understanding that one acquires through education 'are ingredients in one's perception and revelatory of reality' (Dearden, 1986, p. 71). For Peters, to say that learning and knowledge must affect the way one sees the world and *transform* one's perspective on the world has implications for the manner of teaching he wishes to rule out of his definition of teaching. On his view, when teaching is an educational practice, it cannot merely consist in the transmission of knowledge as inert facts and information that the learner receives passively, only to repeat back with accuracy.

With respect to the criteria of educational processes, Peters defines teaching positively in connection with his concept of 'education as initiation'.[9] On Peters' model, teaching is connected to the initiation of others in two respects. First, teaching is 'initiating', as in setting in motion, the learning processes of another person. As Peters writes, 'the tasks of the teacher consist in the employment of various methods to get learning processes going' (Peters, 1967, p. 3; see also 1966, p. 38). Second, teaching involves initiating others in the sense of getting them 'on the inside' of the differentiated modes of human thought and awareness (see Peters 1966, e.g. p. 31). It is this sense of teaching that Peters refers to when he says, 'the learner is initiated by the teacher into something which he has to master, know, or remember' (Peters, 1967, p. 3).

Peters' notion of getting the learner from the 'outside' to the 'inside' of thought and knowledge is central to his understanding the role of the teacher in the learner's transformation through education. However, as I have pointed out thus far, Peters' connections between the ideas of transformation and education have primarily focused on his talking about transformation as a *result* of education. He emphasises that a 'transformed perspective' is a result of education that the teacher should in some way be initiating and seeking out in the learner. But what does this process involve for the learner as the one who is being educated and transformed?

WORLD AS OTHER: TRANSFORMATIVE ENCOUNTERS WITH THE WORLD AS A CHALLENGE TO TEACHER AND LEARNER

The notion of an individual's education as a transformational process has in particular been a theme in the German tradition of educational philosophy brought forth in the idea of *Bildung*. Although Peters' leaves many questions open about his concept of transformation, he does provide some insight into what this process involves in a way that connects to the idea of negativity in learning. Before looking to Peters on this connection, I will point out a few central aspects of the notion of *Bildung* that relate to his work.

Jörg Ruhloff (1993) points out that as far back as the Greek Sophist and Socratic traditions, the category *Bildung* has been utilised to delimit problems of the legitimacy of our basic human dispositions. He explains, '*Bildung*, as a category', thematises and calls into question the apparent self-evidence of 'our perceptions, interpretations, feelings, needs and wishes, our ways of communicating, acting and interacting as well as our intergenerational forms of socialisation, upbringing, and instruction' (Ruhloff, 1993, p. 176).

Questions of how human beings move beyond primary modes of perception and understanding, and with what aims in mind, have become central to theories of *Bildung* in the German tradition of educational philosophy. In his writings on *Bildung*, Wilhelm von Humboldt took up the idea that the world we encounter is something from which we can actively and passively learn. In his short fragment entitled 'Theory of *Education* of Mankind', Humboldt describes *Bildung* as dependent upon the most manifold, 'most general, most free, and most animated interplay between the self and the world' through which both the self and the world change (Humboldt, 1969a, p. 235, see also Humboldt, 1969b p. 64).[10] Humboldt explains that a human being's inner growth and flourishing rely upon this world being something other than himself; the world is thus '*NichtMensch*' (Humboldt, 1969a, p. 235). Humboldt illustrates that inner growth and change is dependent upon encounters with the otherness of the world as follows: just as mere abilities can be developed only in interaction with objects, and just as thoughts can be sustained only in reference to substance, 'so man needs a world outside himself' (Humboldt, 1969b p. 235). Our encounters with the world are transformative in that they are mediated by 'self-alienation', that is, alienation from our taken-for-granted and habitual self-understandings that arises out of recognition of their limits, and a 'return' to ourselves with new perspective and new understanding (compare Humboldt, 1969a, p. 237; see also Reichenbach, 2002). Thus, the 'interplay' Humboldt speaks of cannot be captured in an understanding of the mind as an autopoietic system interacting with itself; rather, it involves the human being's confrontation with an external world that potentially resists his attempts at change and transformation (Meyer-Drawe, 1999).[11]

The philosopher J. F. Herbart (1806/1902) developed a theory of *Bildung* that took account of the fact that the world as 'other' can either help or hinder an individual's education and growth. Herbart's central educational concern was that without the opportunity for free exchange and educative interplay with the world, the learner could develop narrowly and remain in one-sided familiar ways of thinking and acting. He develops a theory of education that inquires into how educators can counteract one-sided and narrow-minded development. On his view, education can bring about two forms of transformation within the individual, one cognitive and one moral. The educator has the task of facilitating cognitive transformation by expanding the learner's 'circle of thought' (*Gedankenkreis*) to incorporate differentiated forms of knowledge and participation. He has the task of facilitating the learner's moral transformation by fostering the learner's reflective self-critique of his own motives and norms of action (Herbart, 1806/1965). For Herbart, the educator is necessary to initiate and cultivate the learner's expansion and critical self-relation, but it is ultimately the learner who decides if, and to what extent, he will *transform* his own old habits and routines and create new understandings and new interests. To this end, Herbart emphasised that the individual learner is the educator's 'point of orientation' (*Indizpunkt*) in all judgements about the efficacy of pedagogical interaction (ibid.; see also English, 2007a).

This connection to *Bildung* allows us to bring forth the idea that in processes of education there is always another 'other' for both teacher and learner, that is, the world, with which the learner learns to engage and find his way around in ways different than that of the teacher.[12] It is unclear to what extent Peters saw his own account of education as in any way connected to this tradition of *Bildung*, but he does address the issue of the learner's confrontation with the otherness of the world and its connection to education. Without reference to Herbart, Peters takes a similar approach to the issue. Early in *Ethics and Education*, he notes the possibility of the individual's narrow, limited and undifferentiated development and emphasises throughout his work that the learning individual needs to be initiated into the differentiated forms of knowledge, awareness and practices that make up the tradition of human thought and activity (Peters, 1966, pp. 47f.). As mentioned above, for Peters this process involves an educator who can facilitate the learner's transition from the 'outside' to the 'inside' of these differentiated modes of human thought and activity. Although Peters remains relatively vague about the individual's process of moving from the 'outside' to the 'inside', his thematisation of learning through the interaction between the child and the world gives insight into his understanding of the transformational aspect of education.

Peters acknowledges that individuals can learn without a teacher, such that the concept of learning is not dependent on the concept of teaching in the same way that that of teaching is on learning. However, his characterisation of the individual's process of development illustrates the problems of learning about the shared world without the teacher as guide and initiator. The shared world, according to Peters, is an 'impersonal' world common to both teacher and learner and made up of a public inheritance comprised of the 'content that is handed on' from generation to generation and 'the criteria by reference to which that content is criticized and developed' (1966, p. 52). The child begins life 'on the outside' of this world, to use Peters' terms, and initially encounters the world without knowledge, language and understanding of human relationships. As Peters puts this, the world of objects appears fixed to the child; few things are for the child's moulding and manipulation (ibid.). On Peters' view, the world of human interaction also appears fixed. Quoting Durkheim, he points out that in the early stages of the child's life, the social world of human interaction, with its rules and set modes of conduct appears to the learner as things (*comme les choses*) that cannot be altered (ibid.).

Following Peters' thinking on the child's development, one could say that the extent to which the child experiences things and human interaction as fixed and unalterable is the extent to which the child is 'on the outside'. In other words, the child does not understand what choices he has or how to participate in and contribute to the strange world he encounters. What is involved in the child's process of getting on the 'inside' of learning? Peters gives initial insight into the child's process of getting from the outside to the inside of this world in his article, 'Education and Seeing What is There'. There he emphasises that the child learns about himself and the world through confrontations with otherness. As Peters explains, in the child's interaction with the world of things, the child comes to know the 'natural order' and learns to distinguish between 'what is real' and 'what is imaginary' and begins to grasp 'causal connections in nature' that are outside of his control and independent of his wishes (Peters, 1973, p. 118). Similarly, as Peters explains, the child comes to know the 'moral order' as distinct from the 'natural order', though often equally out of synch with his 'natural wants and wishes' (ibid.). In these encounters with other people, the child learns to begin to take the 'point of view of the other' into consideration (ibid.).

Though these confrontations take different forms, one with the natural order, one with the moral order of human beings, what is common to them, as Peters is correct to point out, is that both often involve the individual's *resistance* to change, out of fear or inability to go beyond his interests, and both involve learning about the self through encounters with otherness.[13] However, Peters pays little attention to the question of how the child comes from the stage of resistance, where his experience begins, to the stage of new knowledge, in which he realises the difference between himself and the other as external world, or as other human being. How does the learner experience this difference and distinction between his own expectations of the situation and what is possible within the limits of the situation? This is a question of how learning takes place. Though Peters tends to skip over this question, *Ethics and Education* does provide an important insight into his thinking on the matter. In his explanation of the teacher's obligation to recognise the individuality of the learner, he notes that the learner's process of learning and coming to know the world entails experimentation that can involve the learner's 'misdirected ventures' and 'inchoate formulations' of thoughts and feelings (Peters, 1966, p. 59). In this way, Peters emphasises that mistakes are constitutive of learning:

> People learn by committing themselves and finding out where they are mistaken. Much can be done to anticipate criticism by rehearsals in the imagination. But there is a sense in which no one quite knows what he thinks or feels until he has made a view his own by identifying himself with it and defending it in public (ibid.).[14]

There is a certain pragmatism to Peters' account of learning here. He is pointing out that learning processes involve trying out possible ways of being in the world, committing tentatively to certain beliefs and practices, and then, based on the consequences of those beliefs and practices, deciding what one thinks and wants to do. As suggested by this account of learning, through (tentative) commitments learners come to see how their beliefs and actions fit into, or fail to fit into, the shared world.

Peters' point here almost seems so commonsensical that its significance for education may be taken for granted. We commonly speak of 'learning from our mistakes'. But this point is significant for two reasons. First, he is making clear that the teacher must address the individuality of the learner by recognising that, while both teacher and learner are embedded in a strange world, the learner, who is still finding his way to the inside of this world, experiences this world *differently* than the teacher. This difference lies in the fact that the teacher is more familiar with the traditions of human thought and knowledge, but also that he or she knows how to call the validity of thought and knowledge into question. Teaching the learner about the shared world involves helping him find his mistakes by questioning him about his ideas and presuppositions, and in turn helping him to take on 'the questioner in his own mind' (Peters, 1967, p. 20).[15]

Second, he underscores the fact that 'mistakes' are an essential part of the learning process, a statement that points to the discontinuity and negativity constitutive of all learning processes. However, my central contention is that he does not go far enough in analysing this process and thereby overlooks what is involved in 'finding one's mistakes'. What happens *between* the learner's commitment to do or say something in the world and his found mistake? And, what happens when a mistake is found, but the learner does not know how to correct it? How does the learner move from the located mistake to new knowledge and new abilities? What changes in the process of learning when there is no clear right or wrong answer, such that the question of a mistake is out of place?

These questions concern learning as it connects to encounters with the world of objects or with human beings. Both are mediated by the negativity of encounters with otherness, and both involve pre-reflective and reflective forms of negativity of experience. For example, when a student in a science class decides to mix chemicals in a certain way and does not achieve the expected result, then there is initially an interruption in the smooth path of his experience. At this point, he can either choose to find his mistake or not. If he does, then he is engaging in a reflective process of inquiry into the pre-reflective negativity. In the context of social learning the situation looks different. If a student naively *commits* to a controversial viewpoint about a class novel, thinking that the class will agree with her, and then is confronted with unexpected disagreement about her views, she also experiences these initially as an interruption. However, this situation of learning is more complex as there may not be a clear-cut mistake in her thinking, only a sign of a differing viewpoint.

My point is not to say that Peters would not agree with the difference in these situations. Rather it is to emphasise that he tends to oversimplify the process of learning and thus overlooks the pre-reflective negativity of experience constitutive of learning processes. One could say that Dewey draws out the experience of 'finding the mistake' and thereby stretches out and magnifies the part of experience that Peters glosses over. Oddly enough, Peters criticises Dewey for emphasising problem-solving in learning (see Peters, 1981). What he did not see was that, for Dewey, there is more to the process of learning than finding and solving problems. Rather, for Dewey, the productive and educative aspect of this process of learning is that in the reflective process of inquiry, one can decide to change old habits, discover new ways of treating people, find different ideas and ways of thinking about the world that were previously beyond one's grasp, either for oneself alone or for the society as a whole.

IMPLICATIONS FOR TEACHING

According to the view I have put forth here, transformational learning always necessitates the individual's *inward* and *outward* turn. The inward turn happens when the individual begins to reflectively think about the pre-reflective interruption in his experience and thereby to make it into a conscious moment that he can examine. The outward turn involves the changed outlook on the world that arises out of coming to understand oneself—one's wishes, one's capabilities, one's questions, one's needs, one's feelings and one's failures—and the world differently or otherwise than before the learning experience. This new understanding is not necessarily a gain or a loss, though it can feel like either or both to the experiencer, but primarily a different way of seeing and being in the world. In this way, the negativity of experience in learning has many implications for pedagogical interaction. Here, I would like to name three.

(i)   By recognising the negativity of experience constitutive of learners' experience, teachers can begin to orient themselves differently towards them. Teachers can recognise that interruptions in the learners' experiences are part of understanding if and how they are learning. This orients the teacher's practice on recognising the confusion, perplexity, frustration or doubt, or also surprise and awe accompanying learners' experiences of the new and unfamiliar. These moments of confusion or awe occur between the wrong and right answers in the gray zones of thinking and learning. In this way, a central aspect of teaching becomes examining the process and not simply the results of learning. This requires the ability to see if learners are thinking, and how the learners' thought relates to the results of learning.

(ii)   The negativity of experience involved in learning is also part of teacher's experiences. Teacher's experiences are mediated by a double-negativity (Benner and English, 2004). In other words, in teaching, teachers are confronted with the interruptions in learners' experiences that interrupt their own process of teaching. When teachers begin to reflect on the interruptions in their own practice—that is, the unexpected questions and challenges that arise within their interaction with learners—they begin to learn about themselves as teachers and learn how to teach (see, on this point, Meyer-Drawe, 1987; Burbules, 1997; Hansen, 1997; English, 2007b). They learn where the learners' experience needs expansion or modification and how to help learners find ways out of perplexing situations.

(iii)   The otherness of the world and the negative experiences learners encounter are not necessarily educative. These factors may resist the child's attempts to learn about it and potentially change it. To make the world educative, teachers have to help learners take it apart and explore realms that otherwise may be arbitrarily ignored or intentionally avoided out of fear or lack of interest. To do this, teachers have to learn to cultivate situations in which the learners become productively confused, perplexed and puzzled (on this point see, Passmore, 1967; Hare, 2000). By teaching through questioning, teachers create openings in the learners' experience through which they can explore new ways of thinking and reflective acting. Teaching in this way relates to teaching as an inherently moral practice; through the teacher's questions, learners begin to question their own beliefs, think critically and begin to search for new knowledge and to take a stance.

This type of teaching opposes both models of teaching as 'pouring in' to a passively receptive learner and models of progressive education that see the learner as the primary arbiter of what is to count as worth doing. Peters was correct to reject both of these models of teacher-learner interaction. However, he did not go far enough in recognizing the intersubjective space 'between' teacher and learner, where teachers recognise how the child co-constitutes the pedagogical situation. As Meyer-Drawe writes, 'the child sees not "nothing", he also doesn't see everything, he sees things otherwise' (Meyer-Drawe, 1987, p. 72). To see that the child sees things otherwise involves recognition that the voice of the learner is one that educators, at times, have to help them find.

What helping the learner find their voice might mean for the cultivation of transformational learning processes can be illustrated using a passage from the literary theorist Edward Said's autobiography. He paints the picture of his memorable experience with a high school English teacher, Baldwin, as follows:

During the first weeks Baldwin assigned us an essay topic of a very unpromising sort: 'On Lighting a Match'. I dutifully went to the library and proceeded through encyclopedias, histories of industry, chemical manuals in search of what matches were; I then more or less systematically summarised and transcribed what I had found and, rather proud of what I had compiled, turned it in. Baldwin almost immediately asked me to come and see him during his office hours, which was an entirely novel concept, since VC's [Victoria College's] teachers never had offices, let alone office hours. Baldwin's office was a cheery little place with postcard-covered walls, and as we sat next to each other on two easy chairs he complimented me on my research. 'But is that the most interesting way to examine what happens when someone lights a match? What if he's trying to set a fire to a forest, or light a candle in a cave, or, metaphorically, illuminate the obscurity of a mystery like gravity, the way Newton did?' For literally the first time in my life, a subject was opened up for me by a teacher in a way that I immediately and excitedly responded to. What had previously been repressed and stifled in academic study—repressed in order that thorough and correct answers be given to satisfy a standardized syllabus and a routinized exam designed essentially to show off powers of retention, not critical or imaginative facilities—was awakened, and the complicated process of intellectual discovery (and self-discovery) has never stopped since (Said, 1999, p. 231).

The teacher here brings the student out of the type of strategic learning he has become accustomed to, which has only involved looking for the prescribed and pre-defined right ways of doing things according to the teacher's and the school's pre-conceived notions of correctness. His teacher is now asking him to think in some way differently than he had before, to find a voice that is different than the one he had grown accustomed to expressing. In this case, the voice he has been accustomed to expressing has been restricting and confining his way of thinking about the world. The student learns through this interaction in a way that involves the negativity of disillusionment, of the sort that opens up and liberates thinking. He experiences negativity in a way that rearranges, restructures and transforms his entire thinking about what is possible in literary imagination, in self-understanding and within the teacher-learner relation.

ON THE INDISPENSABILITY OF PHILOSOPHY OF EDUCATION FOR TEACHER EDUCATION

The foregoing discussion has implications for how we understand the role of philosophy of education in the education of teachers. For learners to experience the type of transformation Said describes in his own learning history, we must teach teachers how to cultivate such transformations. Thus, learning to teach involves more than learning a subject well: it entails learning to understand and cultivate the interruptions that arise in learners' experiences with the unknown and unfamiliar, such that learners can transform these into something new. On this understanding of teaching, teaching is a certain type of *experimental* practice. Peters' discussion of the role of philosophy in teacher education is illuminating in its emphasis on the experimental aspect of teaching. Here, I would like to point out some central issues Peters brings up on this topic that I deem vital for us as we look to the future of philosophy of education in teacher education programmes.

Peters saw philosophy of education as central to understanding the fundamental questions of education. For this reason, he also viewed it as vital to the education of teachers, who were entering a practice that was interconnected to the education of another person and who would ultimately face the ethical concerns of this practice. He argues against the traditional apprenticeship model as the sole way of learning to teach, as it reproduces teachers with fixed teaching methods, who are unable to think critically about their practice (Peters, 1977, p. 135). He points out that this model is limited because it does not develop teachers who can deal effectively with the changing and varied conditions of modern society, which demand that teachers think critically about and reflect upon what they are doing and why. Peters writes: 'the question, therefore, is not whether a modern teacher indulges in philosophical reflection about what he is doing; it is rather whether he does it in a sloppy or in a rigorous manner' (p. 136). Peters' point is significant because he demonstrates that if pre-service teachers are not exposed to theoretical inquiry into the underlying questions and problems of education—that is, questions that go beyond the scope of knowing their subject—and consequently are not exposed to philosophical methods of analysing those problems, their growth as professional teachers, and thereby their ability to cultivate learning, will be limited in practice.

In this context, Peters emphasises the need for philosophy of education to provide teachers with a way of seeing the connections between theory and practice, and of developing thereby a 'critical experimental attitude' towards teaching (pp. 145f.; see also pp. 165f.). To cultivate this attitude as teachers, Peters explains, teachers must learn to 'think on their feet and experiment with different ways of teaching different types of subjects to different types of children' (p. 165). The attitude Peters has in mind seems to be akin to what Aristotle called *phronesis*, or the art of making informed, wise decisions in the moment. It connects further to Herbart's (1802/1896) concept of 'pedagogical tact' as the ability to respond to educational situations in ways appropriate to the learner and the profession, and to notions of teaching as a 'reflective practice' developed out of Dewey's thinking (see, for example, Schön, 1991).

These views are not arbitrary. They are describing something inherent in the type of teaching that is educative for the learner. When teaching is educative, it is open to the negativity in learners' experiences and sees these moments as guides to where the learning process of this particular learner needs to continue. Within this interaction the learner is guiding the process insofar as it is the learner's perplexities, confusion, frustration that bring the teacher to question whether his plan for teaching still makes sense to follow, or whether he must change, modify or enhance his idea to meet the demand of the other. Peters emphasises that in learning to teach, teachers must also endure a '*transformation*' of their view of 'children, of [themselves], and of the situation in which [they] are acting' (Peters, 1977, p. 163).

Peters' emphasis is important, and it points to open questions for philosophy of education as it relates to questions of teaching. What is involved in the transformation of the teacher? How are we to understand the experimental structure of teaching processes? How can we teach teachers to have a critical experimental attitude towards their practice?

CONCLUSIONS

Peters does not adequately explicate the experimental aspect of teaching. Peters sees that teachers need to have the autonomy of professional judgment that allows them to thrive in an environment fraught with unpredictable and unforeseeable situations. However, he does not go as far as Dewey and later theorists to underscore that the connections between teaching and learning processes lie in the fact that both are imbued with unexpected, disjunctive, and uncertain moments in experience from which *both* teachers and learners learn. Without fully grasping the pre-reflective interruptions that pervades the learner's experiences, and the learner's reflective inner turn towards the interruption, the learner's education will not lead to the new transformed perspective that Peters emphasises. Experimentation in teaching on this account involves experimenting with methods not simply of getting learners to fixed ends, but of engaging learners in such a way that they can turn towards the interruptions in their experiences and in doing so explore and transform the ends of education.

What remains essential in Peters' account of teaching is that teaching is a theory-guided experimental practice. The idea that teaching is a thoroughly theory-guided profession has unfortunately now more than ever become more of a normative than a descriptive claim. At present, with the rise of standardised testing, the practice of teaching is in danger of becoming a mechanical operation. With the increase of standardised assessment and testing, teachers are increasingly being stripped of their authority and their ability to rely on their own professional judgment about how to successfully deal with the learners that they interact with on a daily basis, and the negativity of those learners' experiences. Under these circumstances, learners' experiences of frustration, confusion or difficulty in their encounters with the unfamiliar can only be assessed as either a sign of failure to reach the expected outcomes, or a problem of classroom management.

Philosophy of education needs to provide pre-service and in-service teachers with the theoretical guidance needed to assess the ethical situations they face in their attempt to educate future generations. Peters' work was essential for understanding the need for philosophy of education in teacher education programmes. Sadly, in the present situation, in many countries, as philosophy is decreasingly seen as an essential part of teacher education, it seems that teacher education programmes are suffering from historical amnesia. Peters' early justification for philosophy in the education of teachers reminds us of the need for philosophy of education to assist teachers in finding justifications and criteria for judgment of complex and challenging educational situations in schools. Whatever the popular approach of the day may be—for example child-centred, behaviourist or constructivist—philosophy of education uncovers the reasons, or lack of reasons, for the practical implementation of these approaches. Without the constant questioning and discussion of the central questions and of varied approaches to education, there is danger that educational ideas and theories are put into practice uncritically. Ultimately, it is the responsibility of society—and, specifically, of educators—to provide a space for philosophy of education so that it can consistently and critically assess old and new ideas and concepts of education. It is its responsibility also to allow pre-service and in-service teachers in teacher education and professionalisation programmes to productively contribute to this discussion.[16]

NOTES

1. All translations of the German texts cited in this chapter are mine unless I additionally reference an English translation of the text.
2. On the forms of aporia in the *Meno* and the educative meaning of doubt, see Burbules, 2000.

3. For an extensive discussion of the forms of negativity in this tradition and their relation to critique, see Benner, 2003 and Benner and English, 2004; see also Koch, 1995. On the moral aspects of negativity of experience, see Oser, 2005.
4. To simplify Dewey's theory of learning as learning by doing is to ignore the value placed on the interruptions in experience that arise in encounters with the unexpected and point to the pre-reflective beginning of learning.
5. For his discussion and critique of the idea of negativity in pragmatism and Dewey, see Buck, 1969, pp. 70f.
6. On this concept see also Buck, 1969, p. 44; Mitgutsch, 2008. Rumpf (2008) argues that openings for negativity in learning arise when we do not relativise the process of learning to its results. See also, Biesta's (2006) discussion of the connection between interruption and education; Haroutunian-Gordon (2003) underscores the educative significance of interruptions in listening in classroom dialogue.
7. See in particular passages 515b–517b, in Plato, 1961b.
8. Peters emphasises that the question of what is worthwhile needs to be left open as a question to be dealt with in the on-going discussion about the aims of education (compare Peters, 1967, p. 5; 1966, p. 25). See also Martin's (2009) related discussion of Peters' theory of moral justification as it pertains to the justification of educational interests and aims.
9. In his most succinct definition of education, Peters defines education as 'initiation into activities or modes of thought and conduct that are worthwhile' (Peters, 1966, p. 55).
10. On Humboldt and *Bildung* see also Peukert, 2000; Løvlie and Standish, 2002; Benner, 2008.
11. See also Benner's (2008) discussion of learning from the other.
12. An interesting point to note is that in German when talking about the *other*, it is immediately clear in the definite article whether that 'other' is a person or a thing. The other as world (*Welt*) takes the neutral definite article, so that it is referred to as *das Andere*, and the other as person takes a gendered definite article so that it is referred to as either masculine *der* or feminine, *die Andere*. One way of dealing with this problem in English is to use *Other* for persons, and use *other* for things. Peters distinguishes between both types of other in various ways, including talking about the 'natural order' or the 'social order'. I make clear in the discussion that follows which one I am referring to by using Peters' terminology.
13. See Peters, 1973, pp. 109f., on fear and wishes as part of the human condition.
14. See also 1967, p. 20 for Peters' emphasis on practical experience being required for judgment.
15. Though Peters and Herbart have certain similarities that I have pointed out, I think they differ on this point in that Herbart did not emphasise the role of questioning in instruction as strongly as Peters does.
16. I would like to thank Paul Standish, the editors Stefaan Cuypers and Christopher Martin, and also William Hare for their valuable feedback on earlier drafts of this chapter.

REFERENCES

Benner, D. (2003) Kritik und Negativität. Ein Versuch zur Pluralisierung von Kritik in Erziehung, Pädagogik und Erziehungswissenschaft, *Zeitschrift für Pädagogik*, 46, pp. 96–110.

Benner, D. (2008) Der Andere und Das Andere als Problem und Aufgabe der Erziehung und Bildung, in: D. Benner, *Bildungstheorie und Bildungsforschung* (Paderborn, Ferdinand Schöningh).

Benner, D. and English, A. (2004) Critique and Negativity. Towards the Pluralization of Critique in Educational Practice, Theory and Research, *Journal of Philosophy of Education*, 38.3, pp. 409–28.

Biesta, G. J. J. (2006) *Beyond Learning* (Boulder, CO, Paradigm).

Buck, G. (1969) *Lernen und Erfahrung* (Stuttgart, Kohlhammer).

Burbules, N. C. (1997) Teaching and the Tragic Sense of Education, in: N. C. Burbules and D. Hansen (eds) *Teaching and its Predicaments* (Boulder, CO, Westview Press), pp. 163–74.

Burbules, N. C. (2000) Aporias, Webs, and Passages: Doubt as an Opportunity to Learn, *Curriculum Inquiry*, 30.2, pp. 171–87.

Dearden, R. F. (1986) Education, Training and the Preparation of Teachers, in: D. Cooper (ed.) *Education, Values and Mind: Essays for R.S. Peters* (London, Routledge and Kegan Paul Ltd).

Dewey, J. (1916/1985) *Democracy and Education*, in *The Middle Works*, vol. 9 (Carbondale, IL, Southern Illinois University Press).

Dewey, J. (1933/1989) *How We Think*, in *The Later Works (1925–1953)*, vol. 8 (Carbondale, IL, Southern Illinois University Press).

Dewey, J. (1938/1991) *Logic: A Theory of Inquiry*, in *The Later Works*, vol. 12 (Carbondale, IL, Southern Illinois University Press).

English, A. (2005) Negativity and the New in John Dewey's Theory of Learning and Democracy: Towards a Renewed Look at Learning Cultures, *Zeitschrift für Erziehungswissenschaft*, 8.1, pp. 28–37.

English, A. (2007a) Die experimentelle Struktur menschliches Lehrens und Lernens: Versuche über die Rolle negativer Erfahrung in den Lehr-Lerntheorien Herbart und Dewey, in: R. Bolle and G. Weigand (eds) *Johann Friedrich Herbart. 200 Jahre Allgemeine Pädagogik* (Berlin, Waxmann), pp. 97–112.

English, A. (2007b) Interrupted Experiences: Reflection, Listening and *Negativity* in the Practice of Teaching, *Learning Inquiry*, Special Issue on Listening and Reflecting, L. Waks (ed.), 1.2, pp. 133–42.

English, A. (2008) Wo 'doing' aufhört und 'learning' anfängt: John Dewey über Lernen und die Negativität im Erfahrung und Denken, in: K. Mitgutsch, E. Sattler, K. Westphal and I. M. Breinbauer (eds) *Dem Lernen auf der Spur* (Stuttgart, Klett-Cotta), pp. 145–58.

Gadamer, H-G. (1960/1997) *Truth and Method*, J. Weinheimer and D. G. Marshall, trans. (New York, Continuum).

Hansen, D. (1997) Being a Good Influence, in: N. C. Burbules and D. Hansen (eds) *Teaching and its Predicaments* (Boulder, CO, Westview Press), pp. 163–74.

Hare, W. (2000) Reflections on the Teacher's Tasks: Contributions from Philosophy of Education in the 20th Century, *Educational Research and Perspectives*, 27.2, pp. 1–23.

Haroutunian-Gordon, S. (2003) Listening—in a Democratic Society, in: K. Alston (ed.) *Philosophy of Education Yearbook* (Urbana, IL, Philosophy of Education Society), pp. 1–18.

Herbart, J. F. (1806/1965) Allgemeine Pädagogik aus dem Zweck der Erziehung abgeleitet, in: W. Asmus (ed.) *Johann Friedrich Herbart Pädagogische Schriften* (Düsseldorf, Helmut Kuepper).

Herbart, J. F. (1806/1902) *The Science of Education*, H. M. Falkin and E. Falkin, trans. (Boston, MA, D.C.H. Heath and Co).

Herbart, J. F. (1802/1896) Introductory Lecture to students in pedagogy, in J. F. Herbart, *ABC of Sense-Perception, and Minor Pedagogical Works*, W. Eckoff, trans. (New York, D. Appleton), pp. 13–28.

Humboldt, W. (1969a) Theorie der Bildung des Menschen, in *Werke in Fünf Bände*, vol. 1 (Darmstadt, Wissenschaftliche Buchgesellschaft).

Humboldt, W. (1969b) Ideen zu einem Versuch, die Gränzen der Wirksamkeit des Staats zu bestimmen, in *Werke in Fünf Bände*, vol. 1 (Darmstadt, Wissenschaftliche Buchge-sellschaft).

Kerdeman, D. (2003) Pulled Up Short: Challenging Self-Understanding as a Focus of Teaching and Learning, *Journal of Philosophy of Education*, 37.2, pp. 294–308.

Koch, L. (1995) *Bildung und Negativität. Grundzüge einer negativen Bildungstheorie* (Weinheim, Deutsche Studien Verlag).

Løvlie, L. and Standish, P. (2002) Introduction: *Bildung* and the Idea of a Liberal Education, *Journal of Philosophy of Education*, 36.3, pp. 317–40.

Martin, C. (2009) R.S. Peters and Jürgen Habermas: Presuppositions of Practical Reason and Educational Justice, *Educational Theory*, 59.1, pp. 1–16.

Meyer-Drawe, K. (1982) Phänomenologische Bemerkungen zum Problem menschliches Lernens, *Vierteljahrsschrift für wissenschaftliche Pädagogik*, 58.4, pp. 510–24.

Meyer-Drawe, K. (1984) Lernen als Umlernen–Zur Negativität des Lernprozesses, in: K. Meyer-Drawe and W. Lippitz (eds) *Lernen und seine Horizonte. Phänomenologische Konzeptionen menschlichen Lernens–didaktische Konsequenzen* (Frankfurt am Main, Scriptor), pp. 19–45.

Meyer-Drawe, K. (1987) Die Belehrbarkeit des Lehrenden durch den Lerneden—Fragen an den Primat des Pädagogischen Bezugs, in: W. Lippitz and K. Meyer-Drawe (eds) *Kind und Welt: Phänomenologische Studien zur Pädagogik* (Frankfurt am Main, Athenaeum Verlag), pp. 63–73.

Meyer-Drawe, K. (1996) Vom anderen Lernen. Phänomenologische Betrachtungen in der Pädagogik, in M. Borrelli and J. Ruhloff (eds) *Deutsche Gegenwartspädagogik, Vol. II* (Baltmannsweiler, Schneider-Verlag Hohengehren), pp. 85–99.

Meyer-Drawe, K. (1999) Die Herausforderung durch die Dinge: Das Andere im Lernprozess, *Zeitschrift für Pädagogik*, 46, pp. 329–36.

Meyer-Drawe, K. (2003) Lernen als Erfahrung, *Zeitschrift für Erziehungswissenschaft*, 6.4, pp. 505–14.

Mitgutsch, K. (2008) Lernen durch Erfahren: Über Bruchlinien im Vollzug des Lernens, in: K. Mitgutsch, E. Sattler, K. Westphal and I. M. Breinbauer (eds) *Dem Lernen auf der Spur* (Stuttgart, Klett-Cotta), pp. 263–77.

Oser, F. (2005) Negatives Wissen und Moral, Special Issue Erziehung-Bildung-Negativität, *Zeitschrift für Pädagogik*, 49, pp. 171–81.

Passmore, J. (1967) On Teaching to be Critical, in: R. S. Peters (ed.) *The Concept of Education* (London, Routledge and Kegan Paul Ltd.), pp. 192–212.

Peters, R. S. (1966) *Ethics and Education* (London, George Allen and Unwin Ltd).

Peters, R. S. (1967) What is an Educational Process?, in: R. S. Peters (ed.) *The Concept of Education* (London, Routledge and Kegan Paul Ltd).

Peters, R. S. (1973) Education and Seeing What is There, in *Authority, Responsibility and Education* (London, George Allen and Unwin Ltd).

Peters, R. S. (1977) *Education and the Education of Teachers* (London, Routledge and Kegan Paul Ltd).

Peters, R. S. (1981) John Dewey's Philosophy of Education, in: R. S. Peters (ed.) *Essays on Educators* (London, George Allen and Unwin Ltd).

Peukert, H. (2000) Reflexionen über die Zukunft von Bildung, *Zeitschrift für Pädagogik*, 46.4, pp. 507–24.

Plato (1961a) Meno, in: E. Hamilton and H. Cairns (eds) *The Collected Dialogues of Plato, Including the Letters* (New York, Pantheon Books).

Plato (1961b) Republic, in: E. Hamilton and H. Cairns (eds) *The Collected Dialogues of Plato, Including the Letters* (New York, Pantheon Books).

Reichenbach, R. (2002) On Irritation and Transformation: A-Teleological *Bildung* and its Significance for the Democratic Form of Living, *Journal of Philosophy of Education*, 36.3, pp. 409–19.

Rousseau, J-J (1762/1979) *Emile or On Education*, A. Bloom, trans. (New York, Basic Books).

Ruhloff, J. (1993) Bildung—nur ein Paradigma im pädagogischen Denken?, in *Skepsis und Widerstreit: Neue Beiträge zur skeptisch-transzendentalkritischen Pädagogik* (Sankt Augustin, Academia Verlag), pp. 173–84.

Rumpf, H. (2008) Lernen als Vollzug und als Erledigung—Sich einlassen auf Befremdliches oder: Über Lernvollzüge ohne Erledigungsdruck, in: K. Mitgutsch, E. Sattler, K. Westphal and I. M. Breinbauer (eds) *Dem Lernen auf der Spur* (Stuttgart, Klett-Cotta), pp. 21–32.

Said, E. W. (1999) *Out of Place: A Memoir* (New York, Vintage Books).

Schön, D. (1991) *The Reflective Practitioner* (Aldershot, Ashgate).

Standish, P. (2007) Moral Education, Liberal Education and the Voice of the Individual, in: K. Roth and I. Gur-Ze'ev (eds) *Education in the Era of Globalization* (Dordrecht, Springer).

6

R. S. Peters' Normative Conception of Education and Educational Aims

MICHAEL S. KATZ

Few analytic philosophers have contributed more substantively to advancing the field of philosophy of education than R. S. Peters. Moreover, none has emphasized 'the concept of education' more than he did. In addition, few philosophers of education have done more important work to elucidate its meaning, its connection to other key concepts and its logical terrain than has Peters. In this chapter, I will try to highlight the importance of that analytical contribution in three ways: 1) by explicating Peters' conception of philosophy of education as a field of philosophy and by explaining his approach to the philosophical analysis of concepts—its purpose and its limitations; 2) by highlighting several (normative) features of Peters' conception of education, while suggesting a couple of oversights; and 3) by briefly suggesting how Peters' analysis might be used to reinvigorate a conversation on how we might educate citizens for the 21st century.

I THE NATURE OF PHILOSOPHY OF EDUCATION AND CONCEPTUAL ANALYSIS

When R. S. Peters edited *The Philosophy of Education* in 1973, analytic efforts to make philosophy of education into a respected field for philosophers were in their infancy. While the United States could claim having its own analytic champions in Israel Scheffler, James McClellan, Thomas Green, Paul Komisar, Leonard Waks and others, Peters sought to lead British colleagues such as Paul Hirst, Richard Pring, D. W. Hamlyn, John White and Patricia White in making philosophy of education more intellectually respectable (Waks, 2008; 1968). Of the early British philosophers of education in the 1960s, R.S. Peters became its foremost leader, committed to enhancing the field's philosophical work and improving its stature as a field of inquiry.

How did Peters conceive of the field of philosophy of education? Although Peters did not doubt that philosophy of education was a 'branch of philosophy', he did not see it as having a separate status apart from established branches of philosophy such as epistemology, ethics, and the

Reading R. S. Peters Today, First Edition. Stefaan E. Cuypers and Christopher Martin.
Chapters © 2011 The Authors. Editorial organization © 2011 Philosophy of Education Society of Great Britain. Published 2011 by Blackwell Publishing Ltd.

philosophy of mind. For him, philosophy of education was a field of philosophy that would draw on established branches of philosophy to illuminate critical concepts and issues central to the domain of education—concepts such as education, freedom, rights, teaching, learning, understanding, the curriculum, etc. (Peters, 1973a, p. 2). Peters believed that philosophical work in other fields such as political philosophy, ethics, and the philosophy of mind had to be applied appropriately to educational issues, not in a mechanical way, but in a way that acknowledged the unique qualities of the educational context. Thus, in his preface to *The Philosophy of Education*, he writes about the notion of 'punishment' applied to school settings:

> Most of the work on 'punishment', for instance, has been based on the paradigm of the operation of the legal system. When applied to problems of children in school, there are important differences as well as similarities. Punishment presupposes responsibility for action. But at what stage are children fully responsible for their actions? The school, too, is primarily concerned with education which suggests some kind of improvement in people as its rationale. Must this radically transform arguments which attempt to justify the punishment of children? (pp. 2–3)

However, Peters realised that with a concept like that of 'education' philosophers could not take advantage of established work in philosophy. Such work, he argued, did not yet exist. From this vantage point, he argued that philosophers of education must till new conceptual ground and map out new logical terrain. Peters spelled out what he thinks this conceptual mapping must consist of for the notion of education.

> There are many issues ... on which no work exists at all. What, for instance, is meant by 'education'. This is a question which has not been tackled in any precise way before. Perhaps, it is not amenable to precise analysis. But this cannot be claimed in advance of making an attempt to give an analysis of it. Suppose it is claimed that 'education' involves at least the development of knowledge and understanding. There is then the queer anomaly ... that there is great concentration of work by philosophers on 'knowledge', but precious little on 'understanding'. 'Education' also implies some kind of learning. But there has been little work done by philosophers on the concept of learning and still less on activities such as those of 'teaching', 'imparting', and 'indoctrinating', by means of which learning is promoted (p. 3).

Thus, Peters, it seems, viewed himself as leading others to create a carefully conceived conceptual landscape for careful, informed discussions about important educational issues.

With this view of his starting point, and given the unexcavated terrain of 'education' as a concept, how did Peters conceive of 'conceptual analysis'?

And how would he engage in the process? First, he did not think of the process as one of his early critics, John Woods did—as a rather tightly defined form of logical analysis, one which conforms very closely with the appropriate ways we ordinarily speak, such as how we speak of 'being a bachelor' (Woods, 1973, pp. 29–30). In Woods' paradigm, one spells out the necessary and sufficient conditions for using words properly in one of their senses. Thus, in his article 'The Aims of Education—A Conceptual Inquiry' (Peter, 1973b, henceforth AE) Peters responds to Woods' logical critique of his analysis of education:

> I don't take it to be the philosopher's job, with a concept like 'education', to formulate hard and fast, necessary and sufficient conditions which must always be satisfied if the word is to be used correctly. The point of approaching the concept as I did can be expressed as follows: We have developed certain ways of talking in which we use the word 'education' rather than 'training'. There are clear examples of when we would use one rather than the other: the stock example which I give is the difference between sex education and sex training. Now, given that a way of talking has emerged to mark such a difference, the point of doing what I did is to get clear about the distinctions that lie behind the words. Really, *the main point is to become clearer and clearer about the contours of the concepts which have emerged; we cannot pin them down with a definition* (AE, pp. 44; emphases added).

In criticising Peters' conception of the notion of 'aims of education', Woods argues that Peters provides essentially a *de facto* analysis of how people sometimes use the term 'educational aims' to achieve something far and distant, something that one might seek more specificity about. In response, Peters admits that if that is all he was doing, the analysis would be defective. However, he defends himself by claiming that what he has in mind is exploring the conceptual connections that reveal what he calls 'a more sophisticated notion of meaning'—not something that merely falls under its denotative sense (AE, p. 45).

Here, R. S. Peters implicitly invokes the Wittgensteinean notion of how we use concepts within a purposeful kind of talk, a 'language game'—this language game being viewed as a 'form of life'. Moreover, within this 'form of life', there are dominant ways of using words, and other ways that are 'derivative upon' or 'parasitic upon' these. In his earlier work, *Ethics and Education*, Peters explicitly invokes his debt to Wittgenstein:

> The uses of a word are not always related by falling under a definition as in geometry where definitions are provided for terms such as 'triangle'. Rather they form a 'family', united 'by a complicated network of similarities, overlapping and criss-crossing; sometimes overall similarities, sometimes similarities of detail' (Peters, 1966, p. 23; Wittgenstein, 1953, §32).

In doing conceptual analysis, Peters aims to make useful conceptual connections and illuminate the ways in which concepts are deeply embedded in our normal ways of thinking and talking; however, he does not seek to satisfy the 'ordinary language' purist by merely doing a 'de facto' analysis of the ways in which people do, in fact, generally speak. The main point, as he indicates, is '*to become clearer and clearer about the contours of the concepts which have emerged*' (emphases added).

This kind of analysis aims to elucidate important problems, eliminate conceptual confusion, and make the waters of serious educational discourse less opaque. Peters distinguishes conceptual analysis from philosophical justification. The latter seeks to provide compelling ethical arguments for why we should think of education in a certain way and what the content of that education should consist of.

For Peters, education is a concept with necessary normative connections built logically into it. Although he admits that sociologists and anthropologists may use the term 'education' in a value neutral way to refer to a cultural or social artifact, namely the systematic ways the culture transmits itself to future generations, he argues that even sociologists and anthropologists would acknowledge that, from the inside of the culture or society, people use the term as a normative concept (AE, p. 50). Its central use relies ineluctably on that the sense that in being educated, people are not merely changed, but are made 'better'. Even in his non-justificatory discussion of education, Peters puts some flesh on the bare bones of what education must consist of: for him, certain features constitute the very meaning of 'education': 1) it must initiate people into activities that are worth-while; 2) it must provide people with breadth and depth of knowledge and understanding; 3) it must dispose people to examine their beliefs and conduct critically, 4) it must make people willing to submit to the demands of reason in their efforts to discover what is true; 5) it must be conducted in morally unobjectionable ways; 6) it must enable people to enjoy some activities associated with it, in a non-instrumental way, for their own sake.

As I indicated earlier, Peters clearly seeks to distinguish between conceptual analysis—whose object is to illuminate the connections between concepts within a particular form of discourse—and philosophical justification, which aims to provide compelling ethical arguments for a substantive conception of what educational activities are 'worth-while' and why they are so. Peters provides several justificatory arguments for education in his *Ethics and Education* (see, for example, the contributions of Michael Hand and Christopher Martin to this book), but I will not focus my critique on those arguments, as others do in this volume. What I want to emphasize is that Peters is willing both to clarify and justify his conception of education and that he sees these tasks as fundamentally different, although related. Peters believed that one cannot know where to start one's justification of something without a clear-headed view of what it is that one is justifying.

II PETERS' CONCEPTION OF EDUCATION AND SOME OF ITS NORMATIVE IMPLICATIONS

Peters understood well that words acquire a life of their own in particular forms of discourse, within particular cultures and particular historical periods. For example, he understood that the term 'education' for much of its early history was used to refer to 'training or bringing up children'. But this broader pre-20th century usage also had 'education' referring to bringing up animals and plants. In these earlier senses, the connection of education to breadth and depth of knowledge was minimal. Thus, Peters' writes: 'The Latin word "educere" was usually, though not always used of *physical* development. In Silver Latin "educere" was used to the rearing of plants and animals as well as children. In English, the word "education" was originally used to talk in a very general ways about the bringing up of children and animals' (AE, p. 53). As Peters focuses on the etymological roots of the older, more generalised use of the education as 'training or bringing up', he notes how it is not closely connected with knowledge and understanding; but he appears to overlook, or at least deemphasize, education's central normative focus on what I would call '*proper child rearing*' (emphases added). Moreover, in some of its forms 'proper child rearing' had critical connections to knowledge and understanding, albeit different kinds of knowledge and understanding than those Peters emphasizes. For example, the early Puritans were so concerned that Puritan parents educate their children well, i.e. bring them up as 'good Puritans', that they passed compulsory education laws in Massachusetts Bay Colony in 1642 and 1648. These laws were designed to insure that all children learned to read (the Bible) and to understand the principles of Puritanism and the laws of the Commonwealth (Katz, 1976).

  In discussing contemporary policies aimed at parents in England, Judith Suissa has re-invoked the older notion of education as a form of proper child rearing (Suissa, 2009). Peters rightly concludes that education necessarily makes a person better by initiating her into a worth-while form of life. Thus, it is a fundamentally normative conception of education, not a value-neutral conception. But Peters' focus on the etymological roots of education as suggesting child-rearing is rather dismissive. Thus, he writes: 'Arguments from etymology, of course, establish very little. At best they provide clues which may be worthwhile to follow up. In this case, for instance, it seems the word originally had a very generalized meaning' (AE, p. 53). By discussing education as 'child rearing' in this way, Peters underemphasizes its critical normative force. In my view, his casual dismissal of child rearing as a form of normative education belies Peters' deep appreciation for how words inhabit historical contexts, contexts which give them social and political significance. For the Puritans, the failure to educate their children properly was a serious moral and legal offense; special offices of oversight were established to insure that the offense was not widespread. Today, dissatisfied with public schooling, increasing numbers of parents in the US are home schooling their children. Moreover, state-supported programs for parental education provide testimony to the normative importance parents attach to bringing their children up well—the older pre-20th century notion of schooling. Its older normative force remains significant, even if Peters has chosen to under-emphasize it.

R. S. Peters also notes another important dimension of how we often use the term 'education'—its modern linguistic narrowing to formal schooling. Thus, he writes:

> With the coming of industrialism, however, and the increasing demand for knowledge and skill consequent on it, 'education' became increasingly associated with 'schooling' and with the sort of training and instruction that went on in special institutions. This large scale change, culminating in the development of compulsory schooling for all, may well have brought about such a radical tightening up that we now only tend to use the word in connection with the development of knowledge and understanding (ibid.).

Although Peters acknowledges the emerging association of education and formal schooling, this acknowledgement is not central to his conceptual analysis, However, I believe it warrants some further discussion here because it obscures two important points: 1) the way in which schooling became the only socially legitimated form of education, and 2) the increasing possibility that schooling might be 'mis-educative' rather than educative (Illich, 1970). Peters suggested that we talk primarily of education as schooling because it relates to the development of knowledge and understanding. But another reason seems more critical. We naturally speak of 'education' as linguistically equivalent to 'schooling' because of the way society requires the symbols of educational achievement in schools—diplomas, certificates, and credentials—as necessary for entrance into, and competition within, the socio-economic system. Schooling has become not merely legally compulsory but socio-economically compulsory. In fact, the socio-economic compulsion underlying schooling gives the equation of 'education' with 'schooling' its social-political force (Katz, 2008). Thus, when we ask of someone 'Where did you get your education?', we recognise that society will recognise as legitimate only that kind of formal instruction in schools that has led to a diploma, certificate, or credential. In many industrialised societies, we often value what Thomas Green calls 'the secondary goods' of education—diplomas, certificates and credentials—as more than its primary goods—knowledge, skills and under-standings (Green, 1980).

Green has argued that schooling is not regulated primarily according to any philosophically enlightened view of what a moderately or well educated person should know or understand but rather on what society considers intolerable. The extraordinary regulation of literacy in the US through high stakes testing provides ample support for Green's claim—namely that we regulate schooling to reduce or eliminate the most intolerable social outcomes rather than to foster any elevated form of educational achievement. It is simply not tolerable to give high school diplomas to students who are either illiterate or barely literate, in math and reading.

The fact that education came to be associated with formal schooling is correct on its surface; but it obscures another obvious fact—that 'schooling' often has little to do with the kind of knowledge, understanding and perspective Peters associates with education. In fact, as we know, schools historically have often emphasized memorisation, recitation, and regurgitation of poorly understood bits of verbal information—leading not to the knowledge and understanding central to Peters' conception. Moreover, Donald Arnstine, a contemporary critic of schooling, has argued quite persuasively that contemporary schooling largely mis-educates students rather than educates them. (Arnstine, 1995) Why is schooling so often mis-educative? Simply because it does not cultivate the habits of thought and inquiry, reasonableness and curiosity, reflectiveness, and critical perspective that most would associate with developing an educated person.

Having digressed a bit, let us return to the heart of Peters' conceptual analysis of 'education'. Here one can differentiate between a word's becoming ambiguous and a word's being 'vague' in one of its uses. Ambiguity involves words having different meanings in their various uses. Thus, 'education,' because it has several meanings, remains ambiguous; we can refer to it as 'a field of study.' For example, we can ask someone what s/he is majoring in and get 'education' as an answer. We can also ask how much have we spent on 'education' in the US in the past year? In this question, 'education' denotes a system of schooling. But as a process or a set of processes, 'education' remains vague, not merely ambiguous. Its vagueness has to do with our uncertainty about the proper criteria for its use in one of its senses. This is where Peters' conceptual analysis provides the most force. For Peters, "education' 'cannot logically refer to a particular activity or process but must refer to a family of processes culminating in a person becoming educated and thus made better. The concept of education, as a family of processes, culminates in a person having an outlook and form of life that is in some way desirable (AE, p. 55).

In this sense, Peters' claims that 'education' is a normative term like 'reform' in that it would be a logical contradiction to say 'My son has been educated, but nothing desirable happened to him' just as it would be illogical to say 'my son has been reformed but has changed in no way for the better' (p. 15). Although education implies that one has been changed for the better by becoming educated, Peters emphasizes that what it means to be 'educated' remains vague, for the criteria for judging one to be educated will always be subject to debate. Here his insight remains quite powerful and right on the mark. In clarifying the notion of 'aims in education', he points out that those discussing aims are often asking for more specificity in what educators are actually striving for. Finally Peters argues that the criteria for considering someone well educated will remain largely indeterminate. He writes:

Education, then, like reform, has norms built into it, which generate the aims which educators strive to develop or attain. But the norms in question are highly indeterminate; for what constitutes a person becoming better or having a desirable outlook? Is it the development of critical awareness in the case of education? Or is it sensitivity to others and to significant form? (AE, p. 17).

Although Peters does sketch his own notion of what he thinks those criteria for being educated must include and also tries to justify what he regards as the essential curricular content of education, what seems critical to his conceptual analysis is his conclusion that the aims of education are indeterminate.

Let me summarise the core features of Peters' analysis. First, Peters emphasizes that the notion that education cannot refer to or denote any particular kind of process or activity. Second, Peters reminds us that 'education' like 'reform' is a normative term, one that is a special case of what Ryle calls an 'achievement verb'. He emphasizes that education, unlike other achievement verbs like winning, finding, remembering, etc. does not have a specific activity associated with it, but it must culminate in something of value. Third, Peters views education as an intentional set of processes, albeit not an individual activity. At its core, education aims to initiate people into a worth-while form of life. Fourth, education necessarily is associated with breadth and depth of knowledge and understanding. In being educated, individuals acquire the kind of knowledge and understanding that enables them to assess their choices of activities critically; it also provides them with intrinsic satisfaction as they pursue their chosen activities thoughtfully. Moreover, as Peters argues, an educated person will continue to pursue such life-enhancing activities when s/he is no longer required to do so, i.e. when compulsory schooling has ended. In this regard, education will necessarily transform and enhance the quality of an educated man's life:

> ... for it is by education that mere living is transformed into a quality of life. For how a man lives depends on what he sees and understands, In schools and colleges, there is, of course, a concentration on activities like literature, science, and history, which have a high degree of cognitive content. But an educated person is not one who simply goes on engaging in such activities when he leaves such institutions; he is one whose whole range of actions, reactions, and activities is gradually transformed by the deepening and widening of his understanding and sensitivity. There is no end to this process (AE, pp. 19–20).

For Peters the educated person becomes someone who 'works with precision, passion, and taste at worth-while things that lie to hand' (p. 20). He is not someone who is too narrowly specialised and not someone who sees learning as merely an instrumental vehicle to other social goods like status, wealth, and power.

While education is a normative term connected to an individual's development, it also has normative cultural and social dimensions. Peters emphasizes that education is 'a form of initiation into worth-while activities'. Thus, he recognises that education can be seen as a form of cultural transmission. In this regard, he notes that 'the values of a community provide the background of content' to which pleas for particular emphases or principles can be made (p. 24). And he emphasizes that 'education consists essentially in the initiation of others into a public world picked out by the language and concepts of a people and structured by rules governing their purposes and interactions with others' (p. 27). And in his justificatory arguments for education, Peters emphasizes such critical cultural values as social justice, equality of opportunity, and respect for persons.

Although Peters clearly acknowledges the public, social, and cultural features of education, he focuses most significantly, I think, on the intrinsic goods of being educated, emphasizing the quasi-universal features of pursuing truth and reason, the value of traditional academic subjects like science, literature, art and philosophy—the staples of a liberal arts education. What appears much less prominently is what others have associated with a critical, socially conscious education—namely the ability to see the gaps between public rhetoric and reality, to explode cultural myths, to notice how textbooks provide a distorted view of social history, and to question official forms of political indoctrination in society. Critical theorists like Paulo Freire, Ronald Glass, Michael Apple, Peter McClaren and others urge us to enable our students to do what Peters does not seem to emphasize in his conception of education; namely, to criticise the subtle, taken-for-granted transmission of their own cultures and to notice how cultures often privilege a few, marginalise some, and oppress others (Glass, 2008). In addition, Peters does not emphasize a view of education I would associate with John Dewey, Amy Guttman, or Eamonn Callan—namely developing citizens as active political participants seeking to perpetuate the critical values of democracy (Dewey, 1916; Guttman, 1987; Callan, 1997). Indeed, as Leonard Waks (2009) has pointed out to me, Peters came in for some very harsh, even viciously hostile, criticism for his own emphasis on a more traditional liberal arts education. My point here is simply to have mentioned very briefly not what Peters' conception of education highlights, but what it seems to underemphasize.

III PETERS' INDETERMINACY OF EDUCATIONAL AIMS AND THE NEED FOR SUSTAINED DIALOGUE

In the final section, I shall speculate on how R. S. Peters' analysis might serve a useful purpose today for contemporary educational policy makers: namely, to encourage them to reinvigorate their dialogue about the aims of education. One central virtue of R. S. Peters' conceptual analysis is his distinction between the meaning of education in one of its central uses and the content of education. He argues that education is unlike medicine where there is broad consensus about what it means to be 'cured'; no such consensus exists about what constitutes 'being educated' (AE, p. 52). Peters focuses on two essential but rather vague conditions that are inextricably attached to the notion of education—its desirability and its connection to the depth and breadth of knowledge. Nevertheless, he also argues that the aims of education remain largely indeterminate. As an indeterminate concept, 'education' provides us with a useful starting point for reconsidering how we might develop sensible educational policy. Peters' analysis, I believe, encourages us to rethink the aims of education with each new generation. We must re-examine these aims specifically within our contemporary political, social, and economic contexts. In no other way can we give meaningful substance to our commitment to the ideal of universal education.

Peters has reminded us of something we cannot afford to forget: namely that we need to justify the content of education not once and for all time, but over and over again with each new generation. In this way, we can give political force to his core premise: that the aims of education are fundamentally indeterminate and must be made relevant to each historical period. Peters implied no less than this when he wrote: 'as Dewey shrewdly remarks: "For the *statement* of aim is a matter of emphasis at a given time"' (AE, p. 20). For Peters, the aims of education are both indeterminate and matters of emphasis at a given time. Remembering that can serve a very useful purpose: namely, to remind educators and policy makers that they cannot avoid a sustained, vigorous, and critical dialogue over the purposes and content of education.

Why is such dialogue so critical today? The reason, I think, is straightforward: the cultural realities that we confront—increased threats to our environment, global economic interdependency, increasing cultural diversity, rapid technological change, and widespread international terrorism—are serious. But the educational system that we created at the turn of the 20th century to accommodate industrialisation and urbanisation has acquired a life of its own, one that appears largely resistant to change (Katz and Denti, 1996). In the US it aims, for the most part, to do what it has done so well for the past century: namely, to socialise students to schooling, to sort them by their differing educational achievements, and to assign them to their appropriate slots within a given social structure. These schooling functions have little to do with educating people in the sense R. S. Peters discussed. But Peters was not blind to the crass instrumentalism he viewed among educational policy makers. He clearly acknowledged that many of them had a narrowly economic view of education seen as formal schooling, Thus, he writes: 'A politician or administrator, in an economic frame of mind, might think of education as the means by which a supply of trained manpower is assured' (AE, p. 27). But Peters, while acknowledging this viewpoint, did not regard it as a serious threat to educating people. Thus, he continues: 'Of course, looking at what goes on in schools and universities from this economic point of view is not *necessarily* antagonistic to being concerned with education in the more specific sense' (AE, p. 52). Not 'necessarily' antagonistic.

Here is where R. S. Peters and I part company. The crass economic instrumentalism that Peters did not fear brings me almost to despair. The conventional wisdom informing American education is blinded by such economic instrumentalism. It is based on the notion that schooling's central purpose is to promote economic competitiveness through the production of skilled workers. Accompanying this belief is the view that teachers and administrators cannot be trusted to perform their educational tasks well but must be critically evaluated through only one mechanism: the performance of their students on high stakes tests. The results of these tests, however unrelated they are to the curriculum in the schools, will be the central measure for determining the value of formal schooling. Moreover, the test results are being used in the US to reward or punish schools for student improvement. Schools are labelled as 'underperforming' unless significant year-to-year progress is made by students on these tests. In addition, schools with a great deal of cultural diversity are often punished for their diversity, since the scores on the tests are disaggregated by ethnic and demographic groups, all of which need to make standard forms of progress (Sleeter, 2007).

One could go on, but the point is simple. In the US, at least, we have implemented a set of policies and practices alien to any informed notion of educating people well for the 21st century. Moreover, these policies, practices and the intellectual mindset underlying them have acquired a life of their own that naturally seems to sustain itself. What is even more striking is that these policies and practices have had an even more dangerous consequence: namely, to make having a serious, informed discussion on the aims of education less likely to occur. Now more than ever, we need vigorous a dialogue about the aims of education so that we might subject present educational policies to critical scrutiny. However, in the US no such serious dialogue seems to be occurring among educators, legislators, policy makers and other informed citizens. Rather the economic mindset and the concomitant views of assessment and accountability reinforce an uncritical taken-for-granted view, namely that schooling has as its central purpose the creation of skilled workers.

The present state of affairs in the US may have parallels in other countries, for I suspect that narrow versions of school accountability emphasizing student outcomes by standardised measures is not a uniquely US phenomenon. But it should remind all of us that Peters' earlier analysis of education needs to be transformed into a substantive dialogue about the current aims of education. Peters' analysis of education as initiating us into what is worthwhile requires that we rethink what is really worthwhile and why it is so. Aside from Peters' concern with knowledge and understanding, what kinds of educational dispositions and reasoning skills will people need to flourish in this new world? We cannot afford to neglect these questions if we aim to prepare our children to live intelligently in 21st century. Clearly the world they will inherit will be far different from that which Peters inhabited when he wrote his early essays. It will be a world where we face far too much information and too little time to use it well, a world where widespread indoctrination may still impede the likelihood of informed political judgment, and a world where disparities between the rich and poor will threaten the well being of many groups. Peters reminded us that we not only need to think clearly about what education means, but also need to justify what we regard as its worth-while content. If we take his charge seriously, we will reinvigorate the dialogue over the aims of education in the 21st century. To do less is to dishonour his philosophical legacy.

REFERENCES

Arnstine, D (1995) *Democracy and the Arts of Schooling* (Albany, NY, SUNY Press).

Callan, E. (1997) *Creating Citizens* (Oxford, Clarendon).

Dewey, J. (1916/1966) *Democracy and Education* (New York, Macmillan).

Green, T. with the assistance of Ericson, D, Seidman, H. (1980) *Predicting the Behavior of the Educational System* (Syracuse, NY, Syracuse University Press).

Glass, R. (2008) Education and the Ethics of Democratic Citizenship, in: *Education, Democracy, and the Moral Life* (New York, Springer), pp. 9–30.

Guttman, A. (1987) *Democratic Education* (Princeton, NJ, Princeton University Press).

Illich, I. (1970) *Deschooling Society* (New York, Harper and Row).

Katz, M. (1976) *A History of Compulsory Education Laws* (Bloomington, IN, Phi Delta Kappa).

Katz, M. and Denti, L. (1996) The Road to Nowhere Begins with Where We Are: Rethinking the Future Of American Education, *Interchange*, 27.3 &4, pp. 261–77.

Katz, M. (2008) Is There a Right to Education: A Philosophical Analysis through U.S. Lenses, in: *Education, Democracy, and the Moral Life* (New York, Springer).

Peters, R. S. (1966) *Ethics and Education* (London, George Allen & Unwin).

Peters, R. S. (1973a) Introduction, in R. S. Peters (ed.) *The Philosophy of Education* (Oxford, Oxford University Press), pp. 1–7.

Peters, R. S. (1973b) The Aims of Education—A Conceptual Inquiry, in: R. S. Peters (ed.) *The Philosophy of Education* (Oxford, Oxford University Press), pp. 11–57.

Sleeter, C. (ed.) (2007) *Facing Accountability in Education: Democracy and Equity at Risk* (New York, Teachers College Press).

Suissa, J. (2009) Constructions of Parents and Languages of Parenting. Paper delivered at the Annual Meeting of the Philosophy of Education Society, Montreal, Canada.

Waks, L. (1968) Knowledge and Understanding as Educational Aims, *The Monist*, 52.4, pp. 104–9.

Waks, L. (2008) *Leaders in Philosophy of Education: Intellectual Self-Portraits* (Rotterdam, Sense Publishers).

Waks, L. (2009) Email communication with Michael Katz on May 8.

Wittgenstein, L. (1953) *Philosophical Investigations* (Oxford, Blackwell).

Woods, J. (1973) Commentary, in R. S. Peters (ed.) *The Philosophy of Education* (Oxford, Oxford University Press), pp. 29–34.

7

On the Worthwhileness of Theoretical Activities

MICHAEL HAND

In chapter five of *Ethics and Education* (1966), and again in 'The Justification of Education' (1973), R. S. Peters sets out his arguments for the worthwhileness of theoretical activities. His purpose in setting out these arguments is to justify the enterprise of education. In *Ethics and Education* he describes himself as supplying 'ethical foundations' for the 'matter' of education (Peters, 1966, p. 91), which matter he has already shown to comprise those 'differentiated modes of thought and awareness' that are 'characterized both by a content or "body of knowledge" and by public procedures by means of which this content has been accumulated, criticized and revised' (p. 50). To demonstrate the value of initiation into theoretical activities is, for Peters, to demonstrate the value of education itself.

It would therefore be a mistake to see Peters' arguments for the worthwhileness of theoretical activities as an exercise in curriculum justification. The arguments are *not* designed to show that theoretical activities are more worthwhile than activities of other kinds and thus more deserving of a place on the curriculum. For Peters, the question of curriculum content is settled by conceptual rather than ethical considerations. It is, he thinks, conceptually true that education consists in the transmission of 'knowledge and understanding and some kind of cognitive perspective, which are not inert' (p. 45). Since education *must* involve initiation into theoretical activities, it makes no sense to ask whether or not it should.

For this reason Peters is able largely to avoid the question of the *relative* worth of theoretical activities. The task he sets himself is not to weigh up the merits of rival contenders for curriculum space, but simply to show that educating children—initiating them into theoretical activities—is ethically justifiable. He could, of course, have gone on to ask questions about the place of education in the broader enterprise of upbringing, about how educational processes rank alongside the various other kinds of care, interaction and initiation from which children stand to benefit; but he does not do this. He rests content with arguing for the claim that the matter of education is worthwhile.

Few philosophers of education now share Peters' conviction that questions of curriculum content can be settled by analysis of the concept of education.

Reading R. S. Peters Today, First Edition. Stefaan E. Cuypers and Christopher Martin.
Chapters © 2011 The Authors. Editorial organization © 2011 Philosophy of Education Society of Great Britain. Published 2011 by Blackwell Publishing Ltd.

If, following John Wilson, we suppose that the strongest conclusion conceptual analysis can yield is that education is going on when 'human learning above the natural level is being deliberately promoted in accordance with some general or overall policy' (Wilson, 1979, p. 33), we shall need rather more from our ethical arguments than Peters needed from his. We shall need them to address the question of curriculum content. Insofar as we share Peters' interest in supplying education with ethical foundations, our task will be to show that the curriculum content implied by our preferred 'overall policy' is not only worthwhile, but *more* worthwhile, in some relevant sense, than the curriculum content implied by other overall policies.

What I should like to do in this chapter, then, is reconsider Peters' ethical arguments with this more ambitious justificatory question in mind. I should like to ask whether any of his arguments for the worthwhileness of theoretical activities can be pressed into service as arguments for the claim that theoretical activities have greater worth than activities of other kinds. If they cannot, it hardly reflects badly on Peters: he cannot be chastised for producing arguments that fail to support a claim he did not make; but if they can, it gives them a relevance to contemporary debates about what should go on the school curriculum that is otherwise lacking.

In *Ethics and Education* (henceforth EE) and 'The Justification of Education' (henceforth JE), Peters advances two main kinds of argument for the worthwhileness of theoretical activities: *hedonistic* arguments and *transcendental* arguments. We shall consider each in turn.

THE HEDONISTIC ARGUMENTS

One important way in which activities can be worthwhile for human beings is by giving them pleasure. There is, says Peters, 'some important truth in hedonism, in the context of reasons for action and choice' (EE, p. 148). A measure of the worthwhileness of an activity, he thinks, is the degree to which it succeeds in not being boring:

> An activity must go on for a time and if one is deciding to spend time in one way rather than another surely questions relating to boredom must be relevant. From this point of view there must be some kind of preference for activities which are capable of holding a person's attention for a certain span of time, and which provide constant sources of pleasure and satisfaction ... Anyone, therefore, who is thinking seriously about how to spend his time cannot but go for activities which afford rich opportunities for employing his wits, resources and sensitivities in situations in which there is a premium on unpredictability and opportunities for skill (p. 156).

Peters contends that theoretical activities, like science, history and philosophy, are attention-holding activities *par excellence*. There are at least two reasons for this. First, they offer 'unending opportunities for skill and discrimination' (p. 157). Many activities have 'a static quality about them' (p. 158), in the sense that they aim at predetermined and well-understood ends, achievable by a limited number of means. After a while, those who engage in such activities achieve mastery, at which point they no longer present any serious challenge. But theoretical activities are not like this. We do not know the nature of the truths we have not yet discovered, nor the means by which we will discover them. One never truly masters a theoretical activity, so it always remains challenging and absorbing: 'it is inconceivable that anyone could get bored in the same sort of way with science or philosophy. The nature of these pursuits precludes any such finality with its linked sense of mastery' (p. 158).

Second, the permanence and abundance of truth make its disciplined pursuit a particularly reliable source of pleasure. Unlike other goods we pursue, there is no danger of truth perishing, running out or being bought up by the wealthy. Whereas 'to get attached to pets, people or possessions is a bad bet *sub specie aeternitatis*', to love the truth is 'to have a permanent object which is safe forever' (p. 157).

Various kinds of criticism have been levelled against these hedonistic arguments. R. K. Elliott, for example, challenges Peters' characterisation of theoretical activities as pleasurable:

> A long and difficult enquiry has the character of a venture which comprehensively engages the self of the enquirer. Anxiety is frequently the prevailing mood, and confusion, and dead-ends, disappointments, lack of inspiration, and lack of energy combine to generate wretchedness ... Disagreeable experiences probably occupy more of the total time of the enquiry than agreeable experiences, and, on reflection, it is often hard to believe that their intensity was less (Elliott, 1977, p. 10).

Few who have embarked on long and difficult inquiries will be inclined to quarrel with this description; but it hardly deals a fatal blow to the hedonistic arguments. Elliott's objection is not so much to the claim that theoretical activities have hedonistic appeal as to the account Peters gives of that appeal. Theoretical activities, he contends, are better described as *rewarding* or *satisfying* than as pleasurable or enjoyable. It is the satisfaction of rising to a challenge, of overcoming great hindrances, of feeling oneself 'to be living powerfully as a thinking being' (p. 11), that makes engagement in theoretical activities hedonistically worthwhile.

John Wilson detects certain neuroses in Peters' apparent disdain for activities connected with the satisfaction of bodily appetites and with attachments to perishable objects:

> [I]t is odd to describe the satisfaction of the 'necessary appetites' as *boring* just because there is less opportunity for discrimination, skill and 'standards'. They are boring only to those who insist on such things: and

why should we not represent this as some kind of neurotic compulsion? Similarly, we might say that the avoidance of attachments to perishable objects looks more like some fantasy than like acceptance of the world and of human needs as they actually are (Wilson, 1979, p. 138).

There is certainly something awry with Peters' implied equation of what is interesting with what offers opportunities for skill and discrimination and of what is boring with what does not. Regardless of the degree to which eating and sexual activity have been 'civilised' by the development of rules 'which protect those engaged in them from brutal efficiency in relation to the obvious end of the exercise' (EE, p. 152), these pursuits manifestly give theoretical activities a run for their money in terms of hedonistic appeal. And the fact that people and pets are perishable normally does not, and obviously should not, reduce our inclination to delight in our attachments to them. But, again, these points do not count against the claim that theoretical activities are hedonistically worthwhile: they simply warn against the denigration of activities that afford other kinds of satisfaction and pleasure.

There is not, as far as I can see, very much wrong with Peters' hedonistic arguments, insofar as they are designed to show simply that theoretical activities can be richly rewarding for those who engage in them and are in that sense worthwhile. It is plainly true that one important and valid reason people have for devoting themselves to the theoretic life is that they find it satisfying. The question before us, however, is whether the hedonistic arguments might also warrant the stronger conclusion that theoretical activities are more worthwhile than activities of other kinds. Here, I think, in light of the cautionary points made by Elliott and Wilson, the prospects of an affirmative answer are bleak.

Elliott describes the rewards to be found in the disciplined pursuit of truth by contrasting them with the very different rewards attendant on 'the easy spontaneous way in which Pele plays football'. Theoretical inquiries, he insists, do not qualify as enjoyable because they rarely involve the 'brilliant pleasures' of accomplishing something with 'effortless style' (Elliott, 1977, p. 10); but the clear implication is that some activities *do* qualify as enjoyable in exactly this sense. It is difficult to see why the 'effortless style' kind of rewards should confer any less hedonistic worth on the activities that yield them than the 'living powerfully' kind. The satisfaction of a modest accomplishment in an unmasterable domain is different from, but not obviously greater than, the satisfaction of a superlative performance in a domain one has mastered. Peters makes the point himself when he notes that there is something rather 'exhausting' about the endless pursuit of truth, something that 'smacks too much of the frontier mentality' (JE, p. 250). We ought not to forget 'the conservative side of human nature, the enjoyment of routines, and the security to be found in the well-worn and the familiar' (ibid.).

And Wilson, in drawing attention to the oddity of any suggestion that the pursuit of permanently available truths is to be preferred to the satisfaction of bodily desires or the nurturing of loving relationships, reminds us that there are a good many other kinds of hedonistic worth than the two Elliott contrasts. It is no doubt true that the distinctive rewards of theoretical inquiry are attributable in part to the permanence and abundance of truth, but it is clear that the distinctive rewards of other activities must be explained in quite different terms. Again, Peters is ready to acknowledge the point: 'evanescence', he observes, 'is essential to the attraction of some pursuits. What would wine-tasting or sexual activity be like if the culminating point was too permanent and prolonged?' (ibid.).

Activities, in short, yield too many different kinds of satisfaction for there to be any straightforward ranking of activities by hedonistic worth. Almost all activities make available to those who engage in them some sort of satisfaction, some physical or emotional or intellectual pleasure, some reward in rising to challenges or delight in the exercise of mastery, some interest or excitement or comfort or relief. It is plausible to suggest that hedonistic appeal is one of the criteria we normally and reasonably use to select the activities we will devote most time to; but, when we choose some kinds of satisfaction over others, we surely do so on the basis of our personal tastes and preferences, not on the basis of an objective ordering of pleasures. The hedonistic arguments, then, offer little support for the idea that theoretical activities should take precedence over others in the selection of curriculum content.

THE TRANSCENDENTAL ARGUMENTS

Peters' transcendental arguments for the worthwhileness of theoretical activities trade on a rather different sense of 'worthwhile'. Whereas, in the hedonistic arguments, the term is used 'to indicate that an activity is likely to prove absorbing, to be an enjoyable way of passing the time', in the transcendental arguments it has 'little to do with absorption or enjoyment' (p. 247). It has to do, instead, with the value of the end of the activity, even where the pursuit of that end might be 'a bit boring' (p. 248). The aim of the transcendental arguments is to establish the worthwhileness of theoretical activities by demonstrating the value of truth.

How do the arguments work? What Peters tries to show is that a commitment to truth is presupposed by any serious engagement in practical discourse. A person who professed a serious interest in a practical question, such as 'Why do this rather than that?', but who denied caring about the truth, would be guilty of self-contradiction, of ignoring or failing to recognise the logical implications of her interest. Since we can hardly avoid engaging in practical discourse, as this would involve 'a resolute refusal to talk or think about what ought to be done' (EE, pp. 115–6), we have little choice but to care about the truth.

The two transcendental arguments Peters advances pick out different logical connections between serious engagement in practical discourse and commitment to truth. First, the person who seriously asks 'Why do this rather than that?' must, in order to answer her question, find out what this and that involve. She is committed to investigating the nature of this and that and coming to understand them well enough to assess their relative merits and make an informed choice between them. When she carries out these investigations, she will find herself 'embarking on those forms of inquiry such as science, history, literature and philosophy which are concerned with the description, explanation and assessment of different forms of human activity' (p. 162).

Second, the person who seriously asks 'Why do this rather than that?' must already have made some preliminary assessment of her situation, distinguished this and that as options for herself, and judged the choice between them to warrant careful consideration. Her serious practical question, in other words, must itself arise from a concern for truth: theoretical inquiry is 'involved in *asking* the question 'Why do this rather than that?', as well as in answering it' (p. 164). It is not simply that, having committed ourselves to 'choosing rather than plumping' (p. 121), we are obliged to try to understand the options before us; it is that our commitment to choosing rather than plumping is itself grounded in our desire to make sense of the world:

> [T]he attitude of passionate concern about truth ... lies at the heart of all rational activities in which there is a concern for what is true or false, appropriate or inappropriate, correct or incorrect. Anyone who asks seriously the question 'Why do this rather than that?' must already possess it; for it is built into this sense of 'serious'. It is impossible to give any further justification for it; for it is presupposed in all serious attempts at justification (p. 165).

Peters' transcendental arguments have received a great deal of critical attention and discussion. The most common objection to them is that they merely defer the justificatory problem from why we should value truth to why we should seriously ask practical questions:

> The first problem is concerned with the *ad hominem* nature of the transcendental argument to which we drew attention earlier. It is a justification only to those who already ask 'Why do this rather than that?' ... [But] it is easy, and common, for people to avoid raising this question at all (Downie *et al.*, 1974, p. 46).

> [The transcendental arguments] do not much help us because they are too tightly conceived—that is, they move within too small a circle. If, or insofar as, anyone is serious in the required sense, the conclusions may follow; but

many people are often not very serious, and we want arguments to show why, or how far, or when, they ought to be (Wilson, 1979, p. 137).

It only trivialises education if it is argued that a commitment to certain activities deemed to be educationally valuable is presupposed by the justificatory question. For such an argument does not tell us why education is justified except in the sense that it is necessary to answering justificatory questions. What is needed is an account which will display for us the importance of justificatory questions (Kleinig, 1982, p. 87).

The problem, then, is that having shown commitment to truth to be presupposed by serious engagement in practical discourse, Peters now needs to justify serious engagement in practical discourse. Otherwise he has connected theoretical inquiry with practical deliberation without justifying either. It plainly will not do for him to say, as he does at one point, that 'this book is only written for those who take seriously the question "What ought I to do?"' (EE, p. 116). If it is merely a contingent matter that Peters and his audience are the sort of people who go in for serious engagement in practical discourse, then Downie *et al.* are right to dismiss the transcendental argument as a weak *ad hominem* justification.

But Peters does not regard this as a contingent matter. His considered view, strongly implied in *Ethics and Education* and explicitly affirmed in 'The Justification of Education', is that 'human life is a context in which the demands of reason are inescapable' (JE, p. 253). It is a general fact of human existence that 'any man who emerges from infancy tries to perceive, to remember, to infer, to learn, and to regulate his wants'; and to do these things, Peters argues, 'he must have recourse to some procedure of assessment' (p. 254). Anyone who really tried to opt out of practical discourse, to go through life plumping rather than choosing, 'unreflectively relying on feelings in his stomach or on what other people say', would find himself living by 'procedures which are inappropriate to demands that are admitted, and must be admitted by anyone who takes part in human life' (p. 253).

This argument is perhaps not entirely convincing. Even if the demands of reason are built into the structure of human existence in the way Peters describes, the possibility of ignoring those demands remains. No doubt it would be impossible to ignore them if one took life at all seriously, but, as Wilson observes, 'many people are often not very serious'. It seems at least intelligible to ask for further arguments in support of taking life seriously. Nevertheless, the transcendental arguments cannot fairly be dismissed on the grounds that they merely defer the justificatory problem: Peters does try to complete his justification by showing the inescapability of practical discourse in human life.

Let us assume, for the sake of argument, that Peters succeeds in showing both that serious practical deliberation presupposes the value of truth and that it is inescapable for human beings. He would then have advanced a powerful case for the worthwhileness of theoretical activities. What we must now ask is whether this argument lends any support to the view that theoretical activities are more worthwhile than activities of other kinds. If Peters'transcendental arguments demonstrate the value of truth, do they also demonstrate the ultimacy of this value?

The first point to note is that Peters himself explicitly denies this. To subscribe to his transcendental justification of the value of truth, he insists, is not to say 'that there are not *other* features of life which are valuable—love for others, for instance', or even 'that other such concerns may not be more valuable' (p. 255). He reiterates the point in his reply to Elliott's critique of 'The Justification of Education':

> I do not think, and never have thought, that the values surrounding the concern for truth are the only ones in life. I am not sure, either, whether I think that they are of over-riding importance. There is also the consideration of interests—especially of those who suffer, justice, love, and the more hedonistic or 'vital' values constitutive of people's interests (Peters, 1977, p. 37).

There is, to be sure, some uncertainty here, as if Peters might be somewhat tempted by the thought that truth is a value of 'over-riding importance'; but it is difficult to see how this much stronger conclusion could be derived from the transcendental arguments. One reason for this is that, as Peters argues persuasively in chapter four of *Ethics and Education*, serious engagement in practical discourse implies a commitment to justice as well as truth. Askers of practical questions must be committed to 'the principle of justice' as 'a presupposition of the activity of justifying or searching for reasons for conduct' (EE, p. 125). Indeed, Peters holds that the transcendental form of argument 'is much clearer in its support of the principle of fairness than in its bearing on the worthwhileness of activities which form the main substance of the curriculum' (p. 117). So those social activities and practices which have justice as their end would appear to be at least as worthwhile, in the relevant sense, as theoretical activities.

Like the hedonistic arguments, the transcendental arguments do not help us much with the task of assessing the relative worth of theoretical activities. They show (insofar as they are successful) that truth is an important value capable of conferring worth on activities dedicated to its pursuit. But there are other values in life equally capable of conferring worth on the activities through which they are pursued, and there is nothing in the transcendental arguments to suggest that truth somehow trumps or overrides these other values.

THE INSTRUMENTAL WORTH OF THEORETICAL ACTIVITIES

Neither of the main kinds of argument Peters advances for the worthwhileness of theoretical activities, then, promises to offer us much assistance with the question of what should go on the school curriculum. Theoretical activities cannot plausibly be seen as more worthwhile than other activities in terms of either the satisfaction they afford or the value of their end. Before we abandon our quest, however, it may be worth considering one further kind of argument, a kind that Peters tries hard to play down but to which his discussions can be construed as lending support in several places. What I have in mind here are *instrumental* arguments for the worthwhileness of theoretical activities.

In *Ethics and Education* Peters asserts, rather dogmatically, that considerations of instrumental worth are inadmissible in justifications of the matter of education: 'though most of these activities can be viewed instrumentally, to regard them as having educational value is to rule out such considerations' (p. 144). By the time he writes 'The Justification of Education', his attitude has softened somewhat. He now concedes that 'A strong instrumental case can also be made for the passing on of knowledge and understanding' (JE, p. 243) and that this case might play some role in a fully adequate justification of education. Nevertheless, he insists that instrumental justifications have 'an obvious incompleteness' about them and moves swiftly on to the question of 'whether knowledge and under-standing have strong claims to be included as one of the goods which are *constitutive* of a worth-while level of life' (p. 247).

As we have seen, the difficulty with this strategy is that it is very difficult to compare and rank activities with respect to their intrinsic worth. We may well accept that theoretical activities are intrinsically worthwhile, in both of the senses examined above, but so are a great many other activities. The multiplicity of intrinsically worthwhile activities is not a problem for Peters because he operates with a definition of education that guarantees theoretical activities their privileged place on the curriculum. But for those of us unpersuaded by this definition, the problem is acute. How are we to select from the class of intrinsically worthwhile activities? Instrumental justifica-tions at least hold out the possibility of making meaningful comparisons. If we cannot rank activities with respect to their intrinsic worth, perhaps we can rank them with respect to how well they serve some extrinsic purpose.

A move of just this kind is proposed by John White in *Towards a Compulsory Curriculum* (White, 1973). White is dissatisfied with Peters' hedonistic and transcendental arguments and proposes that we shift our attention from the *intrinsic* to the *educational* worth of theoretical activities:

> [T]he method will be very different from any attempt to prove the intrinsic worth of these activities. The question 'What kinds of activities are worth while in themselves?' is different from the question 'What kinds of activities are educationally worth while?' If it cannot be shown that science and art are intrinsically valuable for everyone, it still remains possible that they are educationally so (White, 1973, pp. 16–17).

The turn to instrumental justification assumes, of course, that an appropriate criterion of educational worth can be identified. White's own suggestion on this score—that we should include in the curriculum those activities which cannot be understood without engagement—is unpromising, and he has long since abandoned it. But there is, I think, a more plausible criterion, which goes something like this: *Given that there are a great many worthwhile activities, and we do not know which ones children will eventually devote themselves to, we should give curriculum priority to those worthwhile activities that enhance, enter into or shed light on all others.*

The rationale for this criterion should be self-evident. Our task as educators is to prepare children for adult life. We cannot do this by initiating them into the activities that will occupy their time as adults because we do not yet know what those activities will be. Instead, we must try to prepare them in some general way, so their education will be useful to them whatever they choose to do with their lives. Insofar as this general preparation includes initiation into activities, we should select those activities that are relevant to all others, that feed into them, lay foundations for them, increase the interest of them or facilitate informed choice between them. We should select activities not for their own sake, but for their instrumental value in relation to other activities.

Now, while Peters has little time for instrumental justifications of this kind, it is striking that a number of the points he makes about theoretical activities in the course of developing his hedonistic and transcendental arguments speak directly to our criterion of educational worth. Indeed, his first transcendental argument, intended to show that anyone trying to make a reasoned choice between this and that is committed to finding out the truth about this and that, can easily be recast as an instrumental argument of just the kind we are looking for. All human activities involve making reasoned choices between alternatives and therefore require the ability to find out the truth about those alternatives. Since finding out truth is the province of theoretical activities, it follows that theoretical activities enter into activities of all other kinds. By imparting to children both wide-ranging knowledge and the ability to acquire new knowledge when they need it, we prepare them well for any activity they may subsequently decide to take up. This, of course, is precisely the argument J. S. Mill advances in support of 'scientific instruction' in universities:

> All through life it is our most pressing interest to find out the truth about all the matters we are concerned with. If we are farmers, we want to find out what will truly improve our soil; if merchants, what will truly influence the markets for our commodities; if judges, or jurymen, or advocates, who it was that truly did an unlawful act, or to whom a disputed right truly belongs . . . Now, however different these searches for truth may look, and however unlike they really are in their subject-matter, the methods for getting at truth, and the tests of truth, are in all cases much the same (Mill, 1867, p. 160).

But this is not the only way in which theoretical activities, on Peters' account of them, are relevant to all others. Initiation into the various modes of theoretical inquiry not only equips people with the wherewithal to make choices encountered in the course of practical activities, but also 'changes a man's view of the world' in such a way as to 'transform everything else that he does':

> [Theoretical activities] are 'serious' and cannot be considered merely as if they were particularly delectable pastimes, because they consist largely in the explanation, assessment and illumination of the different facets of life. They thus insensibly change a man's view of the world. A man who has read and digested Burke finds it difficult to look on Americans in quite the same way; his concept of jealousy develops overtones after seeing Othello. If he is also a trained scientist he scarcely sees the same world as his untrained contemporary; for he is being trained in modes of thought that cannot be tied down to particular times and places. A man who devotes himself to a game, on the other hand, does not thereby equip himself with cognitive content that spills over and transforms his view of other things in life ... A person who has pursued [theoretical activities] systematically develops conceptual schemes and forms of appraisal which transform everything else that he does (EE, p. 160).

The transformative or spillover effects of initiation into theoretical activities described by Peters may be seen as satisfying our criterion of educational worth in two ways. First, people equipped with the conceptual schemes and forms of appraisal yielded by theoretical inquiries are better able to distinguish and make sense of human activities and thus to choose intelligently between them. Theoretical activities have a privileged position among pastimes in that 'they are the main determinants of the conceptual schemes picking out all other pastimes as well as of what is to count as a pastime' (pp. 161–2). By expanding their conceptual schemes, and thus 'enlarging their imagination' (Peters, 1977, p. 37), theoretical inquiries widen the range of activities available to people and deepen their understanding of what those activities involve.

Second, people transformed by initiation into theoretical activities will find their enjoyment of all other activities enhanced. The reason for this is that the interest of a practical activity depends in part on the knowledge and understanding one brings to it. The possession of knowledge 'transforms activities by making them more complex and by altering the way in which they are conceived' (JE, p. 248). Peters elaborates the point in chapter six of *Ethics and Education* when he considers the worthwhileness of practical activities:

> What there is in politics, administration or business depends to a large extent on what a person conceives of himself as doing when he engages in them ... Both Caesar and Pompey were enaged in politics in the dying days of the Roman Republic. But the differences in grasp and conception

between these two contemporaries were so staggering that they were scarcely engaged in the same activity. This was because Caesar was a man of action with wide-ranging theoretical interests. His passion for order and his sense of the ways in which concrete objects could be fitted into a general plan was enlivened by an understanding almost unparalleled amongst his contemporaries (EE, pp. 175–6).

Because practical activities are 'partly dependent, in respect of their quality, on the level of understanding that goes into them' (p. 176), they are richer and more satisfying when pursued by those initiated into theoretical activities. Developing people's 'knowledge, understanding and attitudes as persons', Peters claims, 'should add to their absorption, satisfaction and sense of mastery both in their vocations and in their lives generally' (Peters, 1977, p. 37).

Notwithstanding Peters' aversion to instrumental justifications, then, the account of theoretical activities he develops is just the sort of account one would need to mount a defence of the academic curriculum on instrumental grounds. Theoretical activities, he contends, are activities which enhance, enter into and shed light on all others. They would therefore seem to be at least the right kind of activities to teach children in school, at any rate in societies where it is impossible to predict the activities that will occupy their time as adults. This is what Charles Bailey terms the 'general utility justification' of liberal education: by involving children in 'fundamental understanding of human experience', we educate them in a way that has 'the most general relevance and utility for anything they are likely to want to do' (Bailey, 1984, p. 29).

I do not suggest that Peters says enough to clinch the argument for giving curriculum priority to theoretical activities; still less that I have done so in this chapter. A fuller defence is required of the criterion of educational worth I have proposed and of the claim that it is satisfied by theoretical activities. It needs to be shown, too, that there are not other kinds of activity which satisfy the criterion as well as, or better than, theoretical activities. And attention must be given to the assumption that the question of curriculum content is properly construed as a question about the activities into which children should be initiated, as distinct, say, from the virtues that should be cultivated or the bodies of knowledge that should be imparted. What I do claim is that Peters' rich and complex account of theoretical activities is highly suggestive for the task of assessing their relative instrumental worth and, for this reason, still has much to offer to contemporary debates about what should go on the school curriculum.[1]

NOTE

1. My thanks to Patricia White, John White and Paul Hirst for their patient exegetical assistance. Remaining errors of interpretation are my own.

REFERENCES

Bailey, C. (1984) *Beyond the Present and the Particular: A Theory of Liberal Education* (London, Routledge & Kegan Paul).

Downie, R. S., Loudfoot, E. M. and Telfer, E. (1974) *Education and Personal Relationships* (London, Methuen).

Elliott, R. K. (1977) Education and Justification, *Journal of Philosophy of Education*, 11.1, pp. 7–27.

Kleinig, J. (1982) *Philosophical Issues in Education* (London, Routledge & Kegan Paul).

Mill, J. S. (1867) Inaugural address at St Andrews, in: F. A. Cavenagh (ed.) (1931) *James and John Stuart Mill on Education* (Cambridge, Cambridge University Press), pp. 132–98.

Peters, R. S. (1966) *Ethics and Education* (London, George Allen & Unwin).

Peters, R. S. (1973) The Justification of Education, in: R. S. Peters (ed.) *The Philosophy of Education* (Oxford, Oxford University Press), pp. 239–67.

Peters, R. S. (1977) Education and Justification: A Reply to R. K. Elliott, in *Journal of Philosophy of Education*, 11.1, pp. 28–38.

White, J. (1973) *Towards a Compulsory Curriculum* (London, Routledge & Kegan Paul).

Wilson, J. (1979) *Preface to the Philosophy of Education* (London, Routledge & Kegan Paul).

8

Why General Education? Peters, Hirst and History

JOHN WHITE

I first met Richard Peters in 1960, as a part-time student enrolled in his recently created Joint Honours BA in Philosophy and Psychology at Birkbeck College, London. I found his classes in philosophy of mind, the history of psychology and the history of ethics quite inspirational. When he left us in 1962 to take up a chair at the Institute of Education, I never imagined that three years later I would be joining him as a colleague—or that Patricia, whom I had just married, would be doing so too. But so it turned out.

We were immediately caught up in his all-consuming project of transforming teacher education in England by basing it firmly in the educational disciplines, not least philosophy of education. All this tied in with government policy for an all-graduate teaching profession, based not only on the Postgraduate Certificate of Education, but also on the newly introduced four-year Bachelor of Education degree. Philosophy of education became a prominent feature of both courses. This meant that lecturers had to be trained to teach the subject in both university education departments and in the newly established Colleges of Education. In turn, this demanded a massive amount of work for Richard Peters and us, his colleagues. The new Labour government directly supported our work, by funding a one-year, full-time Diploma in Philosophy of Education at the Institute, specifically designed for schoolteachers who wanted to become college lecturers in our subject.

It may be hard now to imagine the sense we all had in those optimistic days of radical educational reform—it was also the time when secondary schools were becoming comprehensives—that we were engaged in a vitally important public service. Not that this was in the forefront of our consciousness. Rather, it was part of the taken-for-granted background in which we worked. That it was so was largely due to Richard Peters' own deeply-felt belief, shared with his colleague Paul Hirst, that philosophy of education should be brought to bear on matters of public importance. They, like others of us under their tutelage, saw our subject as a handmaiden of an educational service at last becoming reorganised on socially just and rational lines.

Having been brought up to see all my work—in teaching, scholarship and journalism—as intended to serve public ends, I have continued to see it that

Reading R. S. Peters Today, First Edition. Stefaan E. Cuypers and Christopher Martin.
Chapters © 2011 The Authors. Editorial organization © 2011 Philosophy of Education Society of Great Britain. Published 2011 by Blackwell Publishing Ltd.

way through my career, despite the knocks that our discipline has taken since the 1980s and suggestions from governments and the press that it is at best an irrelevance and at worst a drain on the public purse. Other ways of seeing the subject, on the part of its practitioners, have grown up in the last decades. For some, it is harnessed to religious purposes or other deeply-held commitments; for others, it is a branch of philosophical study in its own right, often centred around exegesis and critique of particular thinkers; for others again—and there are overlaps here—its value lies in opportunities to interact with like-minded scholars of the subject across the world. Those of us who still see philosophy of education in the older way, as a vital contributor to the creation of a decent educational system, do well to cling to our perception of it as a public service. If it is to be supported from public funds, it is hard indeed to see what other rationale there could be for it than this.

For me, this is perhaps the greatest legacy of Richard Peters. Many of his specific philosophical arguments have been heavily criticised over the years. The chapter that follows this introduction also pulls no punches. But what has endured, and should continue to endure, is the framework within which Richard Peters set philosophy of education, the taken-for-granted framework of its being an indispensable public service in a liberal democracy committed to justice and freedom. The theme of the chapter that follows, the proper content of a school curriculum, is one illustration of the public focus that has marked all Richard Peters' work.

1.

> Science, mathematics, history, art, cooking and carpentry feature on the curriculum, not bingo, bridge and billiards. Presumably there must be some reason for this apart from their utilitarian or vocational value (Peters, 1966, p. 144).

Peters (1966, 1973) set out to discover this reason. During his enquiry, practical subjects like cooking dropped out of the picture, leaving 'theoretical enquiries' concerned with the pursuit of truth, like science, history and literary studies. Peters also collaborated with Paul Hirst, whose 'forms of knowledge' theory was published earlier, in 1965. This, too, sought to justify theoretical disciplines on intrinsic grounds. Hirst and Peters (1970) took these forms of knowledge as the basis for the curriculum.

With the passing of time, Peters' project, then so influential, seems hard to make sense of. Why start with academic disciplines and seek justifications of them? Logically, curriculum planning has to start with aims, not with vehicles whereby aims may be realised. Looking back, too, there seems to be more to be said than philosophers thought at the time for Michael Young's comment in an early work of his that the prevailing view of the curriculum favoured by philosophers of education (including, incidentally, myself),

> ... appears to be based on an absolutist conception of a set of distinct forms of knowledge which correspond closely to the traditional areas of the academic curriculum and thus justify, rather than examine, what are no more than the socio-historical products of a particular time (Young, 1971, p. 23).

Although Young exaggerates the correspondence he mentions, it is hard not to read the above quotation from Peters as taking the traditional school curriculum as read and assuming there must be good reasons for it.

2.

There is another feature of the Peters project that is hard to fathom. Utilitarian reasons for teaching science, mathematics or history are not hard to find. But the reason he favours is intrinsic. Why? This may not seem to raise difficulties. Aren't teachers justly delighted when a pupil develops a passion for doing science, not out of any instrumental motive, but because it is intrinsically fascinating? I am sure this is right, but it is beside the point. For on Peters' view, pupils are expected to develop an intrinsic interest not only in an area to which they are passionately committed, but also across the board, that is, in every mode of understanding.

This demand for comprehensiveness is fully explicit in the recommendation in Hirst and Peters that pupils be:

> ... significantly introduced to each of the fundamentally different types of objective experience and knowledge that are open to men ... It is therefore not surprising that there is a persistent call that general education shall be maintained for all throughout the secondary school stage (Hirst and Peters, 1970, p. 66).

The same demand is also apparent when, in 1966, Peters writes:

> ... in so far as [a man] can stand back from his life and ask the question 'Why this rather than that?' he must already have a serious concern for truth built into his consciousness. For how can a serious practical question be asked unless a man also wants to acquaint himself as well as he can of [sic] the situation out of which the question arises and of the facts of various kinds which provide the framework for possible answers? The various theoretical enquiries are explorations of these different facets of his experience. To ask the question 'Why do this rather than that?' seriously is therefore, however embryonically, to be committed to those inquiries which are defined by their serious concern with those aspects of reality which give

context to the question which he is asking. In brief the justification of such activities is not purely instrumental because they are involved in asking the question 'Why do this rather than that?' as well as in answering it (Peters, 1966, p.164).

Peters thus favours initiation into a comprehensive range of theoretical enquiries pursued for intrinsic reasons. This means all students taking an intrinsic interest not only in, say, science, but also in a wide range of other disciplines. Psychologically, this is asking a lot of them. No doubt there are occasional pupils who adore everything they learn. But why expect everyone to develop an intrinsic interest in every mode of understanding?

In the light of this, it is not surprising that Peters' various attempts at justifying his 'intrinsic' position are problematic. The most celebrated justification is that quoted above, based on what is presupposed to asking a certain sort of question This is formally similar to Hirst's justification of the pursuit of the seven forms of knowledge (Hirst, 1965, p. 256). Both arguments claim to show that in asking such a question one is already committed to the intrinsic pursuit of a broad range of kinds of knowledge. It is true that in asking 'Why do this rather than that?' or, in Hirst's case, 'Why pursue knowledge?', one wants to know the true, well-founded answer to one's question. If you like to put it this way, the questioner is committed to the pursuit of knowledge on this very specific point. But this does not mean he or she is committed to the pursuit of science, philosophy, literature etc., as Peters' (or Hirst's) position requires (White, 1973, pp.10ff., 78ff.).

Peters' (1973) further wrestlings with the same problem likewise fail to clinch things. In Ray Elliott's words, Peters here claims that:

> ... the educational pursuit of truth in disciplines such as science, philosophy, literature and history is in certain fundamental respects the same as the pursuit of truth in everyday life or any other non-educational context, since in any context the pursuit of truth involves virtues such as truthfulness, clarity, non-arbitrariness, impartiality, a sense of relevance, consistency, respect for evidence, etc. (Elliott, 1977, p. 231).

And further:

> The educational study of the disciplines and their objects is justified on the ground that through it the learner acquires the rational virtues which are essential for reflective thought on matters of a different kind, chiefly what the individual is to do or has done, what he believes and feels about the various matters with which he is existentially concerned, what style of life he is to adopt, and whether the style of life he has adopted is a good one (p. 232).

As Elliott points out, this is a very different kind of justification from that found earlier in Peters. It makes a practically wise life the main function of education, bypassing the earlier emphasis on pursuing science, philosophy etc. for their own intrinsic features.

Turning back for a moment to Hirst's approach to justification, he writes that 'the achievement of knowledge is necessarily the development of mind in its most basic sense' (Hirst, 1965, p. 256). Given this equation, this gives Hirst a way of justifying the pursuit of the seven forms of knowledge that avoids the problem mentioned earlier. Drawing on Greek philosophy, he sees a link between the development of mind and the good life, the latter to be understood in terms of the former (p. 257).

The argument is only sketched in. But it is problematic. Our mental life is various: it includes, for instance, emotional experience as well as states connected with knowledge. Hirst says that acquiring knowledge is the development of mind 'in its most basic sense', but in what way is it more 'basic' than, say, using one's imagination? Again, why is the good life to be understood in terms of mental development (= the pursuit of knowledge), seeing that others have located it in artistic activity, living for others, a mixed life of all sorts of goods, and so on? I come back to the development of mind in Section 7.

Both Peters' and Hirst's justifications for the intrinsic pursuit of intellectual enquiry on a broad front are thus radically problematic.

3.

Ray Elliott also says that although Hirst and Peters (1970) 'emphasise that the forms [of knowledge] are historical institutions, which have undergone a long period of evolution', it is surprising that Peters elsewhere gives such an *a priori* account of them.

> The aims and procedures of historical institutions ... will tend to be extremely complex, and to be discoverable only by resolute and sensitive empirical enquiry ... [Peters] does not anywhere acknowledge that the disciplines stand in need of thoroughgoing interdisciplinary investigation and critique. His attitude seems to be that they are self-correcting and should be trusted absolutely (Elliott 1977, pp. 97–8).

In this connexion, look again at the earlier quotation from Peters: 'Science, mathematics, history, art, cooking and carpentry feature on the curriculum, not bingo, bridge and billiards. Presumably there must be some reason for this apart from their utilitarian or vocational value.' The kind of 'reason' that Peters has in mind concerns justification. But if we want to know why science, mathematics etc. feature on the curriculum, it is more natural to take this as a request for explanation.

I turn now to a historical explanation of the traditional school curriculum. This not only draws attention to its contingent character. It also suggests answers, historically located and not timeless answers, to the questions: Why is comprehensive knowledge—getting inside all the forms of knowledge—educationally important? And why is it important to be intrinsically motivated to have this comprehensive knowledge?

In saying that 'Science, mathematics, history, art, cooking and carpentry feature on the curriculum', Peters was talking about a particular kind of curriculum. In a British context, this was, broadly speaking, the curriculum for so-called 'middle-class schools' proposed by the Taunton Commission of the 1860s and made compulsory for the new state secondary grammar schools introduced in 1904. The 19th-century rival of this 'modern' curriculum had been the classics-based curriculum. This was seen as appropriate for the top public schools by the 1861-4 Clarendon Commission. The third great commission of that class-conscious decade, the Newcastle, proposed a curriculum based on the 3 Rs for the working classes. By the 1960s, when Peters was writing, the victory of the 'modern' curriculum over its rivals was well under way. It was sealed by the National Curriculum in 1988, which imposed it not only on every state secondary school but also on every state primary. The ten compulsory subjects of 1988 were almost identical to those in the 1904 Secondary Regulations.

How did this 'modern' curriculum grow up in the first place? Why, by the 1860s, had it been officially identified with middle-class schooling? Two preliminary points.

(i) Its core had always been knowledge in its different forms. Physical education and more purely aesthetic pursuits had been added in the 19th and 20th centuries, English literature having been part of the knowledge-based core since the 18th century, mined for truths about human nature and society.

(ii) The curriculum had always been based on a notion of general education. Although all kinds of institutions, from 1600 onwards, have taught individual subjects, from Italian to fencing, the modern curriculum that came down to us via Taunton was a compulsory course in a range of types of knowledge.

This curriculum can be traced back before the 1860s. You find it in the newly-founded University of London in 1826 and, after 1838, in the London Matriculation exam required for entrance to the London course but soon used by secondary schools for other purposes. You find it in the English Dissenting Academies, set up after 1662 to provide a higher education or ministerial training for dissenters excluded from Oxford and Cambridge, as well as in dissenting secondary schools. You find it from 1570 onwards in the Scottish universities.[1]

It is no accident that most of these institutions had connexions with English Dissenters and Scottish Presbyterians. These, often with backgrounds in industry and commerce, formed a large part of the 'middling classes' who rose to political power in the 19th century and for whom Taunton's 'middle-class schools' were intended. They were the intellectual descendants of radical protestant reformers, mainly Calvinists, of the 16th century. How is it that these largely Calvinist groups came to be associated with the 'modern' curriculum?

4.

Pierre de la Ramée (Ramus) (1515–1573), a poor boy from northern France, became Regius Professor of Eloquence and Philosophy at the University of Paris in 1551. His central concern was pedagogical. Educated Europeans of his day had been brought up in a tradition of Aristotelian scholarship based on Greek texts and commentaries on them. It was hard for scholars to make headway through the obscurities, and even harder for those unable to afford many years of higher education. Ramus provided them with a swift, manageable, way of mastering what they needed to know in a whole range of subjects and classical authors. (See Hotson, 2007, for material relevant to this Section.)

The key was his idea of the one, single 'method'. This was based on three principles. Items of subject matter had to be all true (unlike dubious material in existing textbooks); they were to be grouped together in their proper categories (so that, for instance, material on geometry would no longer be included in a work on arithmetic); the order of presentation was to be from general to particular (and so more assimilable) (Graves, 1912, p. 5). A logical breakdown of the subject-matter was represented visually as a tree diagram of the main categories, typically with dichotomised branchings taking one towards particularities. Lecture courses led students systematically through the material, with planned private study based on practical exercises, and feedback to the tutor.

Ramus applied his method to the basic teaching of a wider range of subjects than was usual at the time—including arithmetic, geometry, optics, physics and music as well as grammar, dialectic and rhetoric. He created a seven-year curriculum to teach these subjects to boys at a Paris school (Grafton and Jardine, 1986, p. 164).

His pedagogical revolution was continued after his death by three Calvinist scholars at Herborn Academy in northwest Germany. These were Keckermann, Alsted and Comenius, each of the last two the pupil of the preceding one. Together, they pared away inadequate material in Ramus' system, expanding its range to cover more and more disciplines and sub-disciplines, including developments in empirical science from Bacon, Kepler and others. The process reached its culmination in Alsted's comprehensive account in his 1630 Encyclopaedia of all branches of theoretical and practical knowledge, as well as of the mechanical arts.

Comenius carried on the encyclopaedic project under his own label 'pansophism', developing ways of transmitting a vast amount of knowledge in simplified form—for example, via his illustrated *Orbis Pictus* (Comenius,

1658) for younger children. His theoretical treatise *The Great Didactic* (Comenius, 1907) shows the continuity of the Ramist tradition since its founder. It advocates: first, giving children a general outline of a subject; comprehensive coverage of the curriculum; adherence to a single method; elimination of unnecessary content; efficient organisation so no time is wasted; practical application to everyday life.

5.

By 1600 the pedagogical revolution that Ramus initiated became closely associated with Calvinism. Although there was by no means a complete overlap, the emphasis in Calvinism on an ordered system of beliefs, paring away excrescences, simplicity and directness, efficiency and time-saving, reduced reliance on authority, diligence in study, and useful application of knowledge makes its take-up unsurprising. There was a close association between the two movements in Britain, elsewhere in northern Europe, and in New England, where Ramist ideas long remained dominant in Harvard College (founded 1636).

Given the close connexion, how far do religious reasons help to explain attachment to the Ramist tradition? Pre-1600, in the north German context, Hotson (2007) puts most weight on secular motivation. He emphasises the attractiveness of a useful, efficient and relatively inexpensive education to both a mercantile élite and to local princes building up a civil service.

But religious reasons became increasingly important after 1600, as religious divisions sharpened across Europe, not least in Britain where Puritans were gaining strength. The secular hypothesis may well show the appeal of useful knowledge, but does not account for the interest in *encyclopaedic* knowledge. Traditionally, the pursuit of knowledge had been problematic for the Christian, given its role in the Fall. Bacon's *Instauratio Magna* charted a solution that strongly appealed to his puritan disciples. He believed that 'all knowledge is to be limited by religion, and to be referred to use and action'. As Webster says, 'This conclusion was perfectly adapted to the puritan position; investigations conducted into secondary causes, and with utilitarian ends in mind, would incur no risk of transgression, but instead glorify God' (Webster, 1975, p. 22). There is a related view about the Fall that weighed with reformers. Man had been created in the image of God. The Fall meant that there had to be a new 'instauration' in man of this image. Not all had been lost. The human mind still contained 'slender rays of its pristine light', as manifested in its intellectual and volitional abilities (Hotson, 2005, p. 1). The school was the institution in which these abilities could be developed, and therewith the image of God in man restored. The Calvinists Keckermann, Alsted and Comenius all thought this way. It was closely connected with their encyclopaedism. In Alsted's words:

Although God alone is wise and all-knowing, nevertheless he impresses the image of his perfection on men who desire to learn, as is seen especially in those who by vehement force of mind embrace the whole orb of the disciplines, that is to say, what is commonly called the encyclopaedia (Hotson, 2005, p. 11).

Comenius' pansophism and the education he devised to realise it have the same rationale. He writes:

... it is evident that man is naturally capable of a knowledge of all things, since, in the first place, he is the image of God. For an image, if it be accurate, necessarily reproduces the outlines of its archetype, as otherwise it will not be an image. Now omniscience is chief among the properties of God, and it follows that the image of this must be reflected in man (Comenius, 1907, p. 41).

Unlike the secular rationale, this religious argument provides a powerful reason, within its own terms, for an encyclopaedic education. It is man's duty on earth to become as omniscient as possible.

6.

It could be that curricula originally devised for religious reasons by educationalists like Comenius appealed to many students and employers for secular reasons, to do with getting on in the world. But the two motivations are not, in any case, discrete. Calvinism was devoted to diligent social and economic improvement as a sign of devotion to God. The two kinds of reason for a modern, general education interweave through its later history in Britain from the 17th to the 19th centuries.

We find both of them in the extraordinary story of the 'Three Foreigners' who ran educational policy for the Puritans between 1640 and 1660. These were Samuel Hartlib, John Dury, and Comenius himself—all educated by pupils or admirers of Keckermann (Hotson, 1994, p. 45). Comenius, invited to England by Parliament in 1641–2, projected a millenarian reform of English education for the approaching 'last age of the world ... in which Christ and his Church shall triumph[,] ... an age of Enlightenment, in which the earth shall be filled with the knowledge of God, as the waters cover the sea' (Trevor-Roper, 1967, p. 271). To this end, he recommended a national system of education from a central 'pansophical' college down to elementary schools.

After 1660, Anglicanism triumphed. Puritans and other radical protes-tants—e.g. Quakers—who refused to conform were excluded from public life. But the schools and academies that these 'Dissenters' now set up, often illegally, kept alive the modern curriculum. As earlier, religious reasons went along with secular ones.

Three examples of the former. First, Philip Doddridge, writing of students like himself following a modern curriculum at Kibworth Academy around 1720, states that 'they are taught in all the several Branches of their Course to acknowledge God and direct their Enquiries and their Labours to his Glory' (Doddridge, 1728, p. 48). Second, in 1786, Thomas Barnes, principal of the new Manchester Academy, wrote:

> Of all subjects, DIVINITY seems most to demand the aid of kindred, and even of apparently remoter sciences. Its objects are GOD and MAN: and nothing, which can either illustrate the perfections of the one, or the nature, capacities, and history of the other, can be entirely eliminated ... Natural Philosophy, in its widest sense, comprehending whatever relates to the history or properties of the works of Nature, in the Earth, the Air, the Ocean, and including Natural History, Chemistry, &c. has an immediate reference to the one—and to the other belong, all that Anatomy and Physiology can discover relating to the body, and all that Metaphysics, Moral Philosophy, History, or Revelation declare concerning the mind (Sell, 2004, pp. 11–12).

And third, Grove House School, in Tottenham, was a Quaker foundation of 1828. It included natural philosophy (physics) in its broad curriculum, partly for reasons of mental training, but also because it helped pupils to acquire 'a clearer and enlarged vision of the wisdom of the Supreme Being in the wonderful regularity of the Laws of Nature' (Brown, 1952, p. 8).

7.

I come back to Peters and Hirst and the problem of justifying a general, modern curriculum on intrinsic grounds. We saw earlier that their own arguments are problematic. The historical sketch shows us that, in the earlier history of this modern curriculum, there was a good reason, given a certain religious framework, why it (a) should cover the whole range of knowledge, and (b) be intrinsically important.[2] Could there be any echoes of the old religious justification in the writings of the 1960s? In case this seems totally implausible, let's look for a moment at Philip Phenix's theory.

Phenix

Philip Phenix (1964) discusses the ideal curriculum somewhat as Hirst does— in terms of a small number of logically distinct categories of understanding.

Phenix was educated at Union Theological Seminary in New York. In 1961 he wrote that 'the central task of education is religious conversion' (Phenix, 1961, p. 242), and that 'We are reserving the name of religion in the present analysis for a reverential attitude to what is of ultimate value' (p. 237). 'This is the one supreme purpose which unites all the lesser purposes of education: to engender reverence' (p. 252). In 1964 he spelt out his abstract schema for the curriculum, based on six 'realms of meaning': symbolics, empirics, esthetics, synnoetics, ethics and synoptics. The book's first words are: 'It is not easy to sustain a sense of the whole. Many a person pursues his own limited calling with scarcely a thought for his place in the total drama of civilised endeavour' (Phenix, 1964, p. 3). And a little later he writes: 'Students and teachers alike are prone to take the curriculum as they find it, as a traditional sequence of separate elements, without ever inquiring into the comprehensive pattern within which the parts are located' (ibid.). This last quotation assumes that the traditional curriculum does have a comprehensive pattern behind it but has come to be taken as a collection of disparate items. Phenix is a latter-day encyclopaedist, recalling his readers to a wholeness that once lay behind the curriculum's now disconnected parts. At the same time, he does not see this wholeness as an undivided totality: like Hirst, and like the Ramist thinkers, he sees it as subdivisible on logical principles into a number of discrete realms.

Peters

Phenix's emphasis on reverence reminds us of Peters' comment in his transcendental argument that, unlike games, academic disciplines are not 'hived off from man's curiosity about the world and his awe and concern about his own peculiar predicament within it'. He fills this out by a quotation from Whitehead about the value of religion to a human life in merging 'its individual claim with that of the objective universe' (Peters, 1966, p. 164). As Ray Elliott writes, Peters' 'response to Being-in-totality and to human being-in-the-world, on the contemplation of them, is one of piety . . . [H]e attaches what is, according to his own account, a religious significance to that which gives and discovers meaning and which receives and discloses it' (Elliott, 1986, p. 57). When he wrote the passage mentioned above, Peters had been a Quaker for some thirty years. His teaching experience after the war had been in the Quaker school at Sidcot in Somerset, founded in 1699. In 2008 the school's on-line prospectus tells us that 'Education should be a joyful experience of self-development and an inspiring introduction to the wonders of creation'. This reflects, as perhaps does Peters' comment, Quakerism's attachment since its inception to the revelatory power of the natural world and to the role of science in exploring it.

I do not know how much weight, if any, to put on the suggestion that Peters' argument may have some continuity with older religious justifications.

Hirst

One way of coping with some of the problems in Hirst's position would be to fill out his account with arguments taken from the Ramist tradition. But this would be to saddle it with a theological rationale that he would reject.

Three features of Hirst are reminiscent of this tradition. First, both favour an education in every branch of knowledge. As with Keckermann, Alsted and

Comenius, Hirst makes it clear that this ideal can only be realised at the level of general principles, not detailed content (Hirst, 1965, p. 261). Second, the totality of knowledge subdivides by logical principles into smaller categories. Hirst's seven forms of knowledge parallel the academic disciplines identified by Ramus and his successors. In each case, the logical discreteness of these units is stressed. Third, Hirst makes links between (i) the pursuit of knowledge in every domain, (ii) the development of mind (in one place he refers to 'the comprehensive development of the mind in acquiring knowledge' (Hirst, 1965, p. 261)), and (iii) the good life.

The similarities are these. (i) The Ramist tradition prizes encyclopaedic knowledge because (ii) this helps to bring the learner's mind closer to the mind of God as an omniscient being. It furthers, in Alsted's words, the 'instauration of the image of God in Man'. (i) and (ii) are also connected with (iii), the good life. For, assuming the theological framework within which Alsted and others were working, the only good life could be one's existence as an immortal soul after one's salvation, a life freed from the snares of the body and devoted to spiritual activity.

As I have said, Hirst would reject such a rationale. Although he was brought up in a strict evangelical faith, he early abandoned this and saw his theory of liberal education as wholly rationally, not theologically, based (Hirst, 2008).

8.

How significant are parallels between 1960s thinking and the religious tradition in question? I am aware of the temptation to read too much into them and present what I hope is a more rounded historical picture in Section 9. Meanwhile I would like to explore the point about the development of mind in a somewhat different territory.

The development of mind is a key concept for Hirst, as we have seen, and also for Peters. Like Hirst, he links it with learning to operate within the 'differentiated modes of thought and awareness' of a scientific, mathematical, historical, religious, moral or aesthetic sort (Peters, 1966, p. 50).

A predecessor to scientific psychology was pneumatics (or pneumatology). This had to do with the nature of spirits, and was divided into work on the 'powers and faculties' of the human mind, and work on the being of God. It was a staple subject in dissenting academies, Scottish universities, and—often in a different form—in American universities and colleges. In the 19th century, it became secularised as scientific psychology (White, 2006, pp. 100–6). It was also in the 19th century that intrinsic justifications of the academic curriculum begin to appear, based on psychological claims about human faculties. In New England, the 1828 Yale Report justifies its general course in terms of the mental powers that each subject specifically develops: 'In laying the foundation of a thorough education, it is necessary that all the important mental faculties be brought into exercise . . . The mind never attains its full perfection, unless its various powers are so trained as to give them the fair proportions which nature designed.'[3] The Report appeared in the period before the emergence of scientific psychology and traces of New England Puritanism are evident in the passage quoted. It echoes the 17th century notion of the instauration of the image of God in man, already referred to. For Alsted, acquiring encyclopaedic knowledge helps to remedy the defects of our intellectual faculties and thus to restore in us the ruined image of God (Hotson, 2005, pp. 10–11). We find the same idea in John Dury's *The Reformed School*, where he is describing the true end of learning:

> . . . to marshal sciences [i.e. forms of knowledge] rightly that they may be taught orderly and profitably, the subordination of their various ends to each other . . . and the way of teaching the same . . . must be observed . . . For the encyclopaedia of the sciences must answer the wheel of human faculties, and this wheel must answer the circle of creatures [phenomena created by God] whence man is to supply his defects (Dury, 1650/1958, p. 38).

Faculty psychology became influential in the 19th century largely owing to the philosopher Thomas Reid's elaboration of it in his *Essays on the Intellectual Powers of Man* (1785). These powers embraced sense-perception, memory, conception, abstraction, judgment, reasoning and taste. Reid, who had been a Presbyterian minister before becoming an academic, saw his work as a contribution to pneumatology. He wrote that 'The mind of man is the noblest work of God which reason discovers to us, and therefore, on account of its dignity, deserves our study' (Reid, 1785/1941, Preface, p. xxxv). Faculty psychology was used to justify the academic curriculum, not only in the USA but also in Britain. Here justifications in terms of faculties became increasingly applied to modern subjects after 1860. In 1867, J. M. Wilson, science master at Rugby, writes that:

> . . . the mental training to be got from the study of science is the main reason for its introduction into schools . . . The student of natural science is likely to bring with him to the study of philosophy or politics, or business, or his profession, whatever it may be, a more active and original mind, a sounder judgment and a clearer head in consequence of his study (Wilson, in Adamson, 1930, pp. 313-4).

The following year, 1868, the Taunton Report favoured 'the general cultivation of the intellect' or 'powers of the mind':

> In their view the great merit of natural science is that it is 'an important agent in mental discipline', the value of geometry lies in its 'exercise of severe reasoning'; drawing 'strengthens habits of accurate observation' . . .

Latin was to be retained 'partly because all teachers agree in praising its excellence as a mental discipline' (Adamson, 1930, p. 260).

In 1879, the psychologist Alexander Bain published his influential *Education as a Science*. He held that 'the primary, if not the whole, aim of instruction was mental discipline' (Adamson, 1930, p. 476). The 'highest justification' for Mathematics, for instance, has to do with its role in training the 'whole mechanism of reasoning' (Bain, 1879, p. 152). 'The Practical or Applied Sciences', on the other hand—Bain mentions among others navigation, engineering, agriculture, medicine, politics, ethics, law, grammar and rhetoric—'have no purpose beyond their immediate application. None of them can be accounted sciences of Method, Discipline, or Training' (pp. 163–7).

In his preface to the 1904 Secondary Regulations introducing the academic curriculum into state education, Robert Morant underlined the importance of general education. This:

> ... must be such as gives a reasonable degree of exercise and development to the whole of the faculties, and does not confine this development to a particular channel ... Specialisation ... should only begin after the general education has been carried to a point at which the habit of exercising all these faculties has been formed (Board of Education, 1904, Prefatory Memorandum, 5(a)).

Leaving aside problems about how faculties are identified—for Morant is not specific—why did he think it important that all the faculties be developed? He does not say.

Paul Hirst's theory was in part a reaction to the justification found in the Harvard Report of 1946 on *General Education in a Free Society*. This was in the same psychological tradition. The Report argued that a general education based on the natural sciences, the humanities and social studies develops certain mental abilities: 'to think effectively, to communicate thought, to make relevant judgments, to discriminate among values' (Hirst, 1965, p. 249). Although the filling is different, the form of the argument is similar to Morant's. Hirst defined his own position against Harvard's, arguing that the abilities it mentions have a place only within specific forms of thought. What counts as 'effective thinking', for instance, is very different in history and mathematics. Even so, Hirst's position is close to Harvard's (and Morant's) in the place it accords the development of mind in the rationale for a general education.

Whatever the historical links may be between Hirst's and earlier forms of psychological justification, there is no doubt about the originality of Hirst's 'forms of knowledge' argument among accounts of the academic curriculum between, say, 1800 and when he wrote in the 1960s. From the Yale Report of 1828, via Taunton, Morant, the Norwood Report, and through to the

Harvard Report of 1946, these accounts have been largely brief and unsystematic. Hirst's argument is quite different. It presents us with a tightly organised system of categories—the 'forms'—derived *a priori* from the nature of knowledge itself. There has been nothing like this in the history of education since Comenius and his forebears in the Ramist pedagogical tradition.

One last speculation. The latest manifestation of Harvard's ancient attachment to general education are Howard Gardner's eight or nine 'multiple intelligences'. Like Hirst's 'forms', they do not map exactly on to conventional school subjects, but are, even so, close to them. Gardner's writings on the content of education favour the 'general education' tradition. He writes: 'Education in our time should provide the basis for enhanced understanding of our several worlds—the physical world, the biological world, the world of human beings, the world of human artifacts, and the world of the self' (Gardner, 1999, p. 158). He also thinks this understanding should be largely for intrinsic ends: 'I favor . . . the pursuit of knowledge for its own sake over the obeisance to utility' (p. 39).

Does the link that Gardner makes between pursuing this or that branch of knowledge and the development of these or those types of intelligence indicate a revival of the faculty psychology mode of justification? There are question-marks about the ultimate basis of Gardner's theory, just as there are about Hirst's and about Peters'. All three favour the acquisition of comprehensive general knowledge for intrinsic reasons; and all equate this with the development of mind. But their justifications give out at this point.

9.

The Ramist pedagogical tradition had a theological justification for developing the mind/forms of knowledge for intrinsic rather than practical reasons. This keystone, that once held the whole argument together, has long since crumbled away. This did not happen all at once. The original idea that acquiring the whole circle of knowledge remedied the defects of human faculties lived on in the shape of curriculum justifications reliant on faculty psychology, at first within a religious framework, and later in the 19th century within a scientific one. These justifications, although shot to pieces by Dewey and by John Adams among others, lived on into the mid-20th century, supported by Morant in 1904 and the Harvard Report in 1946. Paul Hirst's retention of the development of mind as a justification for an academic curriculum, while rejecting the faculty psychology interpretation of this, was, until the appearance of Gardner's work, the last, now highly abstract, manifestation of this ancient tradition.

As faculty psychology arguments for the academic curriculum grew less influential after 1900, other arguments for its intrinsic value began to take their place. The Norwood Report of 1943, which helped to create the post-war tripartite system, is an important text here. It incorporated another kind of psychological argument—based not on faculty psychology but on the psychology of individual differences championed most notably by Cyril Burt. An academic curriculum, it held, suited a certain kind of secondary pupil only—one with a high level of general intelligence. It claimed that children of this sort were driven by a love of intellectual learning for its own sake. The grammar school, in its eyes, was appropriate for:

> ... the pupil who is interested in learning for its own sake, who can grasp an argument or follow a piece of connected reasoning, who is interested in causes, whether on the level of human volition or in the material world, who cares to know how things came to be as well as how they are, who is sensitive to language as expression of thought, to a proof as a precise demonstration, to a series of experiments justifying a principle: he is interested in the relatedness of related things, in development, in structure, in a coherent body of knowledge (Norwood Report, 1943, chapter 1)

> ... For a mind showing promise of this kind the grammar school has traditionally provided a curriculum which it regards as appropriate (Chapter 2).

Two decades after Norwood, it was left to the new school of British philosophy of education under Hirst and Peters to theorise and justify on philosophical grounds an academic curriculum within the framework inherited from Norwood, but without linking this curriculum only with the most intellectually able and without relying on individual psychology to do so. In Peters' case, but not in Hirst's, there is also a faint echo of an older, religious, justification.

Neither of the two psychology-based justifications, nor the philosophical ones of Peters and Hirst, succeeded in showing why an academic curriculum was worth studying for intrinsic, i.e. non-practical, reasons. After Hirst and Peters intrinsic justifications of any sort, psychological, philosophical or whatever, were rarely attempted.

There is a plausible explanation of this. Already by the end of the 18th century, many English dissenting families, not least those who made use of the liberal academies and Scottish universities, had become wealthy through business and manufacturing. They were often exercised by social status reasons, intent on a liberal education for their sons suitable for a gentleman (Mercer, 2001, p. 50). They saw science as a key component of this. It was 'the mode of cultural self-expression by a new social class who had hitherto felt socially and politically ostracized' (p. 42).

This last point is worth dwelling on. Although some economic historians have seen dissenting academies as utilitarian institutions, preparing their lay students for commercial and industrial careers, there is little evidence for this

(p. 40). What was important was a general education based on modern subjects. The religious rationale that had long lain behind this was joined from the 1780s onwards by the status reason just mentioned (p. 42).

This non-utilitarian reason for favouring an academic education persisted through the 19th century. It was given a boost by the Taunton Report's association of a modern rather than a classical curriculum with the middle classes and also by Morant's introduction of fee-paying state secondary schools for a tiny percentage of the population in 1904. As the 20th century progressed, the position of the academic curriculum was reinforced by the introduction of the School Certificate in 1917, which required a pass in a range of academic subjects; and also by the growth of subject associations and subject departments in secondary schools (Goodson, 1987, pp. 29–30).

One reason why non-utilitarian justifications of the academic curriculum faded away after the 1960s is that, owing to the entrenchment of its position in schools, it was increasingly *taken as read* that an academic education of this sort was a good thing. Socialists from R. H. Tawney (1922) onwards assumed that 'secondary education for all' meant 'academic secondary education for all'. (This is indeed what I myself believed in the 1960s and early 1970s.) Richard Peters, as we saw at the beginning of this chapter, took it for granted that there *must* be some good intrinsic reason for an academic curriculum.

Perhaps the most notorious example of this taking-for-granted is that when Kenneth Baker laid down his ten-subject National Curriculum in 1988, he felt no obligation to provide any reasons why this kind of structure was a good thing. Justification was now otiose.

After 1988, as teachers and others began more and more to ask what the National Curriculum was for, the government produced sets of aims, in 1999 and in 2007, within which the existing subjects were supposed to find a rationale. The era of taking-for-granted seemed to be over. The only problem—a major one, and one with which we are still living—is that, through all the reforms since 1988, governments have insisted that the existing structure of academic subjects is not to be tampered with. Rather than seizing the opportunity to rethink school education as a genuinely aims-based enterprise, they have clung to the centuries-old pattern described in this chapter.[4]

NOTES

1. Here are some early examples of modern curricula. References in White (n.d.):
   - *Melville's Glasgow University after 1574* Year 1: humanities (Greek and Latin) and Ramus' dialectic. 2: mathematics, cosmography, astronomy. 3: moral and political science. 4: natural philosophy (physics) and history.
   - *Keckermann's Danzig gymnasium 1602.* Year 1: logic and physics. 2: metaphysics and mathematics (including astronomy and geography as well as arithmetic and geometry). 3: practical philosophy (ethics, philosophy and economics).
   - *King's College, Aberdeen 1641.* Year 1: mainly Greek and Hebrew. 2: logic, rhetoric

and mathematics. 3: ethics, politics and economics. 4: natural philosophy (including astronomy, geography, optics, music).

- *Doddridge's Northampton Dissenting Academy 1720s.* Year 1: logic, rhetoric, geography, metaphysics, geometry, algebra. 2: trigonometry, conic sections, celestial mechanics, natural and experimental philosophy, divinity, orations. 3: natural and civil history, anatomy, Jewish antiquities, divinity, orations. 4: civil law, mythology and hieroglyphics, English history, history of nonconformity, divinity, preaching and pastoral care
- *Wesley's Kingswood School 1749.* Reading, writing, arithmetic, English, French, Latin, Greek, Hebrew; history, geography, chronology; rhetoric, logic, ethics, geometry, algebra, physics, music.
- *Scottish Universities MA in Arts course, 18th century.* Year 1: Greek tended to be taught. 2: logic and metaphysics. 3: ethics and pneumatics. 4: natural philosophy, probably including some mathematics
- *University of London 1826.* Years 1,2: Latin, Greek and mathematics. 3: logic and philosophy of mind, chemistry and natural philosophy. 4: jurisprudence, political economy, natural philosophy, moral and political philosophy
- *Grove House (Quaker) School, Tottenham 1828.* Latin and Greek, principles of religious liberty and the British constitution, geography and history in relation to the Bible, advanced and applied mathematics, natural philosophy.
- *London Matriculation exam after 1838.* A range of academic subjects close to those taught for the early London BA course—including mathematics, natural philosophy, chemistry, Greek and Latin, English language, outlines of history and geography, and (for Honours) natural history.

2. J. H. Newman was a well-known advocate of the intrinsic value of university education. Although he did not favour a general course, he did say, of the university as a whole, that:

> ... all branches of knowledge are connected together, because the subject-matter of knowledge is intimately united in itself, as being the acts and the work of the Creator ... Knowledge is capable of being its own end. Such is the constitution of the human mind, that any kind of knowledge, if it be really such, is its own reward (Newman, 1854/1976, Discourse 5, Section 1).

3. Available online at: http://collegiateway.org/reading/yale-report-1828/ pp.6–7.
4. This chapter takes much further a theme first explored in White, 2005.

REFERENCES

Adamson, J. W. (1930) *English Education 1789–1902* (Cambridge, Cambridge University Press).
Bain, A. (1879) *Education as a Science* (London, Kegan Paul).
Board of Education (1904) *Regulations for Secondary Schools* (London, HMSO).
Brown, S. W. (1952) *Leighton Park: A History of the School* (London, Leighton Park School?).
Comenius, J. A. (1907) *The Great Didactic*, M. W. Keatinge, trans. (London, Adam and Charles Black).
Comenius, J. A. (1658) *Orbis Sensualis Pictus* Republished 1896 (London, Pospisila).
Doddridge, P. (1728) *Notes on an Educational Method* (GB 0096 MS 609) (London, University of London Library).
Dury, J. [c.1650] (1958) *The Reformed School* (Knox, H. M. ed. (Liverpool, Liverpool University Press).

Elliott, R. K. (1977) Education and Justification, in: Hirst and White (1998) Vol 1

Elliott, R. K. (1986) Richard Peters: A Philosopher in the Older Style, in: Hirst and White (1998) Vol 1.

Gardner, H. (1999) *The Disciplined Mind* (New York, Simon and Schuster).

Goodson, I. (1987) *School Subjects and Curriculum Change* (London, Falmer).

Grafton, A. and Jardine, L. (1986) *From Humanism to the Humanities* (London, Duckworth).

Graves, F. P. (1912) *Peter Ramus and the Educational Reformation of the Sixteenth Century* (New York, Macmillan).

Harvard Report (1946) *General Education in a Free Society* (Cambridge, MA, Harvard University Press).

Hirst, P. H. (1965) Liberal Education and the Nature of Knowledge, in: Hirst and White (1998) Vol 1

Hirst, P. H. (2008) In Pursuit of Reason, in: L. Waks (ed.) *Leaders in Philosophy of Education: Intellectual Self Portraits* (Rotterdam, Sense Press).

Hirst, P. H. and Peters, R. S. (1970) *The Logic of Education* (London, Routledge and Kegan Paul).

Hirst, P. H. and White, P. A. (eds) (1998) *Philosophy of Education: Major Themes in the Analytic Tradition* (London, Routledge).

Hotson, H. (1994) Philosophical Pedagogy in Reformed Central Europe between Ramus and Comenius, in: M. Greengrass and M. Leslie (eds) *Samuel Hartlib and Universal Reformation* (Cambridge, Cambridge University Press).

Hotson, H. (2005) The Instauration of the Image of God in Man, in: M. Pelling and S. Mandelbrote (eds) *The Practice of Reform in Health, Medicine and Science, 1500–2000* (Aldershot, Ashgate).

Hotson, H. (2007) *Commonplace Learning: Ramism and its German Manifestations 1543–1630* (Oxford, Oxford University Press).

Mercer, M. (2001) Dissenting Academies and the Education of the Laity, 1750–1850, *History of Education*, 30.1, pp. 35–58.

Newman, J. H. [1854] (1976) *The Idea of a University* (Ker, I. ed. (Oxford, Clarendon Press).

Norwood Report (1943) *Curriculum and Examinations in Secondary Schools* (London, HMSO).

Peters, R. S. (1966) *Ethics and Education* (London, Allen and Unwin).

Peters, R. S. (1973) The Justification of Education, in: Hirst and White (1998) Vol 1

Phenix, P. H. (1961) *Education and the Common Good* (New York, Harper).

Phenix, P. H. (1964) *Realms of Meaning* (New York, McGraw-Hill).

Reid, T. [1785] (1941) *Essays on the Intellectual Powers of Man* (London, Macmillan).

Sell, A. (2004) *Philosophy, Dissent and Nonconformity 1689–1920* (Cambridge, James Clarke).

Taunton Report (1868) *Report of the Schools Inquiry Commission.*

Tawney, R. H. (1922) *Secondary Education for All* (London, Allen and Unwin).

Trevor-Roper, H. (1967) Three Foreigners: The Philosophers of the Puritan Revolution, in his *Religion, the Reformation and Social Change* (London, Macmillan).

Webster, C. (1975) *The Great Instauration: Science, Medicine And Reform 1626–1660* (London, Duckworth).

White, J. (1973) *Towards a Compulsory Curriculum* (London, Routledge and Kegan Paul).

White, J. (2005) Reassessing 1960s Philosophy of the Curriculum, *Review of Education*, 3.2, pp. 131–44.

White, J. (2006) *Intelligence, Destiny and Education: The Ideological Roots of Intelligence Testing* (London, Routledge).

White, J. (n.d.) *The Struggle for General Education: Ramus, the Dissenters, and the Origins of the National Curriculum.*

Young, M. F. D. (ed.) (1971) *Knowledge and Control* (London, Collier-Macmillan).

9

The Good, the Worthwhile and the Obligatory: Practical Reason and Moral Universalism in R. S. Peters' Conception of Education

CHRISTOPHER MARTIN

When I reread R. S. Peters through the lens of contemporary moral philosophy, I find myself reading him as a moral universalist. He certainly wrote approvingly (though not unqualifiedly so) of much of what universalist moral thinkers such as Kant and Kohlberg had to say. He had a firm grasp of transcendental argument (see in particular Montefiore, 1986; Hirst, 1986; and Kleing, 1973. Further, his work on the autonomy of practical reason has been influential on the universalistic moral theory of Jürgen Habermas (1990; Martin, 2009). Finally, his account of the moral life is most assuredly universalistic, as is clear from Paul Hirst's impressive overview of his work:

> Basic to [his] account is a notion of rational universalistic morality as this has emerged from the clash of codes of living and competing views of the world as a result of social change and economic expansion. Reflecting about which view of the world was true, which code was correct, men came to accept higher-order principles of a procedural sort for determining such questions. By these means matters of morals came to be distinguished from matters of customs of law, codes could be criticised and revised, and men gradually became able to stand on their own feet as autonomous moral beings (Hirst, 1986, p. 31).

As is clear from the above, Peters account of the moral life and the conception of practical reason that informed it was by no means grounded in any speculative metaphysical perspective or noumenal/phenomenal doctrine. Rather, the universalistic core of morality is uncovered through the necessary development of public and discursive means of addressing competing claims of how we ought to live together. Individuals socialised in such a context find that the interests and values defining their own life and community cannot

Reading R. S. Peters Today, First Edition. Stefaan E. Cuypers and Christopher Martin.
Chapters © 2011 The Authors. Editorial organization © 2011 Philosophy of Education Society of Great Britain. Published 2011 by Blackwell Publishing Ltd.

simply be generalised across other communities. Peters' moral universalism is post-metaphysical, appropriately cautious and inclusive in ways that place it in good company with contemporary work in moral philosophy.

It is with some disappointment, then, that an attempt to extend a similarly sophisticated universalism into our understanding of education is not as well received. Here, Peters wishes to develop arguments that demonstrate how education is an enterprise that is separate and distinct from other ways in which persons are shaped and changed (Peters, 1966, pp. 32–35). The implied meaning in the use of the term 'education' is claimed to convey an undertaking directed to the development of a person *as* a person and not for contingent ends. If such an argument were to be successful, one might be able to see education as subject to criteria far more demanding than that to which schooling has been generally associated with. Such an argument, while abstract in nature, is of significant practical importance. If we can show that education entails standards that are not entirely contingent upon current interests, we would have a framework that all institutions seriously claiming to be involved in the enterprise would have to acknowledge. In a more contemporary sense, it might go some way to clarifying how claims about the universal right to an education can mean something more than simply access to free and compulsory schooling—rather, the concept of education would refer to the right to experience an enterprise that is owed to all persons by virtue of being persons. On this view, a well-justified normative account of education could stand as a valuable point of departure for social criticism of our current educational practices.

Nonetheless, while some aspects of Peters' argument may be appealing in this respect, it is difficult to read such a project along lines that are appropriately sensitive to the oft-cited dangers of moral universalism. However, I think a more detailed reconstruction of the relationship between Peters' work in philosophical ethics and his conceptual analysis may go some way in showing how one *can* posit of education as a concept having universalistic connotations. I argue that although many of the criticisms laid at Peters' feet are of merit, they overshadow more potentially useful interpretive moves. Finally, I will suggest that a change in the focus of Peters' account of education and practical reason can provide important resources for engaging in a more plausible exploration of universalistic themes in education.

R. S. PETERS ON THE CONCEPT AND JUSTIFICATION OF EDUCATION

The attempt to establish a general concept of education was by no means unchallenged. W. H. Dray, for example, suggested that Peters' conceptual account of education is more a projection of his own values about what education should be (Dray, 1973, pp. 38–39; Elliott, 1986, pp. 43–44). There is the not unrelated concern that Peters' concept of education was 'essentialist'. These objections are perhaps part of the reason why one might read his work in universalistic terms, yet find that such a reading does not get one very far. On the one hand, Peters wanted to provide a conceptual analysis wherein we can actually understand what it is we are doing (or claiming to do) when we engage in those activities that we call 'educational'. On the other hand, he is too sophisticated a philosopher to be content to offer a conceptual clarification of education and leave it at that. He is well aware that as a *practical* philosophical project, a normative account of education entails more than a description of concepts, and in his reply to Dray he is quick to point out the limits of any singularly conceptual approach (Dray, 1973, p. 43). Even if we are clear on what we are talking about when we speak of education, further work needs to done to show how and to what extent such claims ought to take hold on the lives of developing persons.

This tension between Peters' conceptual analysis and his universalism comes out in two different passages, each of which is worth quoting at length. This first is taken from the 'conceptual' aspect of the spectrum:

> 'Morality' can be used as a classificatory term by means of which a form of interpersonal behaviour can be distinguished from custom, law, religious codes and so on. But in ethics and in the practical task of bringing up children, this does not take us very far; for it would involve us in the most feeble form of the naturalistic fallacy to argue that, because we term a form of behaviour 'moral', this behaviour is one which should be pursued or encouraged. Nothing about what ought to be done follows from the empirical fact that we use a word in a certain way (Peters, 1973, p. 255).[1]

The second passage I see as taken from the 'universalist' aspect:

> It is not to commit some version of the naturalistic fallacy by basing a demand for a type of life on features of human life which make it distinctively human. For this would be to repeat the errors of the old Greek doctrine of function. Rather it is to say that human life already bears witness to the demands of reason. Without some acceptance of such demands their life would be unintelligible (Peters, 1981, pp. 110–111).

I select these passages for their 'comparative' value. Namely, they demonstrate that the conceptual mapping Peters engages in is not restricted to 'educational' terms. Moral language games, like educational ones, can benefit from clarification. The first passage is within the context of a critique of Kohlberg's conception of morality. Here, Kohlberg's usage of the term 'moral' is charged with being unwarrantedly prescriptive by presupposing a usage not always shared by others (note the symmetries with this line of critique, Dray's objection to Peters, and my critique of Peters below). On Peters' view, Kohlberg can only merit such a usage insofar as we understand the more general justificatory framework within which such a language operates—for how else can one rightly say they are making a valid moral claim?

The second passage is a kind of methodological inverse of the first. Here we see that the universalistic framework typically ascribed to Peters' account of the moral life is directly applied to 'education' itself. This latter passage is within the context of an argument about the rationale or justification of education and, more specifically, the value of endeavouring such a justification in the first place. The case is made that there is a deeply immanent connection between educational processes and the justification of those same processes. On this view, to question the substance of the educational account that Peters offers or the value of giving an account *qua* account is to make a demand for reasons—a demand that presupposes the values of rationality that are 'immanent' to the demand for justification itself (Peters, 1973, p. 253). Here, the concept of education and the universalistic framework intersect. What I mean by this is that while practices of justification, generally speaking, presuppose certain values (such as a commitment to truth, for example) education is different in that it seeks to foster such values in persons. Education is on these grounds isolable from other human practices. I might presuppose similar values in other kinds of reason-giving discourse, but education is a different enterprise in that it directly engages with and promotes such values.

If such an account is sound, then we might be able to defend the institutionalisation of educational processes on the basis of their distinct and irreplaceable character. One might even be able to use such an account to advocate access to such a process as a matter of moral right. From a contemporary human rights perspective, this would mean much more than access to 'schooling'. Shouldn't everyone have an opportunity to understand the value of reason-giving, equality and impartiality—values that, on Peters' view, make human community as we know it possible? Human life may always 'bear witness to reason', but education refers to what can move us from passive spectators to active participants. Of course, philosophers with a more contextualist sensibility should be rightly concerned with this line— haven't we heard similar kinds of argument used to defend cultural imperialism, for example? In the next section I would like to give a clearer exposition of how Peters arrives at this position and assess something of its cogency. Does it really have such potential?

EDUCATIONAL VALUES; VALUES OF JUSTIFICATION

Peters is not always straightforward on the connections between his analysis of educational concepts and his universalistic claims about autonomy, morality and practical reason. In *Ethics and Education,* for example, the conceptual analysis of education in the first part of the work seems to jar against the transcendental deduction of principles offered in the second part. Not much is presented in the way of a clear and sustained account of the relationship between the two. In my view, the most significant of what is offered is in the following:

> 'Education' has notions such as 'improvement', 'betterment', and 'the passing on of what is worthwhile' built into it. That education must involve something of ethical value is, therefore, a matter of logical necessity. There is, however, no logical necessity about the particular values ascribed to the variable of 'being worthwhile'. The justification of such values, too, must go beyond the realm of conceptual analysis into that of ethical theory (Peters, 1966, p. 91).

I take Peters to mean that while our talk about education presupposes value, what is of value is to be decided through practical reasoning. It is exactly at this point where the conceptual analysis and the universalistic framework come together. For either the grounds upon which we justify our educational values are fundamentally dependent on the local cultural and historical context or we can make the case that there are certain universal values intrinsic to education. Any conception of education would have to reflect such universal values. On a more contextual conception of education, for example, a sufficient justification for science in the curriculum would be because it somehow reflects our shared, liberal democratic tradition. Having scientific understanding, for example, could be defended on the grounds that there is something about having scientific understanding that could allow one to flourish in modern democratic communities. In the 'universal value' case, the value of science rests on grounds relating to the way in which science reflects values intrinsic to education itself. In this later case, our reasons used to justify the inclusion of science would be more abstract and general in scope, for it would necessarily refer to a standard transcending any particular context. The study of science might, for example, be claimed to result in 'betterment' regardless of time or place. Alternatively, one might argue that participation in scientific discourse is representative of a certain quality in critical thought and reason-giving, a quality of discourse to which all persons with a capacity for practical reasoning should have some exposure. But there is nothing about science that is itself of value in this later case, for there are other pursuits that could achieve the same end. In any case, the kinds of reasons for justifying educational judgements on an intrinsic account would have to extend beyond any and all contexts. In other words, arguments used to rationally justify claims about education would have to appeal to a kind of objective educational principle, similar to the sense in which universalistic moral claims must accord with an objective moral principle.

Such an account cannot be grounded in the conceptual logic of education alone. This is exactly the kind of mistake that Peters sees progressivists as making:

[G]rowth theorists pondered on the concept of 'education' and mistakenly puffed up some minimal conceptual intimations into a procedural principle. More probably their concept of education was moulded by their consciences; for they were morally indignant at the lack of respect shown for children as individuals ... (Peters, 1966, p. 43).

Here the objection is not with progressivism as such, but with a flawed model of justification where certain conditions derived from the mapping of a concept are taken to be ideals to be pursued. So, for example, the fact that the concept of education entails a degree of voluntariness for those involved in an educational process is 'inflated' into the educational ideal that all teaching practices ought always give children the maximum freedom possible.

Even when such pitfalls are identified, such a justificatory project is daunting. If the concept of education is to represent an objective standard, Peters needs to develop an argument showing how his proffered standard for educationally justifiable judgements are not covertly contingent or conventional.[2] Peters' transcendental argument holds some promise here.

Yet, the transcendental theory of justification developed in *Ethics and Education* is not made in reference to any particular conception of education. Accordingly, the moral principles that Peters derives through his transcendental argument could be applied to any kind of rational justification, not just educational justification. Hence the educational relevance of Peters' procedural principles can only be determined through an application of such principles to educational contexts. Objective principles of practical reason regulate *all* action, including action in educational contexts. *Ethics and Education*, for example, devotes large tracts to showing how principles such as the principle of freedom are appropriately applied to classroom practice. For example, one should curtail the immediate desires of children so they can exercise greater freedom in a rich educational context (pp. 192–198). But freedom, like justice, is still 'an independent principle', autonomous from educational concern except as a matter of *post hoc* consideration.

Consequently, while a universalistic account of practical reason is used to justify the moral principles regulating action in educational (and all other) contexts, at this point no case is made showing how or even if education meaningfully connects with objective principles of practical reason. But this is exactly where such an argument is needed. There is an important difference between an argument that shows, on the one hand, how moral-practical considerations place reasoned constraints on a process or action, and on the other hand an argument that shows why the process is itself an educationally worthwhile undertaking. Peters is sufficiently Kantian to hold that any practical activity presupposes the validity of a moral framework in that individuals are to be treated as having equal moral worth. But such a framework by itself tells us nothing about the extent to which the activity is of educational worth in its own right. To rest the case at this point invites objections that are similar to the charge of 'empty formalism'. For example, the categorical imperative that one ought never indoctrinate may be a generalisable and applicable claim, but there is nothing in the imperative that tells us anything about education. It simply means that one ought not indoctrinate. The imperative makes no reference to education as a practice offering reasons for why one ought not to indoctrinate. At most one can simply say that indoctrination in an educational context or any other context are morally impermissible and also irrational. But the normative force of this claim comes from the moral framework, not from any understanding of what education represents as an enterprise. In other words, one cannot derive meaningful educational judgements from an objective practical principle if that principle is a principle expressing an autonomous morality.

Peters seems to think that while a universal, formal moral framework can constrain a practice within certain ethical limits, it does not necessarily offer much in terms of what is of educational worth among these many permissible practices. He wants to show why an activity such as poetry should have greater educational worth than say, children's games (he uses the oft-cited example of doing poetry versus playing push-pin). From a moral point of view, however, poetry and popular children's games are permissible activities. They are of 'equal value' from the standpoint of moral permissibility. So the question remains: are there distinctly educational reasons supporting the recommendation of one of these practices over the other? And could these reasons be grounded in a form of value distinct from mere economic utility or public sentiment?

In other words, a context-transcending justification is necessary for any meaningful universalistic conception of education because otherwise whatever it is we make of education can be adopted or abandoned depending on the sentiments of a society at a particular time and place. It has no obligatory status or normative force. Without such a justification, normative arguments about education ultimately become a matter of prudence or preference as opposed to universal rights or duties.[3] Education might involve an initiation into worthwhile activities, for example, but is education in any way a universally worthwhile activity to the extent that a community could be obligated to undertake that initiation, regardless what their traditions might otherwise recommend?

How Peters handles the case for worthwhileness is crucial to understanding why and how he sees education in universalistic terms. For Peters, education refers to an initiation into worthwhile activities. Yet, the foundationalism within which Peters situates his argument renders any conception of a good education a contextual one insofar as such conceptions rest on values or principles that cannot be generalised. In other words, our chosen conceptions of the good taken by themselves are subjective and cannot be used to establish worthwhileness. Yet talk of worthwhile activities seems to inevitably tie into some objective notion of the good. If education must refer to worthwhileness, and judgements of worthwhileness must presuppose the good, the concept of education must be based on a standard held in common between any and all such conceptions (even when posited in the abstract form of a practical principle). And we have reason to think that this concept of education can accommodate many different conceptions, depending on the culture and traditions at play in particular cases. But there must be some minimal justification or principle for why individuals ought to be initiated into worthwhile activities, whatever they may be and however varying they may be. Does Peters have an argument for this? He certainly attempts as much. Peters grounds the case for what educational processes ought and can do in a positive sense in his well-known transcendental argument. The cogency of a universalisable conception of education rests primarily on this next step. What I aim to show in this next section is that the argument for worthwhileness is best understood as an attempt to establish a general principle of worthwhileness—a context-transcending practical principle having the same universal status as the other practical principles that Peters derives. This principle is the rational standard to which the concept of education is supposed to refer. Accordingly, on Peters' account this principle is an autonomous principle of prudence or goodness, not a universalistic or public morality.

EDUCATION: LOST BETWEEN THE MORAL LIFE AND THE GOOD LIFE?

Peters saw educational processes as constrained by a rational, universalistic morality. This is in part derived from his assertion that any justifiable account of education must be grounded in 'ethical foundations' that are non-arbitrary. These foundational principles are not metaphysical givens, but those that all persons could adopt without contradiction because they are presupposed by any reasoned action. Rendered in this way, however, educational processes stipulate little in terms of positive rights or duties.[4] Education is primarily a matter of goodness or prudence, not moral principle.[5] Moral principles may happen to be instrumentally useful in promoting the good due to their ordering influence, but otherwise have no intrinsic connection to educational processes (Peters, 1966, p. 196).

It is important to be terminologically clear, here. By 'prudence', I (and I also believe Peters) mean questions about the good—of how one wishes to live and flourish. These questions are distinct from questions of moral rightness. Habermas uses a similar distinction, where ethical questions relate to questions of the good, and moral questions refer to questions of moral rightness (Habermas, 1990). Habermas characterises such questions as follows:

One will be able to choose between pursuing a career in management and training to become a theologian on better grounds after one has become clear about who one is and who one would like to be. Ethical questions are generally answered by unconditional imperatives such as the following: 'You must embark on a career that affords you the assurance that you are helping people.' The meaning of this imperative can be understood as an 'ought' that is not dependent on subjective purposes and preferences and yet is not absolute. What you 'should' or 'must' do has here the sense that it is 'good' for you to act in this way in the long run, all things considered. Aristotle speaks in this connection of paths to the good and happy life (1993, p. 5).

These kinds of questions can be distinguished from moral questions:

Only a maxim that can be generalized from the perspective of all affected counts as a norm that can command general assent and to that extent is worthy of recognition or, in other words, is morally binding. The question 'What should I do?' is answered morally with reference to what one ought to do. Moral commands are categorical or unconditional imperatives that express valid norms or make implicit reference to them. The imperative meaning of these commands alone can be understood as an 'ought' that is dependent on neither subjective goals and preferences nor on what is for me the absolute goal of a good, successful or not-failed life (1993, p. 8).

I think that it is the former kind of question that Peters sees education as primarily being responsible for, and this is exactly why he is engaged with important questions of worthwhileness—what objective criteria are there for judging what is worth passing on or worth doing in all cases, and how might this dovetail with what it is we are trying to capture when we speak of education in a general sense? In other words, is there some kind of general procedural principle guiding initiation into the good life? The extent to which our deliberations can be guided by an objective principle is complex. On the one hand, modern pluralism reveals the limited scope of any one conception of the good. On the other hand, conceiving of education as a good-transmitting process is fairly empty if there are no justifiable criteria by which we can judge which goods are to be transmitted.

This is why the worthwhileness argument becomes central. In order to secure the right level of generality and objectivity, educational processes must somehow meaningfully link with practical principles of procedure. Standards of worthwhileness, like standards of moral reasoning, need to be lurking among the foundations of practical reasoning itself. If science is worthwhile, for example, it will be worthwhile because of its immanent connection to universal qualities intrinsic to practical reason. Unlike moral principles whose protective role ensures that developing persons are treated in terms of moral respect simply by virtue of being a person, an objective principle of worthwhileness would refer to the educative role of initiation of persons into certain types of activities.

Why are judgements of worthwhileness in particular and education more generally not simply sublated to the moral sphere? Would it not be more straightforward to leave educational processes as a matter to be regulated by the moral domain? An important development in the move away from this kind of sublation can be found in an earlier paper, co-authored with A. P. Griffiths, called 'The Autonomy of Prudence' (Griffiths and Peters, 1962).[6] As the title suggests, the thrust of the paper is to show that, contrary to the empiricists' readings of Kant's project which would suggest that morality is only practical insofar as it is prudential, judgements of prudence are themselves an autonomous employment of practical reason (pp. 162–163). The argument, briefly stated, is that assessments of the rational force of an action or judgment must be undertaken through an evaluation of the ends (and the means that are employed to achieve that end). This applies to both moral and prudential maxims. However, the kind of prudential judgements that Griffiths and Peters have in mind are claimed to be different from Kant's hypothetical imperative, where the rationality of actions directed to particular ends are assessed by the degree to which the action accords with the practical necessity entailed by the willing of that end. Between an autonomous morality and technical prudence is a practical reason of private prudence: 'Such judgements of private prudence, it is clear, go beyond anything the agent seems himself to want, or actually does want, and concern what he ought to want for himself, and that a wiser person would find satisfaction' (p. 167). This goes squarely against Kant, for Kant sees objective principles of practical reasoning as having two forms alone: either by a hypothetical imperative where an action is good merely as a means to something else, or a categorical imperative where an action is in itself good (Kant, 2008, 25; 4:414–4:415). Griffiths and Peters rightly think that if there is a third objective practical principle by which an individual's ends can be assessed, they can secure the autonomy of prudence and 'the most general procedural principles of technical prudence' (p. 171). They then try to secure the autonomy of prudence by deriving its transcendental necessity: questions of prudence necessarily presuppose the rational assessment of certain wants (p. 175) and that such a rational assessment is possible insofar as there must be certain activities which one must participate in order to for one to be able to engage in this kind of reasoning (activities they claim to be 'formally analogous to itself' (p. 177). On the reading I offer, Peters is here setting out the objective conditions through which a person can learn to rationally assess a plethora of subjective ends.

For Griffiths and Peters, judgements of 'private prudence' are objective, practical, autonomous, but outside the sphere of morality. This early version of the worthwhileness argument will have implications for Peters' later work, for this line of argument leads to the (in)famous transcendental deduction of what are supposed to be universally worthwhile activities—activities such as literature and science that one ought to participate in order to make judgements of 'private prudence'.[7] In this more developed argument, these are the 'formally analogous' activities alluded to in the earlier article. The reasons justifying these activities are autonomous from the moral sphere, and perhaps goes some way to explaining why the moral-practical principles Peters identified in *Ethics* have no internal connection to the concept of education, while the worthwhileness principle does. Here, the transcendental argument derives an objective educational principle showing why one ought to choose end/activity A over end/activity B on 'private' prudential grounds. However, rather than prescribe our ends in a way that would undermine the plurality of particular ends proffered by differing conceptions of the good, the formal character of the principle simply shows that in order to make reasoned prudential judgements between competing ends it is necessary that one first develop a reasoned understanding of judgement itself, and this involves initiation into the theoretical forms of knowledge.

On this view, Peters seems to be relying on what I would call a worthwhileness principle. It is this principle that supplies a missing objective standard for making educational judgements. For example, in leading children though a science experiment the intention, means and end informing my actions can be non-contradictory in a way consonant with the moral law: I treat the children with respect, I teach them in a way that does not undermine the development of their autonomy and so on. But science could be plausibly dropped as an activity and replaced with some other activity without contradicting the moral law. It is difficult to say what might be wrong about this on educational grounds, either. So: why do science? The question remains because, while education may in some way be connected to worthwhileness, we as yet have no reason for why we cannot replace science activities with something else (perhaps anything else) taken to be worthwhile. The worthwhileness principle aims to supply such grounds. Here it is not so much the case of learning science versus bingo, rather, the principle provides reasons for why learning science is something that people should experience if they are to be able to pursue a good life. To deny them science is to deny initiation into a form of knowledge necessary for making judgements about goodness or 'private prudence'. In effect, the practical principle of worthwhileness is the objective educational principle necessary for any intelligible and generalisable conception of education.

If worthwhileness is 'built into' the concept of education and if the initiation into certain worthwhile activities is presupposed in the form of a generalisable principle of worthwhileness, then there are things about educational processes that are themselves universally valid—they are those processes that ensure that such universally worthwhile activities can be accessed by all persons. To say one has a right to learn literature is to make an educationally relevant and generalisable claim. Accordingly, I teach literature because my motive, my means and my end satisfy the educational principle of worthwhileness, not simply because my action is permissible under a formal and general moral law. Such a claim identifies what it is about educational processes that have universal import. Educational processes are universally valid because they are necessary for any form of rational human life (pp. 162–163). On this view, the principle of worthwhileness expresses an aspect of practical reason that has direct educational relevance for developing persons.

This assumes, of course, that initiation in practical reasoning of this sort is universally good. But how well founded is this claim?

A LIFE OF RATIONAL PRINCIPLE: A GENERALISABLE IDEAL?

How defensible is such a reconstruction of Peters' work? Even if we buy into the transcendental argument about worthwhileness, there are other problems. While one can derive practical principles through transcendental argument, Peters see the explicit adoption of those principles as an ethical standard: '[T]o have the concept of a person is to see an individual as an object of respect in a form of life which is conducted on the basis of those principles which are the presuppositions of the use of practical reason' (1966, p. 215). On the one hand, it is possible to interpret the previous passage as simply saying that these presuppositions underlie any form of life, forming the basis of respect for persons. But it can also be taken to mean that one should adopt such principles as an ideal of human flourishing and excellence. Bonnett rightly picks up on this shift and its implications for Peters' account of education as follows:

> The development of mind for Peters then ultimately consists in the internalisation of the standards of rationality where rationality itself, as has been indicated, is seen as a phenomenon in social life ... [E]ducation is certainly not to be construed as consisting in mere sets of abstract principles, but something more akin to a form of life in which they are embedded and which they enable (Bonnett, 1986, pp. 114–115).

Even if we can safely say that the rational principles that Peters derives are objective and generalisable in scope, why does it then mean that a *form of life* based on such principles is a universally valid and applicable? Bernard Williams argues that approaches such as these overstate the role practical reason should have in our lives:

> [T]he drive toward a *rationalistic conception of rationality* ... imposes on personal deliberation and on the idea of practical reason itself a model drawn from a particular understanding of public rationality. This understanding requires in principle every decision to be based on grounds that can be discursively explained (Williams, 1985, p. 18).

There is a great difference between presupposing norms of practical reason versus institutionalising those norms in terms of an ethos to be shared by all communities. What one needs to flourish depends on all sorts of contextual features. Accordingly, an account of educational processes whose universal import is grounded in an endorsement of such a rationalistic ideal of human flourishing is open to objections ranging from its justificatory shortcomings to the moral and political implications of institutionally imposing such a process on more traditional communities that may not see 'the situation of practical reason' as all-defining.

Practical principles can help us to reason out what one ought not do in an educational process (indoctrination, for example, is a self-contradictory violation of norms of practical reason). Reason-giving, deliberation, and the pursuit of worthwhile activities are fundamental to any form of life. Interference with our ability to develop such capacities is morally abhorrent. But positing an educational process that takes such capacities to be of central value in a well-lived life is a different kind of claim.[8] Consider what Peters says regarding the justification of the curriculum in the context of his transcendental argument: 'To ask the question "Why do this rather than that?" seriously is therefore ... to be committed to those inquiries which are defined by their serious concern with those aspects of reality which give context to the question he is asking' (Peters, 1966, p. 164).

Note the shift in the Peters' language. Practical questions presuppose the critical assessment of reasons, but does it also entail a 'commitment to inquiry'?[9] What a principle of worthwhileness suggests at most is that it would be self-contradictory to ask practical questions and ignore relevant information that could lead us to the right answer. It might mean that educational processes cannot legitimately undermine children from developing the ability to ask, answer and assess the evidentiary reasons necessary in the pursuit of such questions. It does not mean that every educational process ought to posit rigorous intellectual scientific inquiry as a life-ideal. Not everyone wants to or ought to live life like a hard-boiled PI or a scientist.

A comparison to the moral law is again useful here—moral deliberation might presuppose the categorical imperative as a objective practical principle of judgement, but we do not infer our moral obligations directly from such a principle. In other words, (at least for Kant) we do not presuppose a particular moral code in the asking of the moral question. Rather, we propose actions and submit them to the CI test. If they pass the test, we may adopt them. Similarly, an objective educational principle of worthwhileness does not directly tell us what is worthwhile. It simply establishes that learning about what is worthwhile between competing alternatives presupposes that one ought to be informed by a reasoned understanding of the various alternatives open to him or her. In the context of a traditional society, for example, such deliberations might mean a reasoned understanding of the many pursuits available to its members (hunting, fishing, gathering, story-telling, carving etc.). It does not necessarily mean scientific reasoning or literary theory. I am not here advocating for an entirely contextualist position. What I am claiming is that what is context-transcendent is at most those formal features of scientific inquiry, not the content of scientific inquiry itself. In a pre-industrial society a similarly reflexive, truth-seeking discourse could occur in the context of their valued pursuits without an explicitly scientific investigation even taking place.[10] Peters shifted the emphasis from the autonomy of morality to the autonomy of prudence in order to provide a more meaningful and substantive account of a general concept of education. In actuality, we seem to have supplanted one kind of empty formalism for another. It is not plausible, in my view, that one can legitimately derive a substantive set of universal educational aims on the basis of an abstract prudential principle any more than one can do so on the basis of an abstract moral principle. One simply ends up projecting one's own conception of the good. It is telling, for example, that after the formalism of his analysis of the worthwhileness principle, Peters characterises our proper understanding of it as a Socratic attitude, where one must have a passionate concern for truth (p. 165). In other words, the fact of practical reason is deftly rendered into a particular conception of the good life.

Peters tried to use the values immanent in the use of practical reason to fill out a quite empty concept—initiation into the good. These values were then used to justify the claim that some aspects of educational processes, such as an engagement with worthwhile activities, have universal import. On the assessment I have offered, such a project is unsuccessful. However, I do think that Peters was moving in the right direction. In this final section, I would like to suggest how Peters' account of ethics could be used to support a generalisable and morally meaningful account of education processes. I argue that Peters thought that the principles he saw as foundational to practical reason could serve as a standard of legitimacy for educational processes, where commitment to such principles secured the necessary conditions for human flourishing. In the account I offer, I would like to show how educational processes themselves can be seen as having a key role in securing necessary conditions for practical reasoning itself. On this view, practical reasoning is a competency to which every person has a moral right to develop. This case cannot proceed without help from Peters, however. While he takes practical principles as setting a standard for excellence in human reasoning, he also assigns to them an important public and communicative role. I argue that a greater emphasis on this communicative aspect of practical reason is a more fruitful way to proceed.

COMMUNICATION AND PRACTICAL REASON: A WAY TOWARD AN EDUCATIONALLY RELEVANT MORAL UNIVERSALISM?

Rather than positing a transcendental ego that imposes structure on experience, Peters is keenly aware of the social development of mind. Yet he also anticipates contemporary thought in Kantian ethics by denying that such a 'detranscendentalised self' entails a completely empiricist account (Peters, 1966, pp. 46–51). More specifically, the self is a socialised and intersubjective self formed through participation in public language and communication (pp. 50–51). On this view, I become aware of myself as a self through reciprocal communication with others.[11] Rather than endorse an atomistic conception of the person, we have an intersubjective self formed through engagement with a social context. The types of practical questions that Peters focuses on in his transcendental analysis (what ought I do?; why do this rather than that?) can be understood as public questions that can only be resolved through deliberation with others.

The practical principles that Peters subsequently identifies are crucial here because they are derived from presuppositions underlying any public communication (Martin, 2009). These presuppositions are communicative and those which persons must make if they are to reach mutual understanding with others.[12] Consequently, they are regulative and constitutive of the public world that all individuals are initiated into. On this view, public practical reason is the means through which persons can become persons and through which they are able to secure their unique identifies. Consider how the principle of worthwhileness works on this interpretation. It becomes clear that when I ask the question 'what is worthwhile?' it makes little sense to posit the question from the standpoint of some solitary, atomistic agent.[13] Activities and practices are social in nature, and so an assessment of their worthwhileness can only take place in a shared evaluative context with other persons. The interpretation of my interests, needs, preferences and long-term goals are formed through my practical deliberation with others. I ask for advice. I contrast possible alternatives and life-experiences. I assess their interpretations within the context of my own unique situation in life. Yet, while the decision to choose one life-plan rather than another takes place within the context of the traditions of my community, the practical reasoning through which such an informed decision is made possible is a far more general competency.

Consequently, a continuing process of open deliberation and reciprocal communication is necessary for the possibility of practical reason (Peters, 1966, pp. 225–226). Through the use of practical reason, one presupposes that there will be properly constituted public procedures of communication and at the same time presupposes these procedures will persist over time. Consequently, practical reason is a kind of universal, context-transcendent tradition that needs to be maintained and handed down. On this view, 'developing centres of consciousness' need to be initiated into such a tradition. Here, a communicative interpretation of practical reasoning is one in which justice-orientated moral norms can be generalised in an open procedure of moral argumentation; a space where informed choices relating to the good life, worthwhile pursuits and one's own self-understanding can only be realised through communicative interaction with others.

I think that starting with this account of initiation is a better approach to conceptualising educational processes. Rather than try to develop an account of education on the basis of activities claimed to be good for the possible flourishing of all persons, we can instead identify those obligations we have to any and all individuals learning to become members of the community of practical reason. Practical reason is that through which persons can become individuals and stand as equal members in a larger moral community. The process as conceived would be representative of a generalisable standard insofar as it does not promote a single conception of the good, but positive insofar as it identifies a kind of initiation to which all persons have a right by virtue of their inclusion in the human community as a matter of principle. We can then distinguish a post-conventional, reasoned education from contingent educational aims by the former's active role in ensuring that such moral obligations of initiation are met. On this view, when we speak of education from a universalistic moral point of view, we are presupposing that our educational institutions and policies are designed in such a way that persons are able to learn to participate in practical reason such that they can capably form their unique identity, freely represent their interests in moral deliberation, and engage in communication aimed at mutual understanding with others.

The principle of consideration of interests serves as one such example. Such a principle *is* educationally meaningful and relevant so long as the validity of a moral judgement rests on the recognition of the needs and interests of others—vulnerable, developing centres of consciousness have a right to learn to be able to represent their interests and the interests of others within moral argumentation. Such a competency is presupposed in the use of practical reason—when I represent my interests I presuppose that I as well as all others ought to be able to learn to represent our interests in a competent way. Similarly, the principle of worthwhileness presupposes that one is capable of rationally assessing the value of competing alternatives. When teachers or policy-makers make judgements about what is a worthwhile activity in an educational context, for example, they also presuppose that all other persons should be able to make informed judgements about worthwhileness. However, as we have seen, this means having an opportunity to communicate with others about such alternatives, to be able to consider the experiences of other persons and to make well-informed judgments on the basis of such practical deliberations. Accordingly, representing interests and evaluating worthwhileness involve demanding competencies not naturally acquired. It requires opportunities to experience a well-ordered social life with other persons where one is free to learn how to reflect and reason about possible life choices, exchange unique perspectives, explore biographical differences and take a critical, post-conventional distance from one's own immediate context. Accordingly, any process that wishes to call itself educational must reflect such demands. The contradiction in denying children these experiences is not that the denial of a particular activity itself that contradicts the worthwhileness principle; rather, to make judgements about what is worthwhile for others without affording them the opportunity to develop similar competencies for judgement is self-contradictory. I think this stricture hits on the right level of formality and generality without being entirely meaningless and irrelevant from an educational standpoint.

All this may seem abstract as rendered, but when we compare the extent to which opportunities for initiation into non-coercive, communicative practical reason is possible within our overcrowded classrooms, narrow curricula and performance-based orientation, we can quickly see the particular ways in which our current institutional arrangements miss the mark, however generally stated these requirements are.

What is offered here is preliminary—if it is of any value, much more work would have to be done. What equitable material conditions must all persons have access to if they are to be initiated into practical reason? What norms must any valid educational process adhere to if it is to meet its moral obligation of initiation into practical reason? The answers to these questions are morally and educationally relevant. They suggest what I would call a morality of development as an area of ethical inquiry. On this view, moral reasoning about the educational process lies not in simply treating it as a means for human flourishing, nor is it to be seen simply as one practice among many to be governed by principles of justice. Rather, educational processes play the positive role of ensuring that persons are initiated into practical reason. Peters' communicative and social account of the development of persons at the hands of this community can help us bridge the gap between morality and prudence, the right and the good. In this important way, Peters' work does provide us with ways in which we can move discussions about the moral domain of education forward, a particularly important contribution in an era where questions of global citizenship, multinational institutions, and human rights are taking on ever-greater importance.

NOTES

1. Peters at times applies this methodological point to his own transcendental deduction of moral principles. See his *Ethics and Education* (1966) and Martin (2009).
2. 'Most writers dealing with "the aims of education" persuasively parade the particular values which they commend such as "the self-realization of the individual"; but they have little to offer in the way of justification' (Peters, 1966, p. 91).
3. As an example see Peters, 1973, p. 28.
4. 'It has been argued that the concept of "education" intimates no special processes, though it may rule out some. Nevertheless, it may be possible to justify on ethical grounds principles such as fairness and freedom in dealing with children' (Peters, 1966, p. 92).
5. 'I take the concept of "education" to be *almost* as unspecific in terms of content as something like "good" or "worthwhile", with the notion of "transmission of" or of "initiation into" prefixed to it' (Peters, 1973, p. 43).
6. I would like to thank John White for directing me to this particular work.
7. I assume a familiarity by the reader regarding this argument.
8. See, for example, John White's *The Aims of Education Restated* (1982).
9. On the moral, social and political limits of such an ideal of human flourishing, see 'Norms and Values: On Hilary Putnam's Kantian Pragmatism' in Jürgen Habermas' *Truth and Justification* (2003).
10. Although it does remain possible that scientific methods could be employed incidentally. I think Peters is open to this interpretation when he says that a person could have their

thinking differentiated into different pursuits such as science or historical awareness, or such forms could 'be only obscurely intimated in an undifferentiated way' (Peters, 1966, p. 164).

11. For a more detailed account of such a process, see the many works by George Mead as well as Habermas' 'Individuation through Socialization' in *Postmetaphysical Thinking* (Habermas, 1992).

12. This is what Jürgen Habermas would refer to as communicative reason. My interpretation of Peters from here on in is largely based on a Habermasian framework. However, I have already noted that both Peters and Habermas take similar positions on public reason and communication.

13. This is in contradiction to Peters' early work on private prudence, where what I 'ought' to want as opposed to what I 'ought' to do morally is distinguished by the fact that in the former, what one ought to do only affects the individual (p. 179).

REFERENCES

Bonnett, M. (1986) Personal Authenticity and Public Standards, in: D. E. Cooper (ed.) *Education, Values and Mind: Essays for R.S. Peters* (London, Routledge), pp. 111–133.

Dray, W. H. (1973) *The Justification of Education* (Oxford, Oxford University Press).

Elliott, R. (1986) Richard Peters: A Philosopher in the Older Style, in: D. E. Cooper (ed.) *Education, Values and Mind: Essays for R. S. Peters* (London, Routledge), pp. 41–68.

Griffiths, A. P. and Peters, R. S. (1962) The Autonomy of Prudence, *Mind*, 71, pp. 161–180.

Habermas, J. (1990) *Moral Consciousness and Communicative Action* (Cambridge MA, MIT Press).

Habermas, J. (1992) Individuation Through Socialization, in *Postmetaphysical Thinking* (Cambridge, MA, MIT Press).

Habermas, J. (1993) *Justification and Application* (Cambridge, MA MIT Press).

Habermas, J. (2003) *Truth and Justification*, B. Fultner trans. (Cambridge, MA, MIT Press).

Hirst, P. (1986) *Richard Peters' Contribution to the Philosophy of Education*, in: D. E. Cooper (ed.) *Education, Values and Mind: Essays for R. S. Peters* (London, Routledge), pp. 8–40.

Kant, I. (2008) *Groundwork of the Metaphysics of Morals*, M. Gregor, trans. (Cambridge, Cambridge University Press).

Kleing, J. (1973) R. S. Peters' Use of Transcendental Arguments, *Journal of Philosophy of Education*, 7.2, pp. 149–166.

Martin, C. (2009) R.S. Peters and Jürgen Habermas: Presuppositions of Practical Reason and Educational Justice, *Educational Theory*, 59.1, pp. 1–15.

Montefiore, A. (1986) Prudence and Respect for Persons: Peters and Kant, in: D. E. Cooper (ed.) *Education, Values, and Mind: Essays for R. S. Peters* (London, Routledge).

Peters, R. S. (1966) *Ethics and Education* (London, Allen and Unwin).

Peters, R. S. (1973) *The Justification of Education* (Oxford, Oxford University Press).

Peters, R. S. (1981) *Moral Development and Moral Education* (London, Allen and Unwin).

White, J. (1982) *The Aims of Education Restated* (London, Routledge).

Williams, B. (1985) *Ethics and the Limits of Philosophy* (Cambridge, MA, Harvard University Press).

10

Overcoming Social Pathologies in Education: On the Concept of Respect in R. S. Peters and Axel Honneth

KRASSIMIR STOJANOV

The concept of respect plays a central role in several recent attempts to re-actualise the programme of a critical social theory. This is especially true with regard to Axel Honneth's approach to the subject of recognition, according to which disrespect—along with lack of empathy, and social disregard—is one of the most crucial forms of social pathology.

Educational theorists and philosophers have until now, however, paid little attention to this new trend in the fields of political and social philosophy. One reason for this may be that in these fields the concept of respect is being used mainly as a synonym for a form of recognition that is linked exclusively to the law. Topics that are central for educational theory and philosophy, such as teaching, cognitive development and human flourishing—that is, topics that are concerned with unique features of the single person and with the unique paths of her development—are left behind by that understanding of respect.

More than forty years ago, however, R.S. Peters did develop a concept of respect as a central educational component. According to him 'respect' is the correct designation for the proper manner of education, and in 'Ethics and Education' he spends much effort in rehearsing the various ways in which respect is of significance in education. But at the time he wrote his main work, the critical potential of the idea was still not really appreciated. So Peters, who obviously had a highly ambivalent relationship to the social-critical approaches of that time, mainly because of their neo-Marxist orientation, did not make systematic use of his concept of respect as a conceptual tool for developing a critical theory of education of his own.

As I already mentioned, Honneth's new critical approach, which—like Habermas' discourse ethics—has overcome the production-centred and functionalist patterns of Marxist and neo-Marxist analyses of capitalist society, is grounded in an understanding of social pathologies that is inherently linked to a concept of respect, even if this is a relatively formal and minimalist one. This leads me to my own attempt, in this chapter, to explore the potential of Peters' more rich and more concrete concept

Reading R. S. Peters Today, First Edition. Stefaan E. Cuypers and Christopher Martin.
Chapters © 2011 The Authors. Editorial organization © 2011 Philosophy of Education Society of Great Britain. Published 2011 by Blackwell Publishing Ltd.

of respect as a means of addressing social pathologies in the fields of education—that is, in order to conceptualise a new critical theory of education.

My argument for treating and explicating Peters' understanding of respect as a conceptual basis of a new critical theory of education involves the following steps. First, I shall refer back to the term 'social pathology' as a grounding category of the new, 'Post-Habermasian' critical theory (in Section 1). Then I shall discuss Honneth's notion of disrespect as a central social pathology. At that point I shall argue that this notion needs further elaboration in order to expand and enrich its meaning in such a way as to enable it to be applied to various aspects and processes of education (Section 2). Peters' educational philosophy offers the best basis for that semantic enrichment. A profound and elaborated concept of respect as proper to education is a central element of his philosophy (Section 3). The concept of respect seems to stand in some tension, however, to Peters' understanding of education as initiation into shared cultural traditions. If we are to replace that understanding with a post-traditional notion of education, the educational significance of the concept of respect will become even greater (Section 4). Finally, I shall try to show how we could use a category of respect elaborated in this way as a means for diagnosing central educational pathologies of our time (Section 5).

1. SOCIAL PATHOLOGIES AS THE FOCUS OF THE NEW CRITICAL THEORY

What distinguishes the new style of critical theory that has been developed by Axel Honneth as an innovative continuation of the tradition of the Frankfurt School is his elaborating of 'social pathology' as a founding term of the whole approach. Unlike the Marxist perspective, which focuses those 'objectively' wrong developments in the economic 'base' that result in a 'super-structure' of 'false consciousness' in different classes, and that can be overcome only by the proletariat, Honneth insists that critical social theory must take as its point of departure those social phenomena that are *directly* (although not necessary explicitly) experienced by *individuals* as harms deriving from society—that is, as obstacles to their social inclusion and to their identity development (see Honneth, 2000, pp. 90–91, 95–96).

At this point Honneth distances himself also from Habermas' model of discourse ethics. According to Honneth, since Habermas' model takes as its main measure for social critique the ideal of communicative understanding in speech, it does not pay enough attention to the critical potential of the subjective experience of deep psychological suffering, as where there is a fracturing of one's identity caused by society. The victims of such suffering do not necessarily experience any failure of implementation of norms of language understanding or of rational discourse as the immediate threat to their selfhood; what they do feel threatened by is lack of empathy, disrespect, and disregard (Honneth, 2000, pp. 96–101).

It is exactly this lack of empathy, disrespect and disregard that are, according to Honneth, the main forms of social pathology in modern, post-traditional societies. This diagnosis rests on the anthropological assumption that the development of identity in the modern individual requires three forms of intersubjective recognition, which enable three basic forms of identity-constituting self-relations. Through the experience of empathy the subject becomes first aware of herself as an independent body-centred entity equipped with her own needs and wishes. The experience of respect enables her to consider herself also as a subject with dignity who is the possessor of the basic right to be treated as a reasonable human being. And finally, the experience of social esteem enables her to access those personal features and abilities of herself on the basis of which she can make her unique contribution to society and thereby become a worthy member of it (see Honneth, 1992, pp. 148–210).

This brief description of Honneth's account of recognition makes clear that for him respect is just one of three normative criteria for diagnosing social pathologies. This criterion applies exclusively to practices of discrimination in their various forms (pp. 173–196, esp. 180–183; pp. 215–216). Emotional neglect and alienation, as well as disregard of people's personal potential should not be spelled out as forms of disrespect, since those practices are (negatively) linked to the norms of empathy and of social esteem, and not to the norm of respect. Hence, if we assume that education is mainly about the development of unique, personalised self-features and abilities whose cultivation requires care and esteem but not necessarily the abstract recognition form of respect, this norm seems to be of only little educational relevance.

However, there are also new approaches in social and political philosophy that spell out respect as *the* central and supreme category for a critical social theory, and especially for a critical theory of justice. According to such approaches based on 'respect egalitarianism', every form of injustice should ultimately be understood as a form of disrespect (see Gosepath, 2004). Indeed, a recent book of essays on critical theory has been published by Honneth in English under the title 'Disrespect' (Honneth, 2007). This requires us to look more carefully at the semantic core of the concept of respect in its relationships to empathy and social esteem, and to explore its relevance for a new critical social theory applicable in education.

2. RESPECT AS A FORM OF INTERSUBJECTIVE RECOGNITION IN HONNETH

As I already stated, according to Honneth respect is, along with empathy and social esteem, one of three forms of intersubjective recognition for which every human individual has a legitimate claim. Honneth spells out this form as being more or less identical with the recognition of law (Honneth, 1992, pp.173–196). On his view, to respect someone means in the first instance not to discriminate against them—that is, to acknowledge that he has the same rights and ultimately the same dignity as every human being.

This recognition of a person as subject to the norms of law presupposes the acknowledgement of her as morally accountable. It presupposes that she is endowed with practical reason—that is, that she is capable of taking the universal moral point of view, of taking responsibility for her own actions and decisions, as well as of deliberating over moral and juristic norms *vis-à-vis* that moral point of view (pp. 173–185). That kind of treatment has regard neither for the *particular* needs for care and concern of the individual, nor directly for his *specific* capabilities and potential. It is concerned only with the formal status of the individual as a reasonable and morally responsible person, who is equal to all other reasonable and morally responsible persons, and who thus has the same rights and duties as them.

For two reasons this concept of respect does not seem to apply to education. First, children obviously cannot yet be taken to be fully reasonable and morally responsible persons. The task of school education is exactly to help them to become such persons. Second, caring for the particular needs and abilities of students is doubtless a very important feature of the proper manner of education. However, exactly this feature is excluded from Honneth's concept of respect.

Now, a concept of 'prospective respect' (Curren, 2007, p. 470) might be helpful in order to overcome the first difficulty. Thus, even if children cannot be taken to be fully capable of reason yet, adults (especially teachers and parents) should recognise them as having the *potential* to become rational persons endowed with moral autonomy. Indeed, this kind of recognition should be understood as a central norm of pedagogical action.

However, what about children with mental disabilities who obviously do not have that potential? There is for sure a large consensus that those children should be treated with dignity. If we are going to follow Honneth, to treat someone with dignity means to respect them—that is, to see them as a morally accountable subject in relation to universal norms of law (Honneth, 1992, pp. 202–204). But in the case of persons with mental disabilities, to respect someone cannot be seen as recognition of their cognitive ability (or potential) or of their moral autonomy. In which sense can we then speak of respect for children with mental disabilities, a respect that is evidently extremely important for their proper education?

Let us concern ourselves now with the second difficulty in applying Honneth's concept of respect to educational contexts. To be sure, Honneth's theory of recognition has much educational relevance, for this theory refers, in flash-back, as it were, to the social and pedagogical conditions of human development, of *Bildung* in general (see Stojanov, 2006). Honneth takes carefully into account, as fundamental prerequisites of human development, the requirements of both attention to the particular needs of those who are growing up, such as love and sympathy, and esteem for their unique abilities and potential. However, these prerequisites are in his view linked to forms of recognition involving empathy and social esteem. The pedagogical relevance of respect is based exclusively on the principle that young people have certain rights—for example, the right not to be discriminated against on racial, sexual or ethnic grounds.

But why, given that the other central aspects of proper pedagogical action such as emotional concern and care, or social esteem, are well conceptualised within Honneth's theory, is it important to enlarge the scope of the recognition form of respect in educational contexts? For surely, whether care and esteem are variations of respect or independent recognition forms seems to be merely a terminological question with no practical impact. Rather, the really important question is whether Honneth's complete typology of recognition forms, including the way in which he spells out the concept of respect, neglects some important intersubjective preconditions of successful educational processes. We can probably grasp what from an educational point of view is missing in Honneth's typology of recognition forms when comparing it with Peters understanding of the proper manner of education. As we will see in the next section, that typology is in fact lacking an educationally crucial form of recognition, which has been described by Peters. This form is at best spelled out as respect, provided that respect is not understood as limited to the sphere of law and not conditional on the person being worthy of respect in virtue of their moral autonomy.

3. RESPECT AS RECOGNITION OF PERSONS AS INDEPENDENT CENTRES OF CONSCIOUSNESS: R. S. PETERS

R. S. Peters formulates three basic criteria of education:

(1) Education must transmit what is worthwhile—that is, content of intrinsic value.
(2) Education must be geared towards the achievement of 'cognitive perspective', which is closely linked with cultivation of knowledge and understanding.
(3) Pedagogical practices that lack reflexivity and voluntariness on the part of learner must be ruled out (Peters, 1966, p. 45).

While the first criterion basically concerns the content of education, the second relates mainly to the impact of education, and the third to its proper manner.

To be sure, pedagogical practices that lack reflexivity and voluntariness on the part of students are partly problematic, because they are unlikely to support the development of understanding and knowledge. However, the most important reason for Peters to dismiss them is that they are not compatible with the norm of respect, which is a positive expression of his notion of the proper manner of education (pp. 35–36). Peters describes respect as follows:

> In general respect for persons is the feeling awakened when another is regarded as a distinctive centre of consciousness, with peculiar feelings and purposes that criss-cross his institutional roles. It is connected with the awareness one has that each man has his own aspirations, his own viewpoint on the world; that each man takes pride in his achievements, however idiosyncratic they may be (p. 59).

What precisely does it mean to treat someone as a (developing) centre of consciousness? It is important to realise that this kind of treatment is not limited to the recognition of the ability of practical reason:

> Choice, which is intimately connected with the exercise of practical reason, is too narrow a concept; for it implies deliberation between alternatives. It does not cover such things as the grasp of rules, as the formulation and statement of intentions and the making of promises by means of which individuals determine the future (pp. 209–210).

Thus unlike Kant (and Honneth) Peters does not spell out respect solely in terms of the recognition of a person's capacity for moral autonomy and accountability *vis-à-vis* the moral point of view. Rather, according to him, there are a number of further features and forms of respect, such as the recognition of someone as possessor of an 'assertive point of view' and as capable of 'judgments, appraisals, intentions, and decisions', or the recognition of him as someone 'who is capable of valuation and choice, and who has a point of view of his own about his own future and interests' (ibid.).

Those features and forms of respect are much broader and much less exclusive than that type of recognition that is founded in the acknowledgment of a person's moral autonomy, in the Kantian sense, to which Honneth refers in his account of respect.[1] They imply, insofar as every human being is the source of a distinct perspective on the world with her own intentions, appraisals and judgments, that she deserves respect regardless of the extent to which she is capable of practical reasoning. This applies also to children with or without disabilities, no matter how reasonable or unreasonable their intentions or choices may appear from an 'objective' point of view. From an educational point of view it is very important to realise that, even when extended in this way, the recognition form of respect remains different from those forms that are based on love and social esteem. To respect someone's intentions, decisions or worldviews does not necessarily imply (although neither does it necessarily preclude) love or sympathy for them, nor any kind of appraisal of their contribution to society. Rather it means taking seriously the intentions, decisions and worldviews that someone may hold—that is, treating them as expressions of a distinctive subjectivity. This is so even where the agent is (still) immature.

So understood, respect becomes both a central ethical norm and a crucial pedagogical maxim. Roughly speaking, there is one way in which the ethical and the pedagogical significance of respect differ, but there is another in which they overlap. They differ insofar as from the ethical point of view respect is understood to have intrinsic value, for this is nothing other than a central case of persons being treated as ends and not as means. They are alike in that respect in education is understood also in extrinsic terms—that is, as an important tool for the fostering of human development. An education-supporting environment is characterised by concern for students' intentions, beliefs and worldviews, where students are encouraged to express these in class, and where teachers foster the judgemental capability of their students by recognising and mirroring their potential ability to justify their intentions, beliefs and choices.[2] Thus understood, respect is none other than that Socratic teaching which aims at the cultivation of reason. Within Peters' approach to ethics and education the significance of the overlap between the ethical and pedagogical dimensions of respect consists in the essential link to the individual's capacity for participation in public discourse. To respect an individual means to grant him access to such discourses, and to recognise his right and his potential thus to participate and thus publicly to articulate his own worldview and concerns and justifications. This is obviously the best way to recognise individuals as distinctive centres of consciousness, as bearers of specific worldviews and as subjects of decision-making and justifications—in short, their membership of the human community. On the other hand, according to Peters, public discourse or rational debate presuppose the mutual respect of their participants as representatives of distinct points of view and as capable of independent claims and justifications (pp. 213–215).

Public discourse, which both is generative of and presupposes respect, plays a crucial role in Peters' conceptions of ethics and of education. In terms of ethics, Peters argues that the common approaches of naturalism, intuitionism and emotivism ultimately fail to justify moral principles. Their common mistake is that they altogether treat the individual 'as an isolated entity exercising his "reason", "feeling", or "intuition"' (p. 114). According to Peters, the only possible positive justification of moral principles is through a form of public discourse within which individuals are reasoning about what they ought or ought not to do (pp. 114–115). About ten years after the publication of Peters' *Ethics and Education* Jürgen Habermas began to extend the same insight to his famous model of discourse ethics, according to which the central moral principles are identical with the rules of moral discourse, including reciprocity, equal access and the acknowledgment of the power only of the better argument (Habermas, 1996, pp. 11–64, esp. p. 49). However, the concept of public discourse plays a crucial role for Peters not only in the justification of ethics but also in his general theory of education. In order to grasp this role we should take a close look at how this theory spells out educational respect with regard both to the content of education (in terms of subject-matter and worthwhile activities) and to its impact (the development of cognitive perspective).

4. RESPECT, DISCURSIVE INITIATION AND COGNITIVE DEVELOPMENT

As I already mentioned at the beginning of the previous section, Peters distinguishes between three core dimensions of education, namely, transmission of what is worthwhile, development of a 'cognitive perspective' and the manifestation of respect. Regarding the relation between those three dimensions in his theory of education, my claim is that respect, as the proper character of education, is not only a moral requirement but also a necessary condition of both the internalisation of worthwhile activities and the development of cognitive perspective. Peters spells out the transmission of worthwhile content as a practice of initiation into certain activities or modes of thought that have intrinsic value within a given community or society. According to him, it is exactly this practice that is to be described as 'education' (p. 55). This understanding of education via initiation into worthwhile activities is grounded in Peters' assumptions about the intersubjective character of the development of the mind. He criticises British empiricism for its focus on the single individual, who develops her beliefs and concepts by a slow process of generalisation from her private impressions and perceptions. Against this empiricist understanding, Peters argues that the mind's development is not something that takes place within the isolated individual (or the individual understood atomistically). It proceeds rather through the child's increasing initiation into the public world, which is for him a world of 'public traditions enshrined in a public language' (p. 49).

Now, this claim can be interpreted in two quite different ways. On the one hand, it can be understood in the sense that education as development of mind requires the individual's internalisation of traditions that determine the horizon of value or worldview of the society in which she grows up. On the ground of this internalisation she begins gradually to communicate with peers and adults in terms of the concepts and rules that are embodied in the traditions of the language community. Communicating these concepts and rules she develops a real understanding of their meanings. On this understanding, the individual's perspective on the world is subordinated to that of her community. In order to become educated the individual just has to internalise a canon of knowledge, values and modes of conduct, a canon that is an embodiment of the community's main traditions. Here the individual cannot be fully recognised as the holder of a distinctive point of view towards the world. Rather, her worldview will appear merely as a concretisation of that of the community in which she has been socialised. Therefore there is a structural tension between the practice of education via the internalisation of public traditions and the principle of respect. Indeed, in *Ethics and Education*, there are several points at which Peters appears to endorse a conservative interpretation of the content dimension of education along these lines. For example, Peters argues that although there are 'individual avenues of initiation', at least at the level of secondary, higher and adult education, they are less important than disciplinary canons (p. 56). Respect for persons and concern for the standards inherent in disciplines appear as competing principles, between which a good teacher will find a proper balance (p. 59). In this same text, however, there is also some suggestion of alternative understanding of education as initiation. Consider Peters' concept of cognitive perspective, whose development, he claims, must be a central impact of that initiation. By 'cognitive perspective' he means the ability of the educated individual not only to grasp the conceptual schemes of the things she is confronted with and to understand the 'reason why' of things, but also her further ability to understand their connection to other entities and their place in a coherent pattern of life (p. 31). To have a cognitive perspective implies being aware of different ways of looking at the world (p. 44), and thus being able to realise that the beliefs and worldviews of one's own community are just possible interpretative schemes, which themselves stand in need of justification. This is to say that having a cognitive perspective presupposes the development of a reflexive relation to such worldviews and beliefs and the critical examination of them in the course of the (discursive) pursuit of truth.

However, initiation into this pursuit of truth, which Peters emphasises at least for higher education (p. 64), is a quite different task from initiation into the public tradition of a particular language community. For initiation into the pursuit of truth cannot be described as an internalisation of context-specific beliefs and values. Rather, it is an initiation into context-transcending practices of argument and a mutual taking of perspectives—practices that probably can best be described in terms of a 'game of giving and asking for reasons', to borrow an expression of Robert Brandom's (Brandom, 1994, pp. 496–497). I think then that the second interpretation of Peters' understanding of the content dimension of education is more compatible with the whole approach of his philosophy of education, for this philosophy surely emphasises the examination of traditions and awareness of the plurality of worldviews as necessary aspects of the process of education. In addition, that interpretation is more appropriate to the conditions of post-traditional societies, within which there is no single cultural canon. Rather, the purpose of educational institutions must be the fostering of key-competences—that is, in literacy, numeracy and science (see OECD, 1999, pp. 20–30).

According to the second interpretation sketched here, it would be better to speak of a 'discursive initiation'—that is, of an initiation into the principles of context-transcending discourses, instead of an initiation into the public traditions of a particular culture, nation or language community. Along such lines, the content aspect of education would not stand in tension or in competition with the principle of respect. On the contrary, discursive initiation and respect appear as two parts of the same story. For cultivating the ability to participate in the game of giving and asking for reasons presupposes both caring for the intentions, beliefs and ideals of the developing individual, and recognising her potential to articulate her intentions, beliefs and ideals discursively through the use of concepts and arguments. These are both exactly the central components of the recognition form of respect.

5. DISRESPECT AS SOCIAL PATHOLOGY IN EDUCATION

On the strength of the discussion in the two previous sections, it follows that lack of respect in educational interactions is not only morally unacceptable but also an obstruction to the cognitive development of student, for cognitive development presupposes what I called, in the last section, 'discursive initiation', where I tried to set, so to speak, Peters against Peters. Hence, disrespect should be seen as a central, indeed perhaps *the* central, social pathology in education.

This pathology has two concrete forms: lack of concern for the particular intentions and points of view of the students, on the one hand, and lack of recognition for their potential discursively to articulate those intentions and points of view, on the other. The first form can be generated institutionally by holding on to a 'leading culture'—that is, to a homogeneous canon of beliefs and rules of conduct students are obligated to internalise regardless of their own intentions, worldviews or ideals. Here students are not recognised as bearers of distinctive and assertive points of view towards the world. Furthermore, the educational canonising of a homogeneous leading culture automatically sets at a disadvantage those students whose patterns of socialisation and upbringing are different from dominant forms. I am thinking, of course, of students from social underclasses and, in particular, of those from immigrant families. The latter group of students is also particularly affected by the second form of the educational pathology of disrespect. With regard to the students from minority groups, this form of disrespect appears often as a practice of their culturalisation. This practice, which seems typical especially of a number of approaches in multicultural education in the United States, deconstructs the notion of a leading culture that is to be transmitted by educational institutions, and it claims that a plurality of culturally different worldviews should instead be acknowledged. However, what matters in those approaches are collective cultural worldviews, patterns of reality perception and learning styles, and not the distinctive points of view of individuals. The latter can be seen to be determined rather by 'cultural standards', which is to say by collective patterns of world- and self-perception and of social behaviour that have been ascribed to their cultures of origin (see Reich, 2002, pp. 175–184). Educational practice of this kind ends up by disrespecting the individual's intentions and points of view. What is even more important here, however, is that it disrespects also the individual's potential for the discursive articulation and justification of his intentions and beliefs. For that discursive articulation and justification presupposes the individual's ability to transcend the limits of her culture of origin, to take the perspectives of the others, to use concepts with trans-contextual validity claims and, thus, in short, to play the game of giving and asking for reasons. Once again, it is respect for that (potential) ability, together with the respect for the individual as a distinctive centre of consciousness, of intentions, of beliefs and of ideals, that should be brought to articulation within the classroom not only because this is a moral requirement in education but also because it is a basic prerequisite for its success.

CONCLUSION

Respect is a key-concept in new critical theory. It serves as a central criterion for the identification and overcoming of social pathologies in the contemporary societies.

In the most prominent version of the concept, which has been developed by Honneth, respect is closely tied to the sphere of law, and it is limited to the recognition of a Kantian-type moral autonomy in the individual. So interpreted, the concept of respect can have only a very limited application in education, where concern for the particular desires, intentions and beliefs of mostly immature persons is at stake. More than forty years ago, however, Peters did develop, as we have seen, an extended concept of respect as proper to the character of education. This concept focuses exactly on those desires, intentions and beliefs, instead of on the very demanding capability of practical reasoning orientated towards the Kantian categorical imperative. According to Peters, to respect a person means to recognise her as a distinctive centre of consciousness, that is, as a subject of intentions, as the holder of a particular point of view towards the world. The tension that I have identified between this concept of respect and Peters' understanding of education as initiation can be overcome if we spell this out in terms not of initiation into the leading traditions of a particular (language) community but of discursive initiation.

Disrespect as a social pathology in education consists both in neglecting the distinctive worldviews and intentions of the students and in treating individuals as culturally determined and culturally bound. These two forms of disrespect are not only morally unacceptable. They are also central obstacles to the success of educational practice in terms of the self-realisation and social inclusion of the individual.

NOTES

1. As Rob Reich convincingly argues, Kant's understanding of individual autonomy is a maximalist (and thus an exclusive) one. The ability to act according to the categorical imperative, thus generating universal laws and obeying them regardless of one's own particular involvements and attachments, might be indeed a noble ideal, but few of us are able (or even willing) to reach it (Reich, 2002, pp. 96–99). This is why Reich offers his own alternative conception of a minimalist autonomy, which consists in an individual's ability to reflect upon her own basic commitments and to choose from a range of meaningful life options (p. 105). I think that this conception of a minimalist autonomy grasps the proper subject of respect precisely.
2. Peters states: 'And they will only really develop as persons in so far as they learn to think of themselves as such' (Peters, 1966, p. 211).

REFERENCES

Brandom, R. B. (1994) *Making It Explicit. Reasoning, Representing, and Discursive Commitment* (Cambridge, MA, Harvard University Press).

Curren, R. (2007) *Coercion and the Ethics of Grading and Testing*, in: R. Curren (ed.) *Philosophy of Education. An Anthology* (Malden, MA, Blackwell), pp. 465–476.

Habermas, J (1996) *Die Einbeziehung des Anderen. Studien zur politischen Theorie* (Frankfurt am Main, Suhrkamp).

Honneth, A. (1992) *Kampf um Anerkennung. Zur moralischen Grammatik sozialer Konflikte* (Frankfurt am Main, Suhrkamp).

Honneth, A. (2000) *Das Andere der Gerechtigkeit. Aufsätze zur praktischen Philosophie* (Frankfurt am Main, Suhrkamp).

Honneth, A. (2007) *Disrespect: The Normative Foundations of Critical Theory* (Cambridge, Polity).

Gosepath, S. (2004) *Gleiche Gerechtigkeit. Grundlagen eines liberalen Egalitarismus* (Frankfurt am Main, Suhrkamp).

OECD (1999) *Measuring Student Knowledge and Skills. A New Framework for Assessment* (Paris, OECD Publications).

Reich, R. (2002) *Bridging Liberalism and Multiculturalism in American Education* (Chicago & London, The University of Chicago Press).

Peters, R. S. (1966) *Ethics and Education* (London, Allen & Unwin).

Stojanov, K. (2006) *Bildung und Anerkennung. Soziale Voraussetzungen für Selbst-Entwicklung und Welt-Erschließung* (Wiesbaden, VS-Verlag).

11

Reason and Virtues: The Paradox of R. S. Peters on Moral Education

GRAHAM HAYDON

A certain story has often been told about the recent course of philosophical thinking on ethics and moral education. In rough outline it goes like this. Until about the early 1980s, the field was dominated by conceptions of ethics as a domain of rules and principles. Such rules and principles could, at least potentially, be given a rational justification, whether by appeal to a Kantian conception of rationality or to an empirical account of human nature: and moral agents could exercise their rational autonomy by following principles that they could see to be justified. Hence the goal of moral education was the development of rational moral agency. But around the early 1980s there began to be changes in philosophical ethics, influencing the philosophy of moral education in turn. If any one book was seminal in this change, it was MacIntyre's *After Virtue* (1981), with its critique of Enlightenment rationality in ethics and its turn to an ethics of virtue. Other influential works appeared around the same time, including in psychology Carol Gilligan's (1982) *In a Different Voice* and in philosophy of education Nel Noddings' (1984) *Caring: A Feminine Approach to Ethics and Moral Education*. There followed an increasing tendency to see moral education through the lens of virtue ethics, or an ethics of care, or some assimilation of the two. The central concern of moral education was seen no longer as equipping agents to answer the question 'What should I do?' but as developing in them the desirable character traits or virtues that would form them as certain sorts of person.[1]

This story—which I shall refer to from time to time as 'the familiar story'—is not fiction, though as outlined here it certainly leaves a lot out, not least the internal variation within one perspective or another, and the complex interconnections between apparently different perspectives, but even over-simplified categories can have heuristic value. We can use this story to ask where the work of Richard Peters on moral education is to be located. More importantly, tracing in Peters' work not only the obvious strand of rationalism but also his thinking on virtues and indeed on care can help us see that the distinctions between different approaches are far less clear-cut than the familiar story suggests.

Reading R. S. Peters Today, First Edition. Stefaan E. Cuypers and Christopher Martin.
Chapters © 2011 The Authors. Editorial organization © 2011 Philosophy of Education Society of Great Britain. Published 2011 by Blackwell Publishing Ltd.

I shall follow Peters' own example in treating as his most significant contributions to the philosophical discussion of moral education a set of papers that he published in the collection *Moral Development and Moral Education* in 1981.[2]

PETERS' PARADOX OF MORAL EDUCATION

What then is the paradox of moral education as I conceive it? It is this: given that it is desirable to develop people who conduct themselves rationally, intelligently and with a fair degree of spontaneity, the brute facts of child development reveal that at the most formative years of a child's development he is incapable of this form of life and impervious to the proper manner of passing it on (Peters, 1981, p. 51).

This quotation is from one of Peters' best known and most discussed papers on moral education, 'Reason and Habit: The Paradox of Moral Education' (first published in Niblett, 1963). In his preface to the 1981 collection Peters does not indicate that any central or special place is to be given to the 'Paradox' paper. I shall follow him in this, for while I am borrowing the term 'paradox' for my title, I think that Peters' main point of substance in that paper is the same point that runs through much of his writing on moral education. This point is simply that the kind of rational morality that Peters sees as a major goal of moral education cannot be taught to children directly through appeal to their reason, but must be approached indirectly through a variety of means, in which habituation is central: children 'can and must enter the palace of Reason through the courtyard of Habit and Tradition' (Peters, 1981, p. 52).

Put like that, one may well wonder where the paradox is. Peters is calling attention to certain 'brute facts of child development' that mean that educators cannot avail themselves of direct appeal to children's rationality and therefore must use an indirect approach in aiming at the development of a rational morality. This seems to be a question of appropriate means towards a desired end and so hardly has even an appearance of paradox.

On the other hand, it is possible to reformulate the statement of something problematical about moral education in a way that at least has more *appearance* of paradox. Thus Peters refers to Aristotle's celebrated claim that 'we become just by doing just acts', which leads Aristotle himself to point out:

The question might be asked, what we mean by saying that we must become just by doing just acts, and temperate by doing temperate acts; for if men do just and temperate acts, they are already just and temperate, exactly as, if they do what is in accordance with the laws of grammar and of music, they are grammarians and musicians (Aristotle, *Nicomachean Ethics*, 1105a).

The solution to the problem, of course, is that the doing of acts that are in accordance with the requirements of justice, while a necessary step towards developing the virtue of justice, is not sufficient for the acts to be the acts of a just person (a person possessing the virtue of justice). Or as Peters put it in a later paper:

> [Aristotle's] paradox of moral education ... is really the paradox of all education. This is that in order to develop the dispositions of a just man the individual has to perform acts that are just, but the acts which contribute to the formation of the dispositions of the just man are not conceived of in the same way as the acts which finally flow from his character, once he has become just (Peters, 1973, p. 242).

This 1973 paper, 'The Justification of Education', was not included in *Moral Development and Moral Education*, presumably because it is not concerned with moral education specifically. As the quotation above shows, Peters thinks the paradox itself is not special to moral education; as he goes on to argue, the activities involved in *becoming* educated, such as doing science or reading poetry, will in an important sense be changed in character once they have come to be the activities of a person who *is* educated.

There is room for debate over whether 'the paradox of all education' in any of Peters' formulations is genuinely a paradox.[3] It would be a paradox if it appeared that two equally inescapable statements about education generated logically incompatible conclusions, such as 'this person is already just' and 'this person is not yet just'. Peters is caught in a paradox if his account of the condition of children outside the gates of reason makes it logically impossible for them ever to enter through those gates (see Luntley in this volume). Similarly he is caught in a paradox if he is accepting two logically incompatible descriptions of the condition of children, one in the language of deterministic psychology, the other in the language of rational agency (see Gardner, 1985, for this interpretation of the paradox as a Kantian antinomy).

To the suggestion that he is caught in a genuine paradox, we can make on behalf of Peters the Aristotelian response that we must 'save the appearances'. It is a fact of experience that children can and sometimes do become (fairly) rational agents and (fairly) educated persons. If a description of the condition of children renders that outcome logically impossible, there is something wrong with the description.

What appeared paradoxical, on Peters' own account, was the relation between certain empirical facts about childhood and a certain goal for moral education. Given that this relationship poses a problem about how moral development takes place and how moral education should be conducted, Peters goes on, in this and several other papers, to propose an answer to the problem. The question is important and it is important to have answers to it: important in practice, rather than because there is some logical conundrum to be resolved.

So far as I can see, Peters is availing himself of a loose ordinary-language sense of the term 'paradox' (and why not, if it makes for a good title?). In this loose sense, it can indeed seem a bit paradoxical that in order to develop a rational moral agent we have to use means that must seem thoroughly indirect and even sometimes apparently contrary to the intended goal. Following Peters' own example in using 'paradox' in this looser sense, I want to draw attention in this chapter to some seemingly paradoxical points about Peters' place in the familiar story.

THE NEGLECT OF PETERS ON MORAL EDUCATION

I said above that 'Reason and Habit: the Paradox of Moral Education' is one of the best known of Peters' papers on moral education. 'Best known' and 'most discussed' are relative terms; this paper has been cited and discussed more than most of Peters' papers on moral education, but those papers as a whole have been cited and discussed much less than *Ethics and Education* (Peters, 1966), and I assume this pattern will continue in the present volume.

In the collection *Virtue Ethics and Moral Education* (Carr and Steutel, 1999), Steutel speaks of *Moral Development and Moral Education* as 'justly celebrated' (Steutel, 1999, p. 125). Yet there is little evidence of this celebrity in the rest of that volume of seventeen chapters: merely that Spiecker refers to Peters' writings on habit (Spiecker, 1999, pp. 213–15); and Carr (1999, p. 143) and Carr and Steutel (1999, pp. 242–43) refer rather critically to Peters' attempt to combine Aristotelian character training with Kohlbergian rationalism (of which more below). Nor is there much if any reference to Peters in other recent philosophical discussions of moral education. In the fourteen chapters of *Education in Morality* (Halstead and McLaughlin, 1999) it is only the editors in their own chapter (McLaughlin and Halstead, 1999) who make any reference to Peters' work on moral education. Noddings and Slote (2003) have only the briefest general reference to Peters, 1973; and I have to admit that I did not mention Peters at all in Haydon, 2003.

Does this lack of attention indicate that Peters said nothing worth reading about moral education, or nothing that had not been said equally well by many others? I suggest that is not the case; rather, it may be that recent writers have not used Peters as a marker in telling their story about the development of the philosophy of moral education precisely because Peters does not fit very easily into the familiar story. I am fairly confident that this is true of my own telling of the story (Haydon, 2003). When I wanted a representative of rationalism about moral education, I cited (early) Hirst; and when one turns to virtue ethics, one can hardly see Peters as *representative* of virtue approaches to moral education. Yet I had already for years been encouraging students of moral education to read Peters on different kinds of virtue (Peters, 1981, pp. 94–9). Peters is a rationalist who gave some quite sustained attention to virtues, long before MacIntyre's *After Virtue*; he sees moral education as crucially involving the development of virtues, yet can say 'I am a staunch supporter of a rationally held and intelligently applied moral code' (Peters, 1981, p. 48). Here is the next paradoxical appearance to be unpacked.

PETERS THE RATIONALIST

If one needs grounds for seeing Peters as a rationalist, then in the claim just quoted, and in similar remarks elsewhere in *Moral Development and Moral Education*, one has it here in his own words. He goes on to spell out what is involved in holding a rational code:

> To hold a rational code a man must subscribe to some higher-order principles which will enable him both to apply rules intelligently in the light of relevant differences in circumstances and to revise rules from time to time in the light of changes in circumstances and in empirical knowledge about the conditions and consequences of their application. The higher-order principles which, in my view, are capable of some sort of rational justification, are those of impartiality, truth-telling, liberty, and the consideration of interests (Peters, 1981, p. 49).

There is no need here to expand on the sort of rational justification that Peters has in mind: it is the transcendental justification that Peters uses in *Ethics and Education*, which is discussed elsewhere in this volume. What is perhaps more striking in relation to the familiar story is the frequency with which Peters, in several papers in *Moral Development and Moral Education*, refers approvingly to rules. Writers sympathetic to virtue ethics have often been sceptical about, if not hostile to, the idea that morality has anything to do with rules (for more on this see Haydon, 1999, pp. 67–75). If one comes to Peters with this stance on rules one will be struck, for instance, by his idea that certain rules are basic to life in society (e.g. Peters, 1981, p. 31); indeed in two places he says 'a society is a collection of individuals united by the acceptance of certain rules' and goes on to mention 'a system of basic rules' (pp. 34, 49). Given this view of life in society, it is not surprising that he sees moral education as partly a matter of perpetuating the rules: 'the educator has ... to make up his mind which *are* basic rules and he has to pass on these rules very firmly at an early age' (p. 34). Moreover, 'It is absolutely essential that in this area of basic rules there should be a high degree of conformity' (p. 179).

Of course, thinking of morality as even partly a system of rules is not sufficient for being a *rationalist* about moral education; for rules could be rationally unjustified (they might be rooted, for instance, in oppressive cultural practices for which no rational defence can be given). Hence the importance of Peters' stress on rationally justifiable *principles*. For Peters, unlike many critics of rule- and principle-based ethics, there is an important distinction to be made between rules and principles. In part this is a difference in degree of specificity; rules are more specific, principles more general. But more important is the different role of rules and principles within what Peters would call a rational morality. Roughly, rules tell one what to do or not do; principles enable one to judge whether the rules are justified. It is not enough that there should be reasons for rules; they need to be good reasons, and principles enable one to distinguish between good and bad reasons, by showing whether certain considerations count. 'A principle is that which makes a consideration relevant' (p. 66); thus principles—such as the ones mentioned above, which Peters claims can be justified by a transcendental argument—'prescribe what sort of considerations are to count as reasons' (p. 65). For example, the principle of consideration of interests shows that considerations about the causing of pain are relevant, which is in turn a step in the justification of rules proscribing particular forms of behaviour liable to cause pain.

Even if one is sceptical about the transcendental argument, those who think of rules and principles as all of a piece would do well to take note of Peters' arguments on the distinction between rules and principles. It is helpful in our thinking about moral agency to be able to make the distinction between specific pieces of guidance which tell one fairly concretely what is to be done—or more often, perhaps, not to be done—and far more general, and in that sense, more abstract, considerations that do and should influence our thinking, while at the same time never telling us exactly what is to be done in any given situation. *Especially* if Peters is right that a society needs certain widely recognised basic rules, then it is vital to a rational morality that there should be the possibility of rational criticism or justification of rules by appeal to more general considerations (see also Haydon, 1999, pp. 81–4).

PETERS THE VIRTUE THEORIST

Is Peters a virtue theorist? Needless to say, it depends on one's interpretation of virtue theory. Certainly Peters does engage in theoretical discussion of virtues. The point is often not noted by commentators on Peters' contribution to the philosophical literature on moral education; attention is more often given to his discussions of the related notions (related within his own account) of character and of habit. The neglect of what Peters actually says about virtues may be largely due to the rather mundane fact that whereas he published papers containing the terms 'character' and 'habit' in the titles ('Moral Education and the Psychology of Character', Peters, 1981, pp. 24–44; and the 'Reason and Habit' paper), his main discussion of virtues comes in a paper called 'Moral development: a plea for pluralism' (Peters, 1981, pp. 83–115). Since this discussion is relatively little known, it will be worth summarising here.

In 'Plea for Pluralism', as in several other places,[4] Peters takes issue with Kohlberg for his dismissive stance towards the idea of character education. This, according to Kohlberg, was an attempt to develop a rather miscellaneous 'bag of virtues'. Kohlberg contrasted the 'bag of virtues' approach to moral education with an approach through the development of rational principles. (This, of course, is ostensibly just the sort of contrast that the familiar story makes between two dominant approaches, that of rational principles until about the 1980s and a virtue-based approach more recently.) Peters himself finds Kohlberg's dichotomy between a principled morality and a morality of character-traits 'a strange contrast' (p. 93). His ensuing discussion calls attention to some differences among character-traits, and this leads him to the conclusion that there are 'distinct classes of virtues' (p. 94). In his own words:

> To summarise, there are (a) highly specific virtues, such as punctuality, tidiness and perhaps honesty, which are connected with specific types of acts, and which lack any built-in reason for acting in the manner prescribed—that is, are not motives, unlike (b) virtues, such as compassion, which are also motives for action. There are, then, (c) more artificial virtues, such as justice and tolerance, which involve more general considerations to do with rights and institutions. Finally, there are (d) virtues of a higher order, such as courage, integrity, perseverance, and the like, which have to be exercised in the face of counter-inclinations (p. 94).

Peters goes on to consider the extent to which virtues of these various kinds could be considered as habits, concluding—contrary, as he sees it, to Kohlberg's sweeping generalisations—that only virtues of class (a) can be so considered (p. 98).

Though it occupies only a short space, it would not be unreasonable to see this account of classes of virtues as 'a systematic and coherent account of virtues', which is one of Carr and Steutel's initial and broad characterisations of virtue ethics (Carr and Steutel, 1999, p. 5). The aim of such an account, they say, would be 'to identify certain traits as desirable, to analyse and classify such traits and to explain their moral significance: more precisely, to justify regarding such traits as virtues' (ibid.). Peters does all this; we shall return to his explanation of the moral significance of the various kinds of trait.

Does this make Peters a virtue theorist in his approach to moral education? Not if we follow Carr and Steutel in interpreting 'a virtue approach to moral education' in a sufficiently narrow way for it to mark something more distinctive. The crux for Carr and Steutel is whether an approach to moral education rests in *virtue ethics*, where virtue ethics takes *aretaic* judgements— judgements about the qualities of character of agents—to be basic. The contrast is with approaches to ethics that take *deontic* judgements— judgements about the rightness and wrongness of actions—to be basic. In the terms of this distinction, Peters does *not* count as taking a virtue approach. While the development of virtues is important to Peters, its importance appears to be in the service of a rational morality, which as we have seen is a matter of adherence to a rationally grounded code. For Peters, the 'moral significance' of traits such as those he identifies, what justifies 'regarding such traits as virtues', is—or so it often appears—that they are necessary to or conducive to a person's acting in accordance with a rational morality.

This is so in several ways, according to the different classes. Virtues of class (a), which can be considered as habits, are valuable because they save us trouble: 'Life would be very exhausting if, in moral situations, we always had to reflect, deliberate and make decisions. It would also be very difficult to conduct our social lives if we could not count on a fair stock of habits such as punctuality, politeness, honesty and the like, in other people' (Peters, 1981, p. 98). Peters is less explicit, I think, on the value of virtues of class (b), but the natural interpretation is that these virtues, such as compassion, are valuable because their built-in motivation makes it more likely that people will act according to the rationally justifiable principles, such as (in this case) the principle of consideration of interests. It is not clear whether Peters thinks people *could* act according to this principle without having any fellow feeling, but he certainly sees it as a welcome fact about human beings that they can have the virtue of compassion, that is they can have the disposition to be moved by their feelings for others (ibid.) to act in the way that a rational morality would prescribe. The development of the capacity for such motivation is thus an important aspect of moral development; a point to which I shall return below in connection with empathy.

Virtues of class (c), such as justice and tolerance, do not, according to Peters, incorporate a natural built-in motivation. They are, as Peters recognises (p. 93), Hume's artificial virtues. Principles of justice and tolerance have value in the regulation of social life; like other principles, they can be internalised, becoming virtues. Finally, virtues of type (d) have value because they enable people to act in accordance with principles in the face of counter-inclinations.

There are, of course, points at which Peters' account of the several types of virtue can be questioned. For instance, in his treatment of type (a) virtues (the ones that can be considered as habits) he arguably over-generalises in two respects in likening honesty to punctuality and tidiness. First, while it is true that punctuality and tidiness have reference to relatively specific kinds of situation, honesty is, or can be, a disposition of much wider relevance. (Peters was perhaps following the Hartshorne-May investigation, which he cites— e.g. p. 92—in interpreting honesty narrowly as non-cheating.) Secondly, while Peters argues that punctuality and tidiness are not motives in their own right, but 'require some further justification in terms of principles' (p. 95), it is not clear that the same is true of honesty; *pace* Peters (p. 99) it appears that it is possible to act *out of* honesty, or at least to refrain, out of honesty, from doing what it might have suited one to do. A principle, or even a rule, once internalised, can have motivating force, even if the motivation is one that has to be developed socially (or 'socially constructed'), unlike compassion, which, it can be argued, is biologically given.

The very fact that Peters' account of virtues is sufficiently complex to allow of detailed criticism indicates that it is more substantial than that of many rationalist and cognitivist interpreters of moral education who preceded him—if indeed his predecessors mentioned virtues at all, which they often did not. It is also clear that, although Peters enters into his discussion of virtues not directly, as it were, by following Aristotle, but rather by critiquing Kohlberg, there are echoes of Aristotle in Peters' account. Indeed it can be argued that in a particular respect he brings something distinctive to broadly Aristotelian (or neo-Aristotelian) accounts of the development of virtues. The account of the development of virtues adumbrated by such theorists sometimes hardly goes beyond broad generalisations about the importance of the learning of habits in the development of virtues. Peters, in setting out four categories of virtues and suggesting that they stand in different relationships to habituation, can encourage us—even if we do not accept all the details of his categorisations—to attempt a more nuanced account.

Yet Aristotle almost certainly should be construed as a proponent of virtue ethics in the more specific sense that Carr and Steutel suggest, whereas Peters, as we have seen, is not. Is Peters getting himself into a paradoxical position here?

IS IT PARADOXICAL TO COMBINE ARISTOTLE AND KOHLBERG?

Carr and Steutel acknowledge that 'perhaps the most influential attempt to turn Aristotelian virtue theory to the purposes of moral education was made by ... Richard Peters'. 'But', they continue, 'Peters seems, somewhat dubiously, to have regarded the Aristotelian emphasis on moral training and character development as a potential addition or supplement, more than an alternative to ... the prevailing post-war moral educational orthodoxy of cognitive development theory' (Carr and Steutel, 1999, p. 242). Carr and Steutel are right that Peters did not see the Aristotelian approach as an *alternative* to Kohlbergian rationalism; but it does not follow that Peters saw the emphasis on character development as merely an addition or supplement. His position, rather, was that indicated by the subtitle of the paper in which he discussed the virtues: a plea for pluralism (not a plea for a supplement to Kohlberg; indeed the paper is quite critical of Kohlberg). Peters was a pluralist about ethics, and therefore about ethical education. Morality, he believes, 'is not as unitary an affair as [Kohlberg] suggests' (Peters, 1981 p. 87). Kohlberg's criticisms of Freud, for instance, may be misplaced because 'Freud was in fact concerned with a different range of questions' (ibid.). In short, 'Kohlberg adopts too simple and too monolithic an approach to moral development' (ibid.).

But not just, we can add, to moral development; it is the ethical aspects of life generally to which Kohlberg adopts too simple an approach. In another important paper, 'Concrete Principles and the Rational Passions' (pp. 61–82), Peters writes of the complexity of the moral life, in which 'at least five facets . . . must be distinguished' (p. 69). The first of these comprises those activities that fall under the concepts of 'good', 'desirable' and 'worthwhile'. Thus he is able to say, echoing a claim that is familiar from *Ethics and Education*, 'Education involves getting people to make something of themselves within activities that are thought to be worthwhile . . . *[A]ll education is, therefore, moral education*, if we are to include the pursuit of good in morals and not just confine it to codes and more general dealings with other men' (pp. 73–4, italics added). The remaining facets of moral life that Peters here distinguishes (corresponding approximately though not precisely to his categories of virtues) are, second, obligations connected with social roles; third, duties related to basic social rules; fourth, wide-ranging goals of life personalised as motives; fifth, very general traits of character relating to the way a person follows his [or her] purposes.

Peters never, to my knowledge, makes any systematic distinction between ethics and morality, or the ethical and the moral. Even the titles of his books *Ethics and Education*; *Psychology and Ethical Development*; *Moral Development and Moral Education*, suggest that he uses the terms interchangeably. Had he been writing a little later, he might well have found it useful to adopt the distinction between morality and ethics that was perhaps introduced into modern philosophical discussion by Bernard Williams (1985) and has been used also by other writers including Charles Taylor (for details see Haydon, 1999, pp. 34–9). In the terms of this distinction, morality—sometimes 'morality in the narrow sense', or, for Williams (1985), 'morality, the peculiar institution'—is the area Peters refers to as 'codes and more general dealings with other men'; while ethics is much wider, including 'the pursuit of good'. It is evident that Kohlberg's concentration was on the former, while Aristotle (as recognised by Williams and many moral philosophers since) was concerned with the latter, much broader, field. Peters, though he does not make the distinction explicit, was concerned with both. He recognises that his advocacy of a rational code applies to that aspect of morality concerning interpersonal conduct; indeed he says at one point, when introducing his own standpoint of advocacy of a rational morality, 'I propose to confine [this standpoint] to the area of morals that is concerned with interpersonal rules' (Peters, 1981, p. 142). At the same time, as we have seen, he sees what would now often be called 'conceptions of the good' as also belonging to the ethical.

Peters' acknowledgement that there is more to ethics than the regulation of interpersonal conduct is, I suggest, the reason why he does not see an Aristotelian approach as an *alternative* to Kohlberg; the two approaches are asking different questions. If a monolithic approach to the whole field of ethics (including but not exhausted by interpersonal morality) is mistaken—a point to which I shall return in conclusion—that will apply to an over-reliance on Aristotle as well as to an over-reliance on Kohlberg.

IS IT PARADOXICAL TO COMBINE VIRTUES WITH RULES?

The suggestion just made implies that, *pace* some enthusiasts for Aristotle, Aristotle did not ask *all* the questions that need to be asked about the ethical life. What might he have missed? According to MacIntyre, 'the most obvious and astonishing absence from Aristotle's thought for any modern reader [is that] there is relatively little mention of rules anywhere in the Ethics' (MacIntyre, 1981, p. 141). (MacIntyre goes on to point out, surely correctly, that the idea that the virtuous person in Aristotle acts 'according to the right rule' rests on a misleading translation of *logos* (p. 143); had MacIntyre adopted Peters' distinction between rules and principles he might have pointed out that 'rational principle' would be a more defensible translation.) MacIntyre, of course, was arguing that the modern preoccupation of moral philosophy with rules reflects a wrong turning taken by the Enlightenment; but it is also in accordance with MacIntyre's recognition that philosophy has sociological implications that we can recognise that rules *do* have a place in society as we know it. That is something amply recognised by Peters in his claim, already noted, that society needs a system of basic rules.

Given that the familiar story about moral philosophy from which I started involves a bifurcation between virtues and rules, we need to ask whether there is anything paradoxical about combining the two. Peters clearly did not think so. And in fact he is by no means alone in this. For instance, as Carr and Steutel recognise (1999, p. 9), Rosalind Hursthouse (1996), undeniably a virtue theorist, sees a place for moral rules both in everyday morality and in moral education—a point with which Peters would certainly agree. Perhaps more significantly for the light it casts on the shortcomings of the familiar story, MacIntyre in *After Virtue*, after pointing out the lack of much explicit attention to rules in Aristotle, argues in his own right that in any society virtues need to be complemented by a morality of rules (or laws, in the case of publicly authoritative norms in a less liberal society than our own). Still more significantly, in his more recent work *Dependent Rational Animals: Why Human Beings Need the Virtues*, MacIntyre argues that living in accordance with the virtues, as a feature of social, not merely individual, life *requires* the acknowledgement and following of rules (MacIntyre, 1999, pp. 109ff.). He uses trustworthiness as an extended example (p. 110). I am trustworthy only if others know that I can be relied on to follow certain rules that are mutually— even if not explicitly—acknowledged. To put the example the other way round, I can recognise that you are trustworthy only if 'I can count on your regarding yourself as bound by certain rules, such rules as those that enjoin us to keep reasonable promises, to be punctual, to tell the truth, never to allow feelings of distaste or distrust to distract us from responsibilities for care, never to disclose confidential information and the like' (ibid.). This account appears very much in line with Peters' conception of the relationship between virtues and rules. He frequently speaks of rules or principles being internalised; general social rules, for instance, 'are personalised as character-traits' (Peters, 1981, p. 69). Once we recognise the factor of internalisation, which means that rules can be followed without explicit articulation, the idea already cited that 'a society is a collection of individuals united by the acceptance of certain rules' (pp. 34, 49) appears much less strange. Implicitly Peters is thinking of a liberal society in which there may not be much agreement on the good, but there still does need to be agreement in practice on some rules of conduct to hold the society together *as* a society. (MacIntyre argues that the same is true even of a community where there *is* agreement on goods; agreement on rules is needed as well: see MacIntyre, 1999, p. 109.) For Peters, the difference between the different categories of virtues corresponds—or so it appears, though he is not as precise in spelling this out as one might wish—to the difference between rules and principles. 'Whether a rule, which can also be regarded as a trait of character if it is internalised, is a principle depends on the function which the rule or consideration, which is personalised in the trait, performs' (Peters, 1981, p. 93).

To return to MacIntyre, his argument is that while conforming to certain rules is a necessary condition of the possession of certain virtues, it is by no means sufficient. There are circumstances where no rule will deliver an answer, and then practical judgment is required. This is, indeed, the familiar point of many virtue theorists, particularly those following Aristotle, that what the moral life requires is not rule-following but practical wisdom. But if MacIntyre, and Peters before him, are right, it is not only possible, but necessary, for both rules and practical wisdom to enter into the moral life. Indeed practical wisdom is essential to right rule-following. And the exercise of practical wisdom, as in Aristotle, cannot be confined to a purely cognitive exercise of the intellect. As Peters puts it, 'sympathy and imagination . . . are necessary also for the sensitive exercise of the judicial function in making relevant exceptions to rules and for seeing situations as falling under different rules' (p. 41). So Peters is at one with MacIntyre in seeing an interrelationship between rules and virtues. Arguably, also, in the distinction between rules and principles Peters has the tools for a more subtle account of that relationship than MacIntyre's.

PETERS AND CARE ETHICS

As noted at the beginning, the turn away from rationalist accounts of morality and moral education has been not only towards virtue ethics, but also towards an ethics of care. In the light of the familiar story, one would hardly expect to find links between Peters and an ethic of care, apart from the fact that care may be considered one virtue among others.[5] And it must certainly be acknowledged both that Peters (like Kohlberg and other writers on moral education at that time) shows no awareness that study of and reflection on the moral development of girls and women could bring a distinctive perspective to the field, and that Peters' language is unremittingly *not* gender-neutral. Peters' thought and language was of its time in those respects, and its time, though not before feminism, was before the impact of Noddings and Gilligan.

But if care ethics began from a distinctively feminist position it is by no means now tied to gender. We cannot rule out in advance that there may be aspects of Peters' thinking that theorists of care ethics could recognise as part of their own thinking too. In fact Peters is no stranger to the use of terms such as 'care', 'concern', 'compassion', 'sympathy' and 'empathy', though he does not analyse the relationships and differences between these notions. We saw above that he sees sympathy as necessary to sensitive rule-following; from this it follows already that the development of sympathy must be part of moral development. Peters also makes an explicit link between care and the principle of justice. In 'The Place of Kohlberg's Theory in Moral Education' he explicitly criticises Kohlberg for neglecting something that is vital even to understanding how the principle of justice can operate (1981, pp. 166–82). We cannot, Peters argues, deploy the notion of justice without there being something *else* of value at stake besides the notion of justice itself. For instance (to use my own example) we *could* claim that we are treating people equally by making them all equally miserable, or all as miserable as they deserve; but, Peters argues, what we are usually assuming in our talk of justice is that other people's interests must count positively in our considerations. Peters complains that there is no account in Kohlberg or in Piaget of how this concern for others is supposed to develop. Thus Piaget, in his account of how a child acquires the ability to take the point of view of another, 'never shows why a child should *care* about the other whose point of view he can take' (p. 172).

More than most philosophical writers on moral education at his time, Peters kept abreast of psychological research, and not only that in a Kohlbergian mode. When he recognised the need for a developmental account of caring he turned to Martin Hoffman's research on the development of empathy (pp. 161, 173–4, 179). Hoffman's research (as summarised in Hoffman, 2000) remains important for some of the writers on care ethics, referred to by Noddings and Slote (2003, pp. 354–5), and given considerable weight by Slote in his own extended treatment of *The Ethics of Care and Empathy* (Slote, 2007, e.g. pp. 12–15, 29–31). It is no coincidence, then, but reflects the breadth of Peters' conception of moral development, that he had already in the 1970s recognised the significance of Hoffman's work and thereby also the importance of the child's early relationships with its carers.

CONCLUSION: PETERS THE PLURALIST

We have seen that Peters calls for pluralism in our approach to moral development and moral education, and indeed in our understanding of the moral—or ethical—life.

He puts stress on the rational holding of a justifiable code, but also stresses the social importance of inculcating that code even if it is not going to be rationally held by all individuals: 'if the ordinary citizen is mugged in the street, how the thief views rules about property is of academic interest to him' (Peters, 1981, p. 157). He takes virtues far more seriously than does Kohlberg, and although his official position appears to be that virtues are important in the service of a rational morality, it is hard not to read him as seeing certain virtues—particularly those such as compassion that incorporate their own motivation—as being desirable in themselves. In stressing the importance, *contra* Kohlberg, of the development of care and concern, he anticipates some of the insights of care ethics. And, as we know well from *Ethics and Education*, he stresses the importance in life of worthwhile activities, and hence of initiation into such activities.

Is there anything paradoxical in one thinker holding such a range of positions, including positions that fall on both sides of the divide indicated by the familiar story? This will only appear paradoxical, I suggest, to someone committed to the belief that there must be one all-encompassing theoretical account of the ethical life. And indeed it is remarkable how much of recent philosophical writing on moral development and moral education has tried to fit all of the phenomena (the Aristotelian appearances) into one mould, even if that, instead of being Kohlbergian, is virtue-theoretical or care-theoretical. The writings of virtue theorists sometimes convey the impression, if not the explicit statement, that the whole Kohlbergian research programme was totally wrong-headed (see many works of David Carr including those cited here). Among theorists of care ethics, Slote goes so far as to claim that 'a fully developed ethics of care' is 'nothing less than a total or systematic *human* morality, one that may be able to give us a better understanding of the whole range of moral issues that concern both men and women than anything to be found in traditional ethical theories' (Slote, 2007, p. 3), and in the course of the book he claims that on a care-ethical basis adequate accounts can be given of all the following: our obligations to others near and far, deontology, autonomy, the shortcomings of liberalism, social justice and practical rationality. Even before any examination of his detailed arguments, one may want to ask '*Why* should we be looking for a total systematic account of something as apparently diverse as human ethical thought and practice?[6]

Peters was more modest in his claims. In the Preface to *Moral Development and Moral Education* he claims that the articles it contains 'are reasonably consistent with each other ... because they stem from a definite ethical theory' (Peters, 1981 p. 8). By 'definite ethical theory' I take him to referring to the stance he develops in *Ethics and Education* on the rational justification of a set of underlying principles. But in the essays of *Moral Development and Moral Education* one does not have the sense that a theoretical structure that works very well in one role is being stretched to explain more than it reasonably can. Peters continues to express the hope that the articles in the book 'will do something to stimulate further reflection and research'. It is regrettable, and a little paradoxical, that philosophers of education who have been stimulated by agreement or disagreement with *Ethics and Education* have for the most part paid rather little attention to the work of the same author on moral education. This, in the end, is the only 'paradox of Peters on moral education' that I have identified.

But the stimulus to further reflection and research is still there. One fairly obvious response to that stimulus is to bring Peters' writing on character, virtues and habituation to the service of the assessment and critique of the notion of character education that has enjoyed continued revival since Peters was writing (see, e.g. McLaughlin and Halstead, 1999). A less obvious focus that is philosophically perhaps more fundamental, on which we could still learn from Peters, is the question of whether it is reasonable to look for a unified theory of ethics and moral education. In the light of 'The Complexity and Concreteness of the Moral Life'[7] (Peters, 1981, p. 68) we should take seriously the possibility that we *need* an eclectic approach because, as Peters argued in criticism of Kohlberg, a monolithic approach must be inadequate.

NOTES

1. Recent tellings of this story include Noddings and Slote (2003) and my own (Haydon, 2003). A writer who has argued in far greater depth for the merits of turning away from Kohlberg towards virtue ethics is David Carr (see Carr, 1996, as well as other works cited below). While Carr does far more than tell 'the familiar story', the contrast he makes between Kohlberg and virtue theory is as sharp as any.
2. This collection is itself, with one exception, a subset of a larger collection, *Psychology and Ethical Development* (Peters, 1974); some of the individual papers in that were first published considerably earlier. Here my page references to papers collected in *Moral Development and Moral Education* are to that collection; other commentators sometimes give page references to the same papers in the earlier book.
3. See several discussions of the 'Paradox' paper that were published in the late 1970s and early 1980s (Kazepides, 1979; Gardner, 1981, 1985).
4. Especially 'The Place of Kohlberg's Theory in Moral Education' (Peters, 1981, pp. 166–82). Unlike the other chapters in *Moral Development and Moral Education*, this chapter was not taken from *Psychology and Ethical Development*, but was first published in *Journal of Moral Education* in 1978.
5. Whether an ethic of care is a form of virtue ethics, or is distinctive in being rooted not in a virtue but in caring relationships, is disputed; see Noddings and Slote (2003). In his fullest account so far of an ethic of care, Slote takes a neutral position on this (Slote, 2007 p. 7). I shall assume the same neutrality here.
6. For two recent recognitions of the diversity of ethical life—very different from each other—see Haydon, 2006, Chapter 2; and Munday, 2009.
7. A section heading from 'Concrete Principles and the Rational Passions'. As suggested above, it might be better to read 'ethical life'—and that is to say nothing here of political life.

REFERENCES

Aristotle (1925) *The Nicomachean Ethics of Aristotle*, D. Ross, trans. (London, Oxford University Press).

Carr, D. (1996) After Kohlberg: Some Implications of an Ethics of Virtue for the Theory of Moral Education and Development, *Studies in Philosophy and Education*, 15, pp. 353–70.

Carr, D. (1999) Virtue, *Akrasia* and Moral Weakness, in: D. Carr and J. Steutel (eds) *Virtue Ethics and Moral Education* (London, Routledge).

Carr, D. and Steutel, J. (eds) (1999) *Virtue Ethics and Moral Education* (London, Routledge).

Gardner, P. (1981) On Some Paradoxes in Moral Education, *Journal of Philosophy of Education*, 15.1, pp. 65–76.

Gardner, P. (1985) The Paradox of Moral Education: A Reassessment, *Journal of Philosophy of Education*, 19.1, pp. 39–48.

Gilligan, C. (1982) *In a Different Voice: Psychological Theory and Women's Development* (Cambridge, MA, Harvard University Press).

Halstead, J. M. and McLaughlin, T. H. (eds) (1999) *Education in Morality* (London, Routledge).

Haydon, G. (1999) *Values, Virtues and Violence: Education and the Public Understanding of Morality, Special Issue of Journal of Philosophy of Education*, 33.1.

Haydon, G. (2003) Moral Education, in: R. Curren (ed.) *The Blackwell Companion to Philosophy of Education* (Oxford, Blackwell).

Haydon, G. (2006) *Education, Philosophy and the Ethical Environment* (Abingdon, Routledge).

Hoffman, M. L. (2000) *Empathy and Moral Development: Implications for Caring and Justice* (New York, Cambridge University Press).

Hursthouse, R. (1996) Normative Virtue Ethics, in: R. Crisp and M. Slote (eds) *Virtue Ethics* (Oxford, Oxford University Press).

Kazepides, T. (1979) The Alleged Paradox of Moral Education, in: D. B. Cochrane, C. M. Hamm and A. C. Kazepides (eds) *The Domain of Moral Education* (New York, Paulist Press).

McLaughlin, T. H. and Halstead, J. M. (1999) Education in Character and Virtue, in: J. M. Halstead and T. H. McLaughlin (eds) *Education in Morality* (London, Routledge).

MacIntyre, A. (1981) *After Virtue* (London, Duckworth).

MacIntyre, A. (1999) *Dependent Rational Animals: Why Human Beings Need the Virtues* (London, Duckworth).

Munday, I. (2009) Passionate Utterance and Moral Education, *Journal of Philosophy of Education*, 43.1, pp. 57–74.

Niblett, W. R. (ed.) (1963) *Moral Education in a Changing Society* (London, Faber).

Noddings, N. (1984) *Caring: A Feminine Approach to Ethics and Moral Education* (Berkeley, CA, University of California Press).

Noddings, N. and Slote, M. (2003) Changing Notions of the Moral and of Moral Education, in N. Blake, P. Smeyers, R. Smith and P. Standish (eds) *The Blackwell Guide to Philosophy of Education* (Oxford, Blackwell).

Peters, R. S. (1966) *Ethics and Education* (London, Allen & Unwin).

Peters, R. S. (1973) The Justification of Education, in: R. S. Peters (ed.) *The Philosophy of Education* (Oxford, Oxford University Press).

Peters, R. S. (1981) *Moral Development and Moral Education* (London, George Allen & Unwin).

Peters, R. S. (1974) *Psychology and Ethical Development* (London, George Allen & Unwin).

Slote, M. (2007) *The Ethics of Care and Empathy* (London, Routledge).

Spiecker, B. (1999) Habituation and Training in Early Moral Upbringing, in: D. Carr and J. Steutel (eds) *Virtue Ethics and Moral Education* (London, Routledge).

Steutel, J. (1999) The Virtues of Will-Power: Self-Control and Deliberation, in: D. Carr and J. Steutel (eds) *Virtue Ethics and Moral Education* (London, Routledge).

Williams, B. (1985) *Ethics and the Limits of Philosophy* (London, Fontana).

12

Autonomy in R. S. Peters' Educational Theory

STEFAAN E. CUYPERS

One of the major themes in Richard S. Peters' work is that of the education and development of the child into a rational autonomous person. In this chapter, I try to unravel some important strands of this complex issue against the backdrop of contemporary educational theory and analytical philosophy. My guideline will be the threefold distinction among autonomy as an actual psychological condition, as a capacity that can be developed, and as an educational ideal.

The chapter is structured as follows. Section I probes the metaphysical foundations of Peters' conceptual analysis of 'freedom' and 'autonomy'. Section II reconstructs this analysis and explores the intricate relation between autonomy and rationality. Section III investigates the development of autonomy, while Section IV deals with autonomy as an educational ideal. Finally, Section V briefly evaluates Peters' legacy on autonomy.

I THE METAPHYSICS OF AUTONOMY

The concept of autonomy belongs to the cluster of concepts around 'freedom'. Rereading Peters on autonomy quite naturally brings to mind the philosophical debate on freedom and determinism today and invites the question whether he was a compatibilist or an incompatibilist. To answer this question, I introduce some basic terminology.

Determinism is 'the thesis that there is at any instant exactly one physically possible future' (van Inwagen, 1983, p. 3). If this thesis is true, the facts of the past, together with the (causal) laws of nature, entail all facts of the present and future. Indeterminism is the denial of determinism. Compatibilism is the view that free will, free action and moral responsibility are compatible with determinism; incompatibilism is the denial of compatibilism.

In Chapter 9, 'Freedom and Responsibility', of *Social Principles and the Democratic State*, Stanley I. Benn and Peters write:

> Causes, being pictured always as internal pushes and pulls, were thought somehow to compel a man. And this picture suggests compulsion whether

Reading R. S. Peters Today, First Edition. Stefaan E. Cuypers and Christopher Martin.
Chapters © 2011 The Authors. Editorial organization © 2011 Philosophy of Education Society of Great Britain. Published 2011 by Blackwell Publishing Ltd.

such causes are properly to be regarded as necessary or as sufficient conditions for human action. Men were therefore regarded as being not free because they were the victims of a peculiar internal sort of compulsion exercised by the causes of their behaviour (Benn and Peters, 1959, p. 205).

In their response to this picture, Peters and Benn make the compatibilist distinction between compelled (or constrained) and ordinary caused behaviour: 'Causes in general must be distinguished from the special types of causes that have unavoidable effects.'[1] Only causes such as irresistible impulses deprive a person of his freedom. Free action is then compatible with the ordinary causal production of behaviour, since caused action does not coincide with unavoidable action. Yet, although they keep causal determination apart from compulsion, Peters and Benn do not seem to go all the way with compatibilism:

> Thus even if all behaviour has causes, in the sense of *necessary* conditions, there are objections to saying that all behaviour—especially rational behaviour—can be *sufficiently* explained by causes of the sort suggested by physical scientists, and by mechanistic philosophers like Hobbes. Whether this means that there is *also* a case for freedom depends on whether 'free' can be equated, in any of its various senses, with 'not sufficiently explained in causal terms' (p. 204).

Spelled out, determinism is the thesis that all events and actions are the necessary consequences of causal antecedents. Assuming deterministic causation, the governing laws of nature consist in the state of affairs that certain antecedents causally necessitate certain consequences. Compatibilism is then, more precisely, the view that although freedom from compulsion does not include freedom from necessitation, freedom is compatible with causal necessitation. On this view, moreover, precisely because a rational action is causally necessitated, it can be *sufficiently explained* in terms of causal factors.

In his early books *Hobbes* (1956, pp. 167–177) and *The Concept of Motivation* (1958, pp. 1–16), Peters argues negatively against this causalism in the explanation of human action and positively for the alternative, purposive rule-following model. In contrast to what happens to a person—passive events—human actions are done after rational deliberation and in accordance with standards, norms, or rules. For this reason, although rational action unquestionably depends on necessary causal conditions (brain-functioning, nerve-stimulation, muscle-contraction, etc.), it cannot be sufficiently explained in causal terms. Since rational canons and behavioural rules are normative, action explanation cannot be based on non-normative processes, such as causal ones. Hence, a sufficient explanation of human action can only be given in terms of the rule-following purposive model.

Non-causalism in action explanation typically goes hand in hand with incompatibilism.[2] Peters also seems to equate 'free' with 'not sufficiently explained in causal terms': 'A man is free or self-determined . . . in so far as his behaviour is explained in terms of his rational decisions rather than in terms of purely mechanical causes' (Benn and Peters, 1959, p. 204). Does this make him an incompatibilist? Although I am inclined to think that, on the basis of his writings, Peters actually can be associated with a non-causalist incompatibilist position in the metaphysics of free will, his being such an incompatibilist (or not) does not have much influence upon his key project of *conceptual analysis* in the philosophy of education, upon which he embarks in the early 1960s. In that heyday of ordinary language philosophy, conceptual analysis had a strongly anti-metaphysical bent. Peters' educational theory is, accordingly, neutral with regard to the metaphysics of free will.

However, Peters' execution of the pertinent project, laying bare the conceptual geography around the concepts of education, development and autonomy, is in itself much more congenial to compatibilism. In his analysis he addresses what David Zimmerman calls the puzzle of naturalised self-creation in real time: 'How do some children manage to develop the capacity to *make up their own minds* about what values to embrace, by virtue of having gone through a process in which they play an increasingly active role in *making their own minds*, a process that begins with their *having virtually no minds at all?*' (Zimmerman, 2003, p. 638) The property of *being autonomous* is not a transcendent (or Kantian transcendental) property in an indeterministic world, but an empirical property in a deterministic world where children causally develop into rational autonomous beings by going through an educational process that starts from heteronomy. Elsewhere, I have argued that Peters' conceptual analysis of 'education', 'development' and 'autonomy' is particularly congenial to an externalist compatibilist metaphysics of free will—that is, a type of compatibilism for which the educational history of a person in the external world is crucial for his autonomy (Cuypers, 2009).

Precisely because Peters' educational theory is metaphysically neutral, it can also be harmonised with compatibilism. I even speculate that Peters could have pledged allegiance to compatibilism if he had taken to heart two milestone papers in the philosophy of mind and action. In his 1963 paper, 'Actions, Reasons, and Causes', Donald Davidson convincingly argues for the causality thesis that reasons for actions—desire-belief pairs—are their causes. Rational explanation of human action is a species of causal explanation. In his 1971 paper, 'Freedom of the Will and the Concept of a Person', Harry Frankfurt persuasively argues, in the tradition of Hobbes, for the compatibilist view that it might be causally determined that a person enjoys freedom of the will. A person enjoys a free will if he has the will—first-order desires—he wants to have and if he can act in accordance with his higher-order desires without internal or external constraints. Both of these landmark papers could have made Peters' insistence on non-causalism and his inclination toward incompatibilism pointless. However, in the 1960s and 1970s Peters was probably too immersed in his own conceptual project in

educational philosophy to pay sufficient attention to these major developments in the metaphysics of action and free will.[3]

In sum, no one should reject Peters' educational theory of autonomy solely
on metaphysical grounds. So, whether you favour a compatibilist philosophy
of education or an incompatibilist one, we can safely turn to the neutral
domain of conceptual analysis.

II FREEDOM, AUTONOMY AND RATIONALITY

The terms 'freedom' and 'autonomy' are sometimes used interchangeably.
Still, the use of the technical term 'autonomy' is primarily limited to
philosophy and the social sciences, while in daily life 'freedom' is used instead.
But even in philosophical analysis, 'autonomy' does not seem to have a single
meaning, apart from the general and vague etymological one: *autos* (= self)
and *nomos* (= law, rule). Joel Feinberg usefully distinguishes between four
interconnected conceptions of autonomy:

> When applied to individuals the word 'autonomy' has four closely related
> meanings. It can refer either to the *capacity* to govern oneself, which of
> course is a matter of degree; or to the *actual condition* of self-government
> and its associated virtues; or to an *ideal of character* derived from that
> conception; ... and the sense, applied mainly to political states, of *de jure
> sovereignty* and the right of self-determination (Feinberg, 1986, p. 28).

Arguably, the conception of autonomy as a *de facto* condition is the central
core underlying applications of the autonomy concept. What it means for a
person to have a capacity for or a right to autonomy, only becomes clear when
that person is in the condition of actually exercising such a capacity or right.
Moreover, the content of autonomy as an (educational) ideal—something
worthwhile to which persons can aspire—is directly derived from the
characteristics of this actual condition of 'self-government'.

Being autonomous is, in this context, a property of a person. Yet, this
holistic property is best construed as the upshot of a collection of atomistic
properties. Whole persons or their whole lives essentially consist in
psychological connectedness and continuity through time (Parfit, 1984,
Chapter 10). A personal history is composed of a succession of person-phases
at different times. These various person-phases are united by the relations of
mental connectedness and continuity into one personal history. In its turn, a
person-phase is composed of a collection of mental states and events at a
certain moment (or during a certain period). These various mental states and
events are united by the relation of co-consciousness into a single person-
phase. So, according to this line of thought, the ultimate building-blocks of a
person's life as a whole are these atomistic mental elements. *Being autonomous*
is, consequently, primarily a property of mental states and events: choices,

decisions, beliefs, desires, preferences, actions, etc. If these parts are autonomous, then the whole into which they are collected—the person— also possesses the property of *being autonomous*. The sum total is autonomous to the extent that the composing elements are autonomous.

What is it, then, for a certain mental state or event to be in the actual psychological condition of autonomy? Peters focuses on man as a chooser and his choices. According to him, autonomy is a component of the analysis of 'freedom' in the broad sense. He writes:

> The lynch-pin of the analysis is the notion of man as a chooser, a rational being placed in what I have called the situation of practical reason ... In education, however, we are usually concerned with more than just preserving the capacity for choice; we are also concerned with the ideal of personal autonomy, which is a development of some of the potentialities inherent in the notion of man as a chooser (Peters, 1973a, pp. 16–17).

As for the notion of personal autonomy, he explains: 'There is ... a gradation of conditions implicit in the idea of autonomy. The first basic condition is that of authenticity, of adopting a code or way of life that is one's own as distinct from one dictated by others. The second condition of rational reflection on rules is one espoused by most believers in autonomy' (p. 16). An autonomous choice is, at least, a free choice. The notion of man as a free chooser in the narrow sense is that of an agent without external and internal constraints—no chains and no compulsion that hinder him. A free choice is, then, a choice over which the agent has *control*. A free agent is an agent who has options open to him and who controls his actions by having control over his will. Here I leave the term 'options' ambiguous between weak, compatibilist options and strong, incompatibilist ones (such as alternative possibilities). That there is *some* control condition on autonomous choice is not controversial.[4]

However, '[t]o be a chooser is not enough for autonomy,' Benn remarks, 'for a competent chooser may still be a slave to convention, choosing by standards he has accepted quite uncritically from his milieu' (Benn, 1976, p. 123). For that reason, the 'autonomous man' is not only a free chooser but also an agent who possesses an authentic code of conduct in the light of which he reflectively makes rational choices. Peters details his authenticity-condition of autonomy further:

> Etymologically, 'autonomy' suggests that a person accepts or makes rules for himself ... It denies that the individual's code of conduct is simply one that he has picked up from others or adopted in any second-hand way. The rules which he lives by are not just those that are laid down by custom or authority ... [T]his is represented as what the individual really wants as distinct from what conformity dictates (Peters, 1973a, p. 15).

Peters' second condition of autonomy—associated with assessment and criticism—is a rationality-condition: 'The individual is conceived of as being aware of rules as alterable conventions which structure his social life. He subjects them to reflection and criticism in the light of principles and gradually emerges with his own code of conduct' (pp. 15–16).

According to Peters, then, a person's choices are in the *de facto* condition of autonomy when they fulfil the following requirements:

A choice of an agent is autonomous, if and only if,

(1) the choice is under his control,
(2) it is authentic, and
(3) he has rationally reflected upon (the principles behind) it.

Before dealing with the authenticity-condition in the next section, I will explore the complex relation between autonomy and rationality in Peters' educational theory. To my mind, the rationality-condition is ambiguous between two interpretations. John Elster (1983, Chapter 1) makes a distinction between the *thin* and the *broad* theory of rationality. In my disambiguation, I will use this terminology but with a different content.

Thin rationality is the type of rationality employed in *deliberative reflection* and *critical thinking*. According to Alfred Mele, deliberative reflection involves the exercising of deliberative capacities, including (a) the capacity critically to reflect on beliefs, pro-attitudes and principles (or rules), (b) the capacity prudentially and morally to assess these elements, and (c) the capacity to change their strength, or to revise and even to eradicate them, or to foster new elements in the light of (a) and (b) (Mele, 1995, pp. 166–172; pp. 183–184). According to Harvey Siegel, the critical thinking capacity comprises, resonantly but perhaps in a somewhat more demanding sense, '(1) the ability to reason well, i.e. to construct and evaluate the various reasons which have been or can be offered in support or criticism of candidate beliefs, judgments, and actions; and (2) the disposition or inclination to be guided by reasons so evaluated, i.e. actually to believe, judge, and act in accordance with the results of such reasoned evaluations' (Siegel, 2003, p. 305). As I construe it, thin rationality is based on a *purely epistemological* theory of rationality (which is fallibilist).[5] Good reasons for beliefs are based on sufficient *evidence*. Such an evidence-based theory occupies a middle-position between a logical theory of rationality as (mere) consistency and a metaphysical theory of rationality as (robust) truth-entailing. The formal consistency criterion for beliefs is not sufficient, whereas the robustly truth-entailing criterion for beliefs is not necessary for deliberative reflection and critical thinking.

Thin rationality does not only apply to the epistemological domain, it also pertains to the *ethical* domain. Given a generalist view on reason assessment and the perspective of rationalist ethics,[6] the assessment of moral reasons—pro-attitudes and rules—in light of ethical criteria is entirely analogous to that of non-moral reasons according to epistemic criteria. Like epistemic criteria, ethical ones also warrant the impartiality and universality of reasons, exposing the arbitrariness of self-interested reasons.

Although the exercising of the capacities for deliberative reflection and critical thinking is a matter of degree, there is some minimal threshold level of thin rationality below which a person would fail to qualify as a genuine reflective deliberator or critical thinker. Since, according to Peters, (thin) rationality is a *necessary* condition for autonomy, such a person would then also disqualify as an autonomous chooser. The crucial question, however, is whether autonomy does require (even) thin rationality? Even though the rationality-requirement is, according to Peters, 'one espoused by most believers in autonomy', Frankfurt and the existentialists, for instance, are important exceptions. I will not attempt to review this discussion here,[7] but limit myself to observing that the thin rationality conception of autonomy is predominantly Kantian because of the essential connection between autonomy and rationality in Kant's account of free will.

Broad rationality is the type of rationality at work in what Peters (1974) calls our *human or cultural heritage* or *public or shared inheritance*. R. F. Dearden articulates the rationality-condition thus:

> The various activities of mind ... constitutive of autonomy [a person's own choices, deliberations, decisions, reflections, judgments, plannings or reasonings] are all essentially linked to the idea of reason ... Choosing, deciding, deliberating, reflecting and so on are possible only because relevant considerations can be brought to bear in these activities ... Implicitly or explicitly there will be criteria which pick out ... the considerations which we take into account (Dearden, 1972, p. 66).

Peters gives the following specification of these criteria: 'What we call "standards" represent the various demands made on us by the use of reason in its different forms, which is articulated in different ways by the concerns which underlie the various humanities' (Peters, 1974, p. 425). Let me unpack this.

The concerns of human life inexorably present themselves when human beings are confronted with the givenness of the natural and social world. The givenness of *la condition humaine*—natural laws, death, over-population, pain, violence, power, social laws, etc.—triggers equally given human responses. As rational beings we are creatures who live under the demands of reason, while as social beings we are prone to shared reactive attitudes and feelings. Now, according to Peters (1974), education, especially in the humanities, has to be set squarely in these dimensions of the human condition, for education is the search for a quality of living. The humanities, evidently in tandem with the natural sciences, constitute the rational attempt of mankind to deal with the pressures of the human predicament in their search for well-being. The cultural heritage of the humanities encompasses the ways in which man cares about the more permanent and all-pervasive concerns of mankind. At the same time, this shared inheritance comprises man's feeble endeavours to rationally build a human world. The use of reason in the different branches of the humanities—the social sciences, history and literature, philosophy and religious studies—is a public inheritance of critical procedures and standards. These procedures and standards, historically enshrined in the humanities, warrant, if only fallibly, objectivity and non-arbitrariness. Observing these rational standards is intimately connected with the quality of life because they represent the time-honoured ways of dealing adequately with the problems and predicaments of human life.

As I interpret it, broad rationality has its place in a *cognitive virtue* theory of rationality (which is also fallibilist).[8] What Peters tries to bring out is a conception of *human wisdom* embedded in the humanities:

> In science, history, psychology and philosophy the 'goal' is truth . . . the aim is to increase sensitivity and understanding; but this is to be interpreted in terms of values such as clarity, coherence, consistency, relevance, non-arbitrariness, humility, accuracy, precision, truthfulness, sincerity, percep-tiveness and so on. These intellectual virtues are definitive of the search for truth and exert a constant pressure on our struggles for understanding and insight (p. 426).

Whereas choices, deliberations, decisions, beliefs, principles, etc., are thinly rational insofar as there is good evidence for them, these elements are broadly rational insofar as they meet the standards which represent the various demands of reason as articulated within the various humanities. Therefore, given that, according to Peters and Dearden, (broad) rationality is a *necessary* condition for autonomy, an autonomous choice is only possible against the backdrop of shared standards and criteria which belong to our human heritage. The vital question, however, is whether autonomy is (even) compatible with broad rationality? On the face of it, there appears to be a conflict between the broad rationality-condition and autonomy's authenti-city-condition.[9] Peters gives the impression of downgrading subjectivity, creativity and individuality, at least in their extreme forms, when he writes: 'in estimating anything rationally [in the broad sense], identity is as irrelevant as time and place' (Peters, 1974, p. 428). Nothing authentic seems to be left over after a person has complied with the social requirements of reason: 'A reasonable man is one who is prepared to discuss things, to look at a situation impartially from the point of view of others than himself, to discount his own particular biases and predilections. As G. H. Mead put it, he can adopt the point of view of the "generalised other"'(p. 425). Indeed, one can justifiably ask: what then remains of 'doing one's own thing'? How can a broadly rational choice be autonomous if it has to be authentic as well?

III THE DEVELOPMENT OF AUTONOMY

The problem of educational authenticity is a much more pervasive problem. It not only involves the apparent conflict between 'doing one's own thing' and the mediating public inheritance, it also concerns the very idea of 'having it one's own way'. How can there be any authenticity in education at all?

As education is a process of deliberate moulding or intentional influencing, it necessarily involves *interferences*.[10] It requires instilling in the young child, among other things, salient choice-guiding elements such as values and other pro-attitudes, deliberative and other principles. However, the acquisition of these elements totally bypasses the child's rational capacities of reflective assessment and criticism because these capacities are absent or latent at this early stage of development. If such elements are just causally 'implanted', then how is the child's 'adopting a code or way of life that is one's own as distinct from one dictated by others' even possible? As the requisite, pertinent interferences during any process of education seem no different in kind than those of behaviourist conditioning and extreme paternalism which appear to subvert autonomy, these necessary educational interferences also seem incompatible with authenticity. Hence, some may argue, authoritarian indoctrination is unavoidable and, despite our initial intuition to the contrary, an authentic education is impossible and just a pipe-dream.[11]

Peters calls this problem of authentic upbringing 'the paradox of moral education' (Peters, 1963). One formulation of it runs as follows:

> I am not saying, of course, that any sane parent or teacher will, in the early stages, make a child's acceptance of the reasons a condition for his [the child's] doing what is sensible. All I am saying is that rules can be presented in a non-arbitrary way *before* children are capable of accepting them for the reasons given, to help them to get to the stage when they follow rules because of the reasons for them. But it does not follow from this that, on many occasions, parents and teachers may not have to insist on certain forms of conduct even though the children do not accept the good sense of it. Indeed this is a common feature of the 'good boy' and 'rule-conformity' stages of morality (Peters, 1973a, p. 24).

How can a rational or authentic code of conduct be acquired in a non-rational or inauthentic way? Throughout his thinking about this issue, Peters basically uses the same strategy in his attempt to resolve the paradox. He distinguishes between earlier developmental stages of extrinsic (or, more generally, non-intrinsic) motivation and a later stage of intrinsic motivation— that is to say, between heteronomous stages in which the child only acts *in accordance with* moral rules and an autonomous stage in which he acts *on* or *out of* them. The adequate transition from the one to the other phase is made possible by developmental and educational processes that facilitate or, at least, do not stultify the acquisition of a rational or authentic code of conduct. Let me detail this strategy a bit further.

Within the framework of Piagetian-Kohlbergian developmental moral psychology, to which Peters in the main subscribes,[12] one can distinguish roughly between the pre-conventional (egocentric), conventional (conformist) and post-conventional (autonomous) stages. The sequential development of the *forms* of moral rules (or beliefs)—the way in which they are conceived independent of their content—is culturally invariant. Appropriate 'cognitive stimulation' triggers the unfolding of a universal form of moral development. Typical of the last stage is the emergence of rational reflection—that is, the capacity for *thin* rationality. During the transition to autonomy, the 'learning' processes on the side of the child have to correlate with adequate educational processes on the side of the parents and teachers. Educators should not arbitrarily present moral rules to children or, even worse, causally implant them by way of conditioning or some morally illegitimate procedure. Peters calls attention, for instance, to the fact that the processes of training by which moral habits are inculcated should have the necessary plasticity and open-endedness to be conducive to reason and rationality (Peters, 1963, pp. 277; 1967b, pp. 14–16).

There are no less than three serious problems with Peters' attempt to resolve the paradox of moral education. First, the Piaget-Kohlberg framework, which dominated developmental moral psychology in the 1960s and 1970s, has been superseded by an alternative approach to the emergence of the affective and cognitive capacities in the course of child development.[13] This new model challenges, among other elements, the status of the egocentric pre-conventional and conformist conventional stages of Kohlbergian moral developmentalism. Recent research suggests that toddlers, and even children within the first year of life, manifest a range of pro-social behaviours—like helping, comforting, and sharing—that are presumed to derive from innate empathy (of the contagion variety). Also contrary to Piaget and Kohlberg, even preschool children discriminate between moral and conventional rules, and accordingly, between moral transgressions (e.g. pushing someone off a swing) and non-moral ones (e.g. wearing pyjamas at school). Although Peters himself criticises and supplements Kohlberg's stage theory, his model for thinking about the development of autonomy never radically departs from Kohlbergian moral developmentalism (Peters, 1971, 1978).

Second, Peters' model is overly rationalistic. As a consequence of his allegiance to the Piaget-Kohlberg framework, which basically conforms to the Kantian paradigm, his approach to the development of autonomy culminates in the thin rationality conception of autonomy as rational reflection. In contrast, the alternative approach of care ethics, for example, brings to bear empathy and sentimentality in the constitution of autonomy.[14]

Third, and most seriously, the basic problem of authentic upbringing remains unsolved. I agree with Peters that the assessments of and possible subsequent changes in a person's code of conduct—his rules, values, and other pro-attitudes—are authentic if they are effectuated by exercising his own deliberative reflection and critical thinking capacities. Whatever happens under the aegis of a person's own rational reflection is authentic. However, this line of thought does nothing to solve the problem of the authenticity of *initially acquired* pro-attitudes. The reason is that, as observed earlier, the initial acquisition of such attitudes totally bypasses the child's capacities for rational deliberation because these capacities are absent or latent at this early stage. A young child initially acquires not only a set of pro-attitudes but also a set of (beliefs about) deliberative principles. How can these sets be instilled authentically? How can educators authentically inculcate, for example, *the belief that critical self-assessment is important* at a stage where the capacity for rational reflection is inoperative?

A solution to this fundamental authenticity problem seems also required in order to deal with the issue of the compatibility of autonomy with *broad* rationality. How can there be an *authentic* initiation into our cultural heritage? How can one 'do one's own thing' after incorporating the standards of the 'generalised other'? Moreover, one cannot possibly expect a person to critically assess *all* of his public inheritance since most of it will remain in the dark and will not ever see the light of rational reflection. Are we then inevitably condemned to inauthenticity?

Elsewhere, I have proposed in detail a forward-looking account of educational authenticity to resolve Peters' paradox of moral education (Cuypers, 2009).[15] Here I only sketch the main contours to adumbrate an answer to the questions above. On the view that I (and my co-author) defend there is no such thing as plain authenticity or authenticity *per se* or *sans phrase*. Rather, I defend a relational view of authenticity, according to which elements of a code of conduct, such as beliefs and pro-attitudes, are authentic or inauthentic only relative to whether later behaviour that issues from them is behaviour for which the agent, into whom the child will develop, can shoulder *moral responsibility*. My view on authentic education is in this sense forward-looking: although pertinent psychological elements instilled in the child at an early stage are not authentic *per se*, they can be authentic-with-an-eye-towards-future-moral-responsibility. So, on my relational conceptualisation of authenticity, elements constitutive of an initial code of conduct are not authentic in their own right, but only authentic relative to future responsibility. Let me elaborate a bit.

On Peters' view, authenticity is a component of autonomy (freedom), whereas on mine it is a component of moral responsibility. This is not, however, an important difference because his analysis is included in mine. The sort of autonomy Peters is interested in is *responsibility-grounding autonomy* and, accordingly, autonomy—which, according to him, comprises rationality besides control and authenticity—is a necessary condition for moral responsibility. Apart from general agency requirements—such as being capable of intentional action, rational deliberation and evaluative judgment—

moral responsibility specifically has epistemic, control, and authenticity requirements. Its analysis runs as follows:

An agent is morally responsible for a particular action, if and only if,

(1) the agent knows, or believes, that he is doing wrong (or right) in performing the action,
(2) he exercises responsibility-relevant control in doing it, and
(3) the action stems from psychological antecedents, or elements of a code of conduct, that are authentic.

Why is moral responsibility educationally so important? It is undeniable that a primary aim of educating children is to make sure that they become moral agents. However different in other respects, other diverse views concerning the aims of education rest on a *presupposition* that has received insufficient attention: children must be raised so that they develop into free agents who are capable of shouldering moral responsibility for their behaviour. Even communitarians, many of whom regard liberal education as inimical to a valued way of life, do not—indeed cannot—deny that a pivotal goal of education is to turn children into morally responsible agents. A distinguishing mark of moral persons, as opposed to mere members of the species *homo sapiens*, is that persons are responsible agents. So, whatever other secondary goals, such as autonomy, critical thinking, well-being, or democratic citizenship, one wants to promote (see, for example, Marples, 1999; Winch, 2006), fully-fledged personhood seems indisputable as a primary goal of education.

Regarding the child's acquisition of an initial code of conduct, I argue for the view that its constituent elements can be relationally authentic in this manner: they can be authentic relative to respecting or ensuring future moral responsibility. Educators can only succeed in authentically implanting pertinent cognitive and pro-attitudinal elements if these elements play an appropriate role in the child's development into a morally responsible agent (and continue to play that role after the child has become a minimally competent moral agent). Authoritarian indoctrination or harsh paternalism (when responsibility-thwarting), unlike authentic ways of instilling salient psychological elements, make use of ways that undermine such *responsibility-relative authenticity*. To appreciate this strategy, reflect on mental illness, coercion, or deception, factors all parties readily grant frequently affect moral responsibility. Such factors subvert moral responsibility, when they do, if they undermine one or more of the requirements of responsibility, such as epistemic or control requirements. If a person acts on the basis of a belief that is false, the belief having been acquired as a result of deception, then (assuming that the person is non-culpably ignorant) the person is 'off the hook'. Similarly, if a person acts on a surreptitiously implanted desire that is irresistible, so that action issuing from the desire is action that is not under his control, then once again the person has a genuine excuse.

Against the backdrop of these considerations, I propose that a cognitive or pro-attitudinal element, or its mode of acquisition, is *inauthentic* if that psychological element, or the way in which it is acquired, will *subvert* moral responsibility for behaviour, which owes its proximal causal genesis to the element of the agent into whom the child will develop. Subversion of moral responsibility would occur as a result of either the epistemic or control requirement—*independently*, of course, of the authenticity requirement itself—of moral responsibility being thwarted. I recommend, then, the following criterion as one that governs responsibility-relative authenticity of *initial* codes of conduct of children in the early stage(s) of their development.

Criterion of Authenticity: A child's initially acquired code of conduct is responsibility-wise authentic if its elements (1) include all those, if any, that are required to ensure that the agent (into whom the child will develop) will be morally responsible for its future behaviour; (2) do not include any that will subvert the agent's being responsible for future behaviour that issues from these elements; and (3) have been acquired by means that, again, will not subvert the agent's being responsible for its future behaviour.

With this *Criterion* in place, we can address the basic problem of authentic upbringing. Solving this problem involves making a distinction, by means of the *Criterion*, between necessary educational interferences that are authentic (authentic education) and inauthentic ones (authoritarian indoctrination). To ensure that the child matures into a moral agent, certain cognitive and pro-attitudinal elements must be instilled in the child, such as the elementary moral concepts of right, wrong and obligation, (beliefs about) deliberative principles, intrinsic values and attitudes toward the good life and well-being. Yet neither these instilled elements nor their mode of instilment need subvert the child's being morally responsible, at the age when he will be so responsible, for behaviour that causally issues from these instilled elements. The crux of the *Criterion* is that the child's initial code of conduct is not the child's own, only if its cognitive and pro-attitudinal elements subvert, to a substantial degree, moral responsibility for later behaviour that issues from these elements. For example, offensive manipulation, harsh paternalism, hideously depraving conditions, or experiences traumatic to the child may undercut moral responsibility for later behaviour by undermining the fulfilment of necessary requirements of responsibility other than the authenticity requirement itself. If they do (and empirical evidence is required to confirm whether they do), then in these sorts of case, the instilled elements are (relationally) inauthentic—not truly the child's own. So, instilling pertinent beliefs or desires is authentic, if their acquisition does not subvert moral responsibility for later behaviour that issues from these elements because it does not compromise either the epistemic or the control requirement of responsibility. These instilled elements are, then, relative-to-future-responsibility authentic and gradually build up a child's authentic initial code of conduct.

As a corollary, we can also conclude that education as initiation is authentic as long as the instilment of (parts of) our cultural heritage in children complies with the *Criterion of Authenticity*. Shared standards can thus authentically belong to a child's initial code of conduct and continue to be so authentic after the child has developed into a moral agent in full possession of a capacity for rational reflection. So, invoking the *Criterion* helps to understand how autonomy can be compatible with *broad* rationality and, consequently, how broadly rational choices of an agent can be autonomous in Peters' educational theory.

IV AUTONOMY AS AN EDUCATIONAL AIM

From Peters' analysis of autonomy as an actual psychological condition, there can be derived an ideal of character. Such an ideal amounts to an educational aim, that is, something worthwhile to which educators direct youngsters. The content of this aim depends on whether one interprets the rationality-condition of autonomy in the thin or broad sense. Typically, liberals defend a thin interpretation. In children's education they promote the ideal of the self-governing individual as the rational chooser and critical thinker. I will not consider here 'atypical' liberal positions such as the following. First, some liberals do not argue that education should promote autonomy. Rawlsian political liberals, for example, usually limit (fairly substantially) their educational aims to claims about educating for citizenship. Second, other liberals who do argue in favour of educating for autonomy do not, however, view autonomy as the one and only overarching aim of education. John White (1990), for example, considers autonomy to be subordinate to well-being: '... there do seem to be *positive* grounds in favour of some non-autonomous conceptions of well-being' (p. 25).

Peters never defended liberal autonomy as the overriding, ultimate educational ideal. I remarked above that personhood—becoming a morally responsible agent—is a primary goal of education, while autonomy, critical thinking, well-being, and democratic citizenship are secondary ones. Although 'education' is an essentially contested concept, it would, according to Peters (1979, p. 33), be a mistake to limit education's target to such a minimal goal. Throughout his career, he singled out the initiation into different forms of knowledge and understanding, especially of the human condition, as *a* bedrock aim of education, and at times even as *the* overarching aim (Peters, 1966, Chapter 1, 1967a, 1970a, 1974, 1979, pp. 43–46; Hirst and Peters, 1970, Chapter 2). Since this overall cognitive aim is foundational or, at least, the 'first among equals', Peters' view on the aims of education can be summarised in the following thesis:

> All other educational aims *asymmetrically depend upon* the basic aim of initiation into different modes of knowledge and understanding, especially of the human condition.

In the light of this asymmetrical dependency thesis, liberal autonomy, as well as closely related aims such as self-origination, self-determination and self-fulfilment, cannot be realised unless the aim of initiation into the cognitive framework of the 'humanities' is realised first. This explains Peters' scepticism about extreme forms of individualism and his criticism of progressivism (see, for example, Darling, 1994). Progressive education should, however, not be rejected outright but properly contextualised: 'The romantic protest, in other words, presupposes some kind of classical background' (Hirst and Peters, 1970, p. 32).

The asymmetrical dependency thesis is, for instance, clearly at work in Peters' discussion of the ambiguities and dilemmas in 'liberal education' (Peters, 1977a, 1977b). He distinguishes between three interpretations: liberal education as (a) knowledge for its own sake, as (b) general, non-specialised education and as (c) non-authoritarian, progressive education. As to the latter, 'liberalistic' conception, Peters claims that:

> ... the liberal ideal of autonomy for the individual will be empty unless his capacity for choice is enlarged by information, imagination, and critical thought. Unless, therefore, an individual is definitely put in the way of relevant studies in literature, history, geography and parts of the natural and social sciences, he may be severely handicapped in respect of many of the choices which he may have to make (Peters, 1977b, p. 80)

Initiation into the human heritage is a necessary precondition for autonomous choice. As a consequence, Peters acknowledges autonomy as *an* educational aim, but only on the *broad* interpretation of the rationality-condition of autonomy. Broadly rational choices are autonomous precisely because they respect the standards inherent in the 'humanistic' modes of knowledge and understanding. According to Peters, education as initiation into our public heritage is not so much restricting as it is liberating: 'On this view the development of the free-man is not necessarily impeded by instruction from others, by public traditions and the example of others. Indeed it would be argued that the development of mind is inexplicable without reference to such social transactions which the extreme liberal regards as restrictions' (Peters, 1977a, p. 63).

The acceptability of Peters' view on the place of autonomy as an educational aim rests on the validity of the asymmetrical dependency thesis. And the validation of this thesis is, of course, immediately connected with another of his central projects: the justification of education (Peters, 1966, Chapter 5; 1973b). Peters' educational theory is dominated by two key questions: (1) What do you mean by 'education'? and (2) How do you know that 'education' is 'worthwhile'? The first is a question of conceptual analysis, while the second is a question of justification. What then justifies the claim that initiation into different modes of knowledge and understanding is the foundational educational aim or supreme value in education? Although some theorists (for example, White in this book) despair of ever giving an adequate justification and acquiesce in just (historically) *explaining* why comprehensive knowledge and understanding have such a prominent place in the curriculum, I still think that the justificatory programme should be taken up in the hope of satisfactorily executing it. Yet, since this is too large an issue within the confines of this chapter, I limit myself to some intimation of the sort of research line that looks most promising.

Some educational goals are worthy of pursuit, others not, and some more worthy of pursuit than others. Identifying, selecting and justifying bedrock as well as subsidiary educational aims, invariably demands that we tread into the deep waters of *axiology* or *theory of value*. The justification for a candidate educational aim can be sought in an instrumental or non-instrumental style; it can be given in terms of extrinsic or intrinsic value or goodness. The bedrock educational goals Aristotle identifies in Book I of the *Nicomachean Ethics* concern what is good for both individuals and society at large; these aims have to do with what it is to flourish as persons and as citizens. It might be ventured that education's primary aim should be to produce good citizens, but there is no guarantee that if success in this respect were to be achieved, the personal welfare of the relevant subjects would also be enhanced. So we need minimally, first, to get clear on when a person's life is good in itself for that person (in what does personal welfare consist?) and what makes a world intrinsically better than another (or in what does world-betterment consist?). We may refer to an axiology that addresses welfare as a 'life-ranking axiology' and to one that assesses worlds as a 'world-ranking axiology'. Then, second, we need to show how a candidate educational aim is aptly related to these accounts of well-being and world-betterment. Hence, any discussion of the justification of educational aims is inherently associated with the debate concerning alternative life-ranking and world-ranking axiologies.[16]

V PETERS' LEGACY ON AUTONOMY

Peters offers us a complex and inspiring educational theory of autonomy, even if at some places somewhat ambiguous and unfinished in the last analysis. Its major advantage, to my mind, consists in being a counterbalance against too radical versions of individualism, liberalism and child-centred progressivism. Peters' insistence on initiation into public modes of experience, knowledge and understanding of the human predicament in order to become a rational autonomous person remains particularly important for present-day educational theory. Its major drawback is perhaps the out-dated framework of the Piaget-Kohlberg developmental moral psychology as the backdrop to his thinking about autonomy. However, this standard framework of the 1960s and 1970s is only contingently related to the *structural* design of Peters' educational theory of autonomy. As I tried to show in section III, the development of the 'free man' can be accounted for in terms of my *Criterion of Authenticity*, independently of whatever particular developmental moral psychology is espoused.

In conclusion, I identify two future tasks for the educational theory of autonomy, which should supplement Peters' groundwork. First, as I remarked earlier, in contrast to the Kantian approach of the Piaget-Kohlberg framework, the *alternative* approach of care ethics, which brings to bear empathy and sentimentality in the constitution of autonomy, should be worked out further. In addition, the social-relational aspects of autonomy should be explored in detail to build an educational theory that is viable in the present-day context of feminism, multiculturalism and globalisation (see, for example, Cuypers, 2001, Chapter 6; Oshana, 2006). Second, in view of Feinberg's distinctions, Peters' theory is restricted to autonomy as an actual psychological condition (or capacity) and as an ideal of character. Although it also includes a perspective on the development of (the capacity for) autonomy, the theory remains silent on the *right to autonomy*. Contemporary educational theory of autonomy should fill this lacuna with a critical examination of the moral and political status of the child not only in Western liberal democracies but also throughout the world (see, for example, Archard and Macleod 2002; Archard 2003).[17]

NOTES

1. The *locus classicus* of this distinction is Ayer, 1946.
2. For such a non-causalist incompatibilism, see, for example, Ginet, 1990, Chapters 5–6. Note that although all non-causalists in action explanation are incompatibilists, not all incompatibilists are non-causalists. For instance, both incompatibilists, the probabilistic causalist Kane (1996) and the agent causalist Clarke (2003), agree on a causal account of action explanation.
3. In his comment, 'Reasons and Causes', Peters (1970b) remains silent on Davidson. Seven years after 'Actions, Reasons, and Causes', he still writes: 'Of course [causally] explanatory and [rationally] justificatory discourse can co-exist. But the traditional problem of "reasons" and "causes", . . . is in no way illuminated by making this move' (p. 41). Admittedly, my speculation about Peters as a causalist compatibilist is certainly not compelling because even the Davidsonian received view has its critics; see, for example, Schueler, 2003.
4. For several different compatibilist and incompatibilist notions of control, see Cuypers, 2009.
5. See also, Siegel, 1997, especially pp. 17–23 and 101–110.
6. There is an important debate between proponents of a 'generalist' view and those of a 'specifist' view as to whether or not reason assessment skills apply across a broad range of contexts and circumstances: to what extent are assessment criteria *generalisable*? For a concise treatment of this debate, see Bailin and Siegel, 2003, pp. 183–186.
7. For some problems with Frankfurt's hierarchical model and the existentialist conception of autonomy, see Cuypers, 1992. For further discussion, see Bonnett and Cuypers, 2003.
8. For a 'thick' version of virtue-epistemology that is congenial to Peters's position, see Zagzebski, 1996.
9. For an interesting analysis of this conflict, see Bonnett, 1986.

10. Let 'interference' be a general term for things like suppression of innate propensities and dispositions, or implantation of certain beliefs, desires, habits, values and principles, or deliberate lack of instilment of various cognitive and pro-attitudinal elements.
11. For my own solution of the problem of non-indoctrinative, authentic education, see Cuypers and Haji, 2006 and 2007.
12. See, for example, Hirst and Peters, 1970, Chapter 3.
13. For a philosophically relevant survey of this approach, see Dwyer, 2003.
14. For this alternative approach, see Noddings and Slote, 2003 and Slote, 2007.
15. This account of educational authenticity forms an integral part of the theory of moral responsibility—in particular its authenticity condition—that I developed together with Ishtiyaque Haji, especially in Haji and Cuypers, 2008a.
16. For attempts to realise this axiology approach with regard to the justification of autonomy as an educational aim, see Cuypers and Haji, 2008 and Haji and Cuypers, 2008b.
17. I want to express my gratitude to Ishtiyaque Haji for his extremely valuable comments on the penultimate version of this chapter.

REFERENCES

Archard, D. W. (2003) *Children, Family and the State* (Aldershot, Ashgate).

Archard, D. W. and Macleod, C. M. (eds) (2002) *The Moral and Political Status of Children* (Oxford, Oxford University Press).

Ayer, A. J. (1946) Freedom and Necessity, reprinted in: A. J. Ayer, *Philosophical Essays* (London Macmillan, 1959), pp. 271–284.

Bailin, S. and Siegel, H. (2003) Critical Thinking, in: N. Blake, P. Smeyers, R. Smith and P. Standish (eds) *The Blackwell Guide to the Philosophy of Education* (Oxford, Blackwell), pp. 181–193.

Benn, S. I. (1976) Freedom, Autonomy and the Concept of a Person, *Proceedings of the Aristotelian Society*, 76, pp. 109–130.

Bonnett, M. (1986) Personal Authenticity and Public Standards: Towards the Transcendence of a Dualism, in: D. E. Cooper (ed) *Education, Values and Mind. Essays for R. S. Peters* (London, Routledge & Kegan Paul), pp. 111–133.

Bonnett, M. and Cuypers, S. E. (2003) Autonomy and Authenticity in Education, in: N. Blake, P. Smeyers, R. Smith and P. Standish (eds) *The Blackwell Guide to the Philosophy of Education* (Oxford, Blackwell), pp. 326–340.

Benn, S. I. and Peters, R. S. (1959) *Social Principles and the Democratic State* (London, George Allen & Unwin Ltd).

Clarke, R. (2003) *Libertarian Accounts of Free Will* (New York, Oxford University Press).

Cuypers, S. E. (1992) Is Personal Autonomy the First Principle of Education?, *Journal of Philosophy of Education*, 26, pp. 5–17.

Cuypers, S. E. (2001) *Self-Identity and Personal Autonomy* (Aldershot, Ashgate).

Cuypers, S. E. and Haji, I. (2006) Education for Critical Thinking: Can It Be Non-Indoctrinative?, *Educational Philosophy and Theory*, 38, pp. 723–743.

Cuypers, S. E. and Haji, I. (2007) Authentic Education and Moral Responsibility, *Journal of Applied Philosophy*, 24, pp. 78–94.

Cuypers, S. E. and Haji, I. (2008) Educating for Well-Being and Autonomy, *Theory and Research in Education*, 6.1, pp. 71–93.

Cuypers, S. E. (2009) Educating for Authenticity: The Paradox of Moral Education Revisited, in: H. Siegel (ed.) *The Oxford Handbook of Philosophy of Education* (New York, Oxford University Press), pp. 122–144.

Darling, J. (1994) *Child-Centred Education and its Critics* (London, Paul Chapman).

Davidson, D. (1963) Actions, Reasons, and Causes, reprinted in: D. Davidson, *Essays on Actions and Events* (Oxford, Clarendon Press, 1980), pp. 3–19.

Dearden, R. F. (1972) Autonomy and Education, in: R. F. Dearden, P. H. Hirst and R. S. Peters (eds) *Education and Reason. Part 3 of Education and the Development of Reason* (London, Routledge & Kegan Paul), pp. 58–75.

Dwyer, S. (2003) Moral Development and Moral Responsibility, *The Monist*, 86, pp. 181–199.

Elster, J. (1983) *Sour Grapes. Studies in the Subversion of Rationality* (Cambridge, Cambridge University Press).

Feinberg, J. (1986) *Harm to Self* (New York, Oxford University Press).

Frankfurt, H. G. (1971) Freedom of the Will and the Concept of a Person, *Journal of Philosophy*, 68, pp. 5–20.

Ginet, G. (1990) *On Action* (Cambridge, Cambridge University Press).

Haji, I. and Cuypers, S. E. (2008a) *Moral Responsibility, Authenticity, and Education* (New York, Routledge).

Haji, I. and Cuypers, S. E. (2008b) Authenticity-Sensitive Preferentism and Educating for Well-Being and Autonomy, *Journal of Philosophy of Education*, 42, pp. 85–106.

Hirst, P. H. and Peters, R. S. (1970) *The Logic of Education* (London, Routledge & Kegan Paul).

Kane, R. (1996) *The Significance of Free Will* (New York, Oxford University Press).

Marples, R. (ed.) (1999) *The Aims of Education* (London, Routledge).

Mele, A. R. (1995) *Autonomous Agents. From Self-Control to Autonomy* (New York, Oxford University Press).

Noddings, N. and Slote, M. (2003) Changing Notions of the Moral and of Moral Education, in: N. Blake, P. Smeyers, R. Smith and P. Standish (eds) *The Blackwell Guide to the Philosophy of Education* (Oxford, Blackwell), pp. 341–355.

Oshana, M. (2006) *Personal Autonomy in Society* (Aldershot, Ashgate).

Parfit, D. (1984) *Reasons and Persons* (Oxford, Clarendon Press).

Peters, R. S. (1956) *Hobbes* (Harmondsworth, Penguin Books).

Peters, R. S. (1958) *The Concept of Motivation* (London, Routledge & Kegan Paul).

Peters, R. S. (1963) Reason and Habit: The Paradox of Moral Education, reprinted in: R. S. Peters, *Psychology and Ethical Development. A Collection of Articles on Psychological Theories, Ethical Development and Human Understanding* (London, George Allen & Unwin Ltd, 1974), pp. 265–280.

Peters, R. S. (1966) *Ethics and Education* (London, George Allen & Unwin Ltd).

Peters, R. S. (1967a) Aims of Education—A Conceptual Inquiry, in: R. S. Peters (ed.) *The Philosophy of Education* (Oxford, Oxford University Press, 1973), pp. 11–29.

Peters, R. S. (1967b) What is an Educational Process?, in: R. S. Peters (ed.) *The Concept of Education* (London, Routledge & Kegan Paul), pp. 1–23.

Peters, R. S. (1970a) Education and the Educated Man, reprinted in: R. S. Peters, *Education and the Education of Teachers* (London, Routledge & Kegan Paul, 1977), pp. 3–21.

Peters, R. S. (1970b) Reasons and Causes: Comments, in: R. Borger and F. Cioffi (eds) *Explanation in the Behavioural Sciences* (Cambridge, Cambridge University Press), pp. 27–41.

Peters, R. S. (1971) Moral Development: A Plea for Pluralism, in: T. Mischel (ed.) *Cognitive Development and Epistemology* (New York, Academic Press), pp. 237–267.

Peters, R. S. (1973a) Freedom and the Development of the Free Man, in: P. H. Hirst and P. White (eds) *Philosophy of Education. Major Themes in the Analytic Tradition. Volume II: Education and Human Being* (London, Routledge, 1998), pp. 11–31.

Peters, R. S. (1973b) The Justification of Education, reprinted in: R. S. Peters, *Education and the Education of Teachers* (London, Routledge & Kegan Paul, 1977), pp. 86–118.

Peters, R. S. (1974) Subjectivity and Standards, reprinted in: R. S. Peters, *Psychology and Ethical Development. A Collection of Articles on Psychological Theories, Ethical Development and Human Understanding* (London, George Allen & Unwin Ltd, 1974), pp. 413–432.

Peters, R. S. (1977a) Ambiguities in Liberal Education and the Problem of Its Content, in: R. S. Peters, *Education and the Education of Teachers* (London, Routledge & Kegan Paul), pp. 46–67.

Peters, R. S. (1977b) Dilemmas in Liberal Education, in: R. S. Peters, *Education and the Education of Teachers* (London, Routledge & Kegan Paul), pp. 68–85.

Peters, R. S. (1978) The Place of Kohlberg's Theory in Moral Education, reprinted in: R. S. Peters, *Essays on Educators* (London, George Allen & Unwin Ltd, 1981), pp. 113–127.

Peters, R. S. (1979) Democratic Values and Educational Aims, reprinted in: R. S. Peters, *Essays on Educators* (London, George Allen & Unwin Ltd, 1981), pp. 32–50.

Schueler, G. F. (2003) *Reasons And Purposes: Human Rationality and the Teleological Explanation of Action* (Oxford, Clarendon Press).

Siegel, H. (1997) *Rationality Redeemed? Further Dialogues on an Educational Ideal* (New York, Routledge).

Siegel, H. (2003) Cultivating Reason, in: R. Curren (ed.) *A Companion to the Philosophy of Education* (Oxford, Blackwell), pp. 305–319.

Slote, M. (2007) *The Ethics of Care and Empathy* (London, Routledge).

Van Inwagen, P. (1983) *An Essay on Free Will* (Oxford, Clarendon Press).

White, J. (1990) *Education and the Good Life. Beyond the National Curriculum* (London, Kogan Page).

White, J. (this book) Why General Education? Peters, Hirst and History.

Winch, C. (2006) *Education, Autonomy and Critical Thinking* (New York, Routledge).

Zagzebski, L. T. (1996) *Virtues of the Mind. An Inquiry into the Nature of Virtue and the Ethical Foundations of Knowledge* (Cambridge, Cambridge University Press).

Zimmerman, D. (2003) That Was Then, This Is Now: Personal History vs. Psychological Structure in Compatibilist Theories of Autonomous Agency, *Noûs*, 37, pp. 638–671.

13
Richard Peters and Valuing Authenticity

M. A. B. DEGENHARDT

PHILOSOPHIES AND PHILOSOPHERS

It can seem odd that many philosophers regard studying the lives of other philosophers as an integral part of their work. Why should disciplined inquiry, involving high levels of abstraction and generalisation, and aspiring to objectivity and impersonality, be concerned with the personal lives of particular thinkers? There are two reasons in particular.

First, *elucidatory*. We can read philosophers but have difficulty in understanding them if we do not know what problems concerned them and why. Biographies can shed light here though the necessary labour may be huge, as in *Wittgenstein's Vienna* by Allan Janik and Stephen Toulmin [1973] (1996). There is controversy over whether and how knowledge about persons can help us understand their philosophies. Possible relevance varies between cases and there are also different views rooted in different theories. James Conant describes a continuum of positions ranging between two poles (Conant, 2001). Thus *reductivist* views hold that by knowing enough biography we can discern the true meaning of a philosopher's work, even in ways that he or she cannot. So Freudian or Marxist accounts (or travesties of these) might reduce a philosopher's doctrine to symptoms of psycho-pathology or to manifestations of false class-consciousness. On the other hand *compartmentalist* views hold that anything relevant to understanding a piece of philosophy is to be found only in the work itself, quite compartmentalised off from personal traits or a philosopher's experience of things like education, political upheavals and intellectual or cultural movements. Views of both kinds quickly fall into absurdity. Fortunately there are intermediate positions, with less theoretical prescription, which recognise philosophers as having significant freedom of thought, but do not turn them into disembodied intellects. I shall seek to follow such less formal middle ways when I try to resolve a paradox regarding Richard Peters' view of authenticity.

Second, *idealistic*. Though it is rarely made explicit, it seems to be the case that when we attend to philosophers' biographies we are often giving expression to an ideal. We like to anticipate certain continuities between

Reading R. S. Peters Today, First Edition. Stefaan E. Cuypers and Christopher Martin.
Chapters © 2011 The Authors. Editorial organization © 2011 Philosophy of Education Society of Great Britain. Published 2011 by Blackwell Publishing Ltd.

philosophers' lives and their philosophising. While we know better than to commit howlers like citing hypocrisy as evidence that a view is mistaken, we do like to find a harmony between philosophy and philosopher that might be said to evidence authenticity. When, instead, we find discontinuities between the life and thought of a philosopher we esteem, we are puzzled and probably disquieted. Words like 'insincere', and 'lacking authenticity' may come to mind.

The work of the philosopher and historian Pierre Hadot evidences both these motivations (Hadot, 1995). He seeks to free us from false views about much past philosophising, consequent on our failures to understand what the ancients took to be the nature of their discipline. These in turn can lead us to misinterpret their work. In Western antiquity, he holds, to be a philosopher meant, primarily, to belong to a school or community of lovers of wisdom, to follow a way of life intended to liberate the mind from what is alien to it, and to render it receptive to philosophical motives and insights. A way of living or *being* was as definitive of philosophy as was any doctrine. So by describing the lives of philosophers Hadot pursues an improved understanding of their philosophies. At the same time, while making no proposal to put the clock back, he makes it clear that he thinks something is lost when we moderns aspire to philosophise independently of our *being*. That is, he expresses an ideal.

PETERS' AUTHENTICITY

If many of us are unsure what to think on such matters, that may explain why readers were both startled and intrigued by some things Ray Elliott said in his remarkable essay on Richard Peters (Elliott, 1986). After finding fault with much in Peters' philosophy, Elliott discerns in it 'an aspect of greatness'. This is there, he says, because Peters renders his work authentic by revealing himself in his philosophy, and because, in doing this he gives a powerful new expression to the stoic mind set. Not an imitation, he says, but 'a new creation in the grand style', brought about 'partly because Peters was to some extent unaware of himself creating a philosophy of this kind' (p. 65). This seemed paradoxical to many of us who had studied with Peters and been taught to strive for objectivity and to eschew personal expressiveness.

Elliott makes his commendation for authenticity also sound like a rebuke for inadequate self-knowledge. And there are occasions when Peters' self-descriptions do not seem to entirely match his achievement. Thus in his inaugural lecture, 'Education as Initiation', he introduces himself as a professionally trained analytic philosopher, in contrast with his predecessor, L. A. Reid, who was sympathetic to laymen's views and saw the philosopher's task as probing the meaning of life and providing people with 'some kind of synoptic directive for living' (Peters, 1964, p. 8). He seems to endorse the view of those professionals who see their task as 'the disciplined demarcation of concepts and the patient explication of the grounds of knowledge'. And he describes himself as 'most at home in social philosophy and philosophical psychology—those branches of philosophy . . . in which concrete problems of human nature and human conduct loom largest' (pp. 7–8). Much rigorous analysis follows and is shown to have educational import. But then comes a concluding fanfare where he cites Whitehead on 'a quality of life which lies always beyond the mere fact of life,' and tells us that:

> The great teacher is he who can convey this sense of quality to another, so that it haunts his every endeavour and makes him sweat and yearn to fix what he thinks in a fitting form. For life has no one purpose; man imprints his purposes upon it. It presents few tidy problems; mainly predicaments that have to be endured or enjoyed. It is education that provides that touch of eternity under the aspect of which endurance can pass into dignified, wry acceptance, and animal enjoyment into a quality of living (Peters, 1964, p. 48).

Great stuff, no doubt; but hardly analysis. Indeed it might seem to present difficulties for Elliott's commentary. For it may sound unconvincing to commend a body of work for revealing the self, if what is revealed contains striking inconsistencies. However, such judgment may be too speedy. For no selves are without inconsistency, and fluctuations in a philosopher's methods and doctrines are compatible with having lasting and deeply felt philosophical concerns, and with being so anxious to get things right that more than one approach is tried. I have suggested elsewhere that Elliott's account of authenticity in Peters', or anyone's, philosophy should be supplemented (Degenhardt, 2003). First, it must be seen as a two-way affair. The philosophy should reflect or reveal the self and the philosophising should also come to inform and help make the self. It would be a shallow rather than an authentic philosopher who carefully developed and published insights and analyses but in himself was quite unchanged by them. Second, Elliott speaks, as we often do, of self and philosophy as distinct entities. But there must not just be the self *plus* the philosopher's way of teaching and of living, all in accord and mutual influence. I think Elliott would have agreed that their relationship must be organic to a point where they can be properly seen as aspects of the one *being*. The greater the organic integration the greater the authenticity. This alone is not enough to make a great philosopher, but getting close to it is surely a *sine qua non*. (Similar points hold for other disciplines of course: something overlooked in the horrible philistinism of contemporary proposals to periodically 're-skill' members of the learned professions.)

On this sort of view, Peters is, I believe, a highly authentic philosopher, though some kinds of evidence on the matter are not readily available. For, consistently with his stoic mind-set, Peters rarely tells readers a lot about himself. However there is one brief but invaluable exception. In 1950, before he was much involved with philosophy of education, he gave a short talk on

BBC Radio entitled 'I Was Twenty Then', which told of his experience of, and response to, the outbreak of World War II and what followed (Peters, 1974, pp. 464–8). I will now note some remarkable continuities between the young man he recollects having been and the educational philosophy he developed in maturity: continuities which surely license talk of 'authenticity'.

In his second year at Oxford, he recalls, he was shocked by the war—not just by the sight of London burning but also by the evident hypocrisy of the allies who seemed really to care little about the horrors of Nazism and how to stop them, until the realities of power politics demanded action. His education had not equipped him to think about such matters. Politics were not discussed at home. At school, 'political education' came only from occasional visiting lecturers who did things like lauding Mussolini or having the class sing jingoistic ditties. (I suspect that actually he did gain some political understanding from studying history, Shakespeare and classics.) At the same time he became seriously interested in religion. Having been an adolescent atheist who enjoyed shocking his teachers in the manner of Bernard Shaw, in the Sixth Form he was stirred by St John's Gospel. This stimulated a solo search for religious truth and eventually led to involvement with the Quakers. In politics and religion he did his thinking mostly on his own, and not just from necessity. 'I thought one had to work out one's personal attitude, standards, and beliefs more or less in isolation', only occasionally peeping out 'from my cell of self-sufficiency' (p. 465).

He became dissatisfied with this approach when he had to face horrific tasks as a full-time recruit to the Friends' Ambulance Unit and, later, doing relief work among victims of bombing in the East End. He found himself trying to help people in ghastly situations beyond his experience and ability to cope. 'People—bombed out, bereaved, lost, cold and hungry—impinged on me in a way they never had before with problems too large and complicated and terrible for me to comprehend properly'. Now he felt a different kind of isolation. He was working with the less well-off but 'had been brought up in a tradition of middle-class security which verged almost on snobbery. The habits and ideas I soaked up in school put me in a particular class and put a barrier between me and other people' (pp. 465–6). As a Christian he knew this was wrong but did not know how to break the barrier. By what turned out to be good fortune he was asked to supervise the development of a youth centre. Things changed. He was working *with* other people, not just *for* them. They shared everything: experiences and thoughts as well as razor blades. Differences between them ceased to matter. It was no longer as if he were a builder and they were his bricks. 'They *and* I were part of the design which we were shaping together—and which was shaping us as we worked ... My feelings and my beliefs came together and the conflict which had started at Oxford when I was twenty worked itself out' (p. 466).

In due course he returned to Oxford. Then he took to school-mastering and revelled in an 'idyllic breathing space of construction and co-operation—a youth centre in ideal surroundings' (ibid.). But he missed the variety in experience and background he had encountered in youth work. Moving to teach philosophy at Birkbeck College, he found these but missed the sense of community. Reflection on this alerted him to the importance of certain traditions and institutions in our culture, some of which had been eroded in the centuries since the break-up of the close knit communities of the middle ages. His immediate personal solution was to move to a small country town where he could be active in the local community and commute to lecture in London. But his thinking and studies were also adjusted and developed as he worked to understand the life and preservation of communities and institutions.

It is illuminating to read these memoirs after having studied his educational thought. We can see a continuity between the two which fills out the picture of Peters' authenticity in a way compatible with, and complementary to, what Elliott saw. The stoic mind-set is there when a young man with little preparation faces the dead and dying, and works out what he *can* do about them, rather than indulge in complaint and despair. Also, motivating his grappling with religious puzzles, is the concern for truth and the dislike of muddle that became recurring, explicit motifs in his later philosophising.

He did, in time, change his approach in two fundamental ways. He ceased to pursue truth according to a supposed epistemic virtue of solitary self-sufficiency. His wartime experiences in problem-solving team-work helped him to see the opposite possibility. His philosophical studies probably helped him as well; he does not actually say this, but he sometimes talks of being much influenced by Bacon and Popper. Understanding inquiry as a largely social enterprise calls for co-operative discussion, criticism and checking among fellow researchers. This extends to learning from thinkers of past ages, other cultures and opposed viewpoints. So, not surprisingly, in his later lecturing career he set much store by conferences and seminars; and his philosophical writing showed remarkable erudition. He would look to past thinkers not as antiquarian curiosities but as vital contributors to present inquiries. Doing this, even when it was rather unfashionable, authentically expressed the concerns that had originally brought him to philosophy, and united what he had learned in the world as well as in the library. (I do not know why he neglected non-Western thinkers. He does like to have an argument to grapple with, but perhaps he was unable to recognise the arguments that they produce. And of course none of us gets to read everything we think we ought to.)

In 1962, when Peters was appointed to the London chair of Philosophy of Education, people wondered why he should forsake his Readership at Birkbeck where there were able, responsive students and good research opportunities, for a post where he would have to devote much time to administration and committee work. This, however, involved him working with a mixed array of colleagues and students, with other institutions, government departments, politicians and teachers, all concerned to improve education in Britain and beyond. Surely there was nothing puzzling about this change. Was it not the most authentic career move he could have made—what he had been looking for ever since he left the youth club?

Turning now to some of the ways in which Peters evidenced authenticity in his work as professor, I will switch briefly into autobiographical mode. For it was shortly after he took up the chair that I enrolled to study with him, eventually also working with him as a colleague in various enterprises. So by observation I learned about his ways of teaching and working with people. Looking back now, with more knowledge of his developing educational thinking, I can see his teaching approaches as authentic expressions of just this thinking.

From the first it was clear that he took teaching very seriously. It was not just that he carefully planned his lectures to present ideas at a level that students could grasp, evaluate and build on. It was also that in presenting us with philosophical ideas and puzzles, and with the attempts of himself and others to resolve them, he was at pains to engage us in thinking about them. He did this not only through the normal practice of insisting on follow-up discussion. Sometimes as he lectured he would think of a new point and try to explore it. Once when he did this I quite lost track of what he was saying but it was an excellent lesson in what it can be to *do* philosophy. Philosophy got caught as well as taught. Some of us found he had a charismatic effect on us. Not, that is to say, that he drew us to respond uncritically to a dazzling performance but that he made us want to join in thinking with him. Certainly there were none of the attention-grabbing displays that have earned complaints about lecturers keeping students awake for an hour by sending them to sleep for a lifetime. All this I soon came to see as continuous with the idea of education as initiating us into the great traditions of creativity and understanding, and also as intended to afford learners wittingness and willingness to reflect on and judge what they were taught. And all this evidenced his concern to have people work together to pursue truth, clarity and wise decision-making.

Initially it seemed to me that Peters got rather grumpy if one of us missed the point. Later on I realised that he made high demands on himself and was probably as grumpy about his own teaching as about our obtuseness. There was, however, no problem of interpreting his distaste if he thought someone guilty of showing off or being frivolous. He welcomed independent thinking but two things displeased him and could be received unsympathetically.

First, he disliked expressions of existential dread or despair. It did worry me that he seemed not to take seriously views that proposed the pointlessness of things—views that have been embraced by some impressive thinkers and that some of us in the class found it hard to overcome. However Elliott, who did take such outlooks seriously, explains the awe which Peters feels towards the fact that we all have to make sense of our lives for ourselves, and then points out that:

> ... a person of Stoical disposition ... cannot be expected to attach any importance to an acknowledgement which would be emotionally disturbing and yet lack point. What work would it do? ... [I]t is the individual whom

Peters has always in mind, and the life he has to lead. From the standpoint of his benevolent practical concern, he cannot blamelessly allow himself to be distracted by idle speculations. Whether it is to our taste or not, we need to recognise that he is a philosopher in an older style, and the style is Stoical, as he himself acknowledges (Elliott, 1986, p. 58).

Again, Peters' position is shown to be authentic, which is one good reason to go on wondering whether it is right.

Second, he also disliked claims that deep, widespread differences between people's judgments of facts and values imply a thorough-going relativism in knowledge and values. What worries him here is not just the blatant *non-sequitur*, but also that it is a view that make the search for truth and justification incapable of success, and so renders the philosophical enterprise quite pointless. In his abhorrence for it (and for the fashion in many educational circles for teaching it with smug self-assurance) Peters is authentic to the very concerns that first led him into philosophy and education, both of which pursue better understanding as an aid to rational living. This is at the core of the paradox to be explored shortly. For his distaste here is for a mind-set that is often represented (or misrepresented) as being essential to authenticity and to the acknowledgment of everyone's right to think for themselves.

Famously, as a professor, Peters displayed one great intellectual virtue for which we seem to have no name—the virtue of active concern for the wellbeing and wider impact of one's discipline. There are familiar, if exaggerated, accounts of the poor state of philosophy of education prior to the increased activity of the 1960s. It was certainly no highly respected area of study then, but things had begun to improve remarkably in the USA by the time Peters came to the London chair. He used this ideal position to work extremely hard, with others, to promote philosophical thinking about education, through publishing, forming a society and launching a journal. Again, he was doing something authentic to, or expressive of, his early recognition of rational, interpersonal deliberation as the way to approach puzzling questions bearing on practical action. His enduring hope was that educators in general could learn to be better participants in just this.

WHY VALUE AUTHENICITY?

I have been discussing authenticity as instanced in the work of Richard Peters. This, I hope, will bring out important points about the nature and value of authenticity in teaching and inquiry. I do not, of course, hope to demonstrate great general truths by focusing on the work of one person alone. However, though the word 'authenticity' enjoys wide and varying applications, most of them have a common reference to some person or thing or idea being somehow true to some other person or thing or idea. This makes room for distinct and individual achievements of authenticity in many areas, including philosophising and teaching. The topic has stimulated excellent general studies (e.g. Trilling, 1972; Cooper, 1983; Taylor, 1991). And this leaves room for more attention to individual cases and the development of individual minds. Moreover, resolving a paradox about Peters and authenticity promises to be rewarding, as we shall see later.

Hitherto I have tended to describe instances of authenticity, and take it for granted that they are good things—partly because these were instances where to describe something seems also to be to reveal its value. However I shall now try to strengthen the case by referring back to examples considered in the previous section and reflecting on what is lost when one does not achieve authenticity in each of the particular ways described. Thus lack of strong, lasting concern for a particular topic or question, and of any deep re-thinking and maturation, would evidence fundamental indifference to the matter involved. The apparent interest in the matter would not be authentic. Similar points hold for internal inconsistencies and shifts in thinking, when not attributable to a resolve to try many possibilities in order to get things sorted. Shallowness and low personal involvement are also indicated when the authenticity only goes one way, so that the philosophy expresses the self but the self is untouched by the philosophy.

Those who do not out-grow (or out-learn) a belief that they can progress in understanding by working solo rather than co-operatively, have either been deprived of important learning opportunities or are prey to egotistical arrogance. It seems not unlikely that one infected with the latter vice will also evidence cultural arrogance or temporal chauvinism, or both, in their failure to allow that there may be things to learn from other cultures, traditions and eras. Such failings are forgivable folly in the young, for it takes a while to grasp the importance of learning from and with others, and to come to see this as a means of strengthening rather than abdicating personal judgment. Never to learn this is disastrous.

Finally, the inauthenticity evidenced by scholars who do not care for the wellbeing of their discipline, reveals churlish indifference to the traditions of learning and creativity that have helped to make them what they are. It also shows irresponsibility concerning the contributions their subject could and should make to common goods. And teachers who pretend to love their subject but do not care about teaching it, do not really love it. Perhaps they just enjoy or use it.

AN APPARENT PARADOX: PETERS' EXPRESSED DISDAIN FOR AUTHENTICITY

I will attend shortly to claims for a higher and more general value of authenticity, but first I must consider the already noted puzzle regarding Peters' view of the matter. The instances of authenticity evident in

Peters' work were discerned by reflecting on, and building from, Elliott's identification of a central authenticity in that work. Yet authenticity seems not to be favoured by Peters himself. David Cooper notes something that makes the paradox even more striking: that Peters rarely uses the word, and in 'Ambiguities in Liberal Education and the Problem of its Content', he actually expresses hostility (Cooper, 1983, p. 20). Thus Peters says:

> Extreme versions of modern individualism stress the importance of everyone doing his own thing, of being 'true to himself'. Self origination is interpreted in terms of authenticity, of not copying others or conforming to social roles, whether of being a woman or being a waiter. Thus any processes of education which involve being told things by others, being initiated into public traditions, or being influenced by example, are thought of as constricting the individual's development. He must find his way by his own experience and discoveries and eventually learn to be himself, do his own thing, even, in some versions of this doctrine, construct his own reality (Peters, 1977, pp. 62–63).

It is not hard to think of tendencies in our culture that are well described by these complaints. Peters' own preference is for a less extreme individualism with less stress on individual choice and more on reason informing choices.

> The emphasis is on autonomy as well as on authenticity. In other words the importance of first-hand experience, of beliefs which are not second-hand, and codes of conduct that are not accepted just on authority, is granted. But stress is placed on the role of reasoning in achieving such independence of mind ... [T]he development of the free man is not necessarily impeded by instruction ... What is crucial is the encouragement of criticism in the individual so that he can eventually accept or reject what he hears, sees or is told, on the basis of reason (Peters, 1977, p. 63).

But if Peters condemns authenticity, and others have admired him precisely *for* his authenticity, then how are the two views to be approached and compared? The talk seems to be at cross purposes, with favourable and unfavourable comments referring to significantly different things. What is needed is clarification of the concept of 'authenticity'. And since authenticity is for many an important human value with a rich if surprisingly short history, then a synchronic analysis that attends only to present day usages will not be adequate. Only a diachronic analysis, attending to changing uses over time, their differences as well as their interconnections, is likely to get at the moving spirit of the concept, and the developments in understanding and values informing the changes. Attempting this for 'authenticity' is no easy task but fortunately Charles Taylor has already done helpful work for us (Taylor, 1991).

Taylor finds the idea of authenticity becoming very important in the late 18th century through the work of the Prussian, Johann Herder. Herder's philosophy involved a remarkable new kind of subjectivism which affords a new moral significance to the differences between human beings. 'There is a certain way of being human that is *my* way. I am called upon to live my life in this way, and not in imitation of anyone else's. But this gives a new importance to being true to myself. If I am not, I miss the point of my life, I miss the point of what being human is for *me*' (Taylor, 1991, pp. 28–29).

In a relatively short time, Taylor believes, this new ideal, this new picture of what a better or higher mode of life would be, has entered deeply into modern consciousness. Just how deeply is perhaps brought home to us if we reflect on the difficulty we now have in imagining how previous visions of the good life could have found no place for people to do something like striving to recognise and fulfil their own unique way of being human. To do this we need to be reminded not only of the strong pressures to social conformity present in much of human history, but also of the fact that for most pre-moderns the struggle to preserve one's life left little time for extended reflection on what to actually make of it. This has recently been well documented regarding England by Keith Thomas (2009, especially Chapter 1). Herder, it seems, came on the scene just as circumstances were becoming propitious for him to be heard.

It can seem quite natural to modern readers first encountering Herder to take him to be adumbrating ideals of complete personal freedom for everyone to think, believe and choose how to 'make themselves' entirely as they wish. These do come together today in a widely spread mind-set that engenders active enthusiasm among many as well as outraged criticism from others. However, for Herder the business of getting to know oneself, and then living accordingly, is no soft option. Moreover his intense disapproval of individuals or institutions which oppress or interfere with the authentic development and expression of other groups or individuals, implies important constraints on how one ought to set about living a life of self-fulfilment alongside other human beings doing likewise.

At the same time Herder's thoughts do have important affinities with today's enthusiasms for relativism, subjectivism, permissiveness, and self-fulfilment through 'doing one's thing'. Taylor shows that there is historical continuity between the two. But at the same time, Herder's original vision has developed and changed in interaction with other movements in the culture such as subjectivisms and relativisms so uncompromising that they constitute a total moral and epistemological scepticism. Alongside these there has developed an individualism that slides into egotism and leaves no room for higher purposes, for objective values, or for moral strivings and heroism. Often these revisions have drawn support from versions of existentialism and postmodernism. But on Taylor's account the original and admirable vision of authenticity has often taken on degraded, absurd or trivialised forms which have become part of a new and importantly different culture of authenticity.

This has been subjected to powerful criticism, and its educational repercussions were harshly surveyed in Allan Bloom's best seller, *The Closing of the American Mind* (1987). Taylor is more balanced in recognising good and bad elements in modern ideals of authenticity, but if anyone doubts that they sometimes manifest themselves perniciously in popular culture they might note how the focus on self as the fundamental justifier is unintentionally satirised in the pompous righteousness with which Frank Sinatra croons the continuingly popular, egotistical and morally corrupt doggerel of 'My Way'.

This brief venture into some large themes in our cultural history can now be used to resolve the apparent paradox that Peters disdains a quality for which he has been esteemed. It is not that he and Elliott are in discord. It is that they are talking about two related but importantly different things. As Taylor helps us to see, Elliott is talking of authenticity as something recognisably close to Herder's ideal. Peters, however, has encountered and is troubled by the subsequent developments of the authenticity ideal. The point can be missed because the importantly different ideas have historical connections, some similarities and a shared label.

Moreover, Peters' understanding of religious awe and Christian love seems to harmonise well with Herder's view of self-making. The two are not identical but can probably be set side-by-side with no great difficulty or discomfort. He writes:

> What is called Christian love can be understood as an intensified and particularised form of this generalised respect for the individual and awe that is felt for the predicament of any man trying to make something of his life. We are born. We grow up and gradually our predicament dawns upon us. We have to make something of the brief space of years that is our lot, with the variable and partly alterable equipment with which we are blessed. To view anyone trying to make something of himself in this context, and to be intensely concerned about him is to love him in the Christian sense (Peters, 1973, p. 110).

CONCLUSION

I began by noting two reasons why philosophers may take an interest in the lives and persons of other philosophers. Exploring some ways in which Peters evidences authenticity in a good sense served both purposes: improving our understating of his work and celebrating a thinker who evidences an organic unity of self, philosophy and professorial work. His expressed disdain for authenticity confirmed that we are dealing with no simple concept but with an evolving, ambiguous one that has not always stayed authentic to its own moving spirit. There seem to be at least two distinct kinds of advocacy of authenticity: one that some hold should be preserved and revisited as involving important values for philosophy and for human living, and one that incorporates other more controversial and potentially harmful supposed values. Taylor warns us against thinking of them in terms of straightforward opposition. Our task is not like steering between dangerous fixed points like Scylla and Charybdis but more like navigating the floating, changing masses of the Sargasso Sea. So it is important to understand the development and ambiguities of authenticity as an ideal for living, as a preliminary to working out what versions, or what combination of bits of versions, of authenticity should be treasured in a culture and nurtured by educators.

I have indicated some starting possibilities for reflection on this: but such reflection soon leads on to other matters including the question: if we recognise authenticity as a value, or group of values, then with precisely what kind of values should we take ourselves to be dealing? Since they relate to matters of how we live and behave, then they might seem to be straight-forward moral values. But, as Taylor's account reveals, authenticity came on the scene as a protest at the dominant view of moral values and duties as being somehow objectively determined from outside of us. Authenticity as an ideal then becomes a matter of rejecting or relaxing the demands of these in favour of pursuing a state I can and should achieve and that satisfies me as being uniquely appropriate to myself. This is hardly what we normally understand as a matter of duty. So it might be suspected that authenticity is not part of morality but another kind of value altogether. However, I think there is a preferable interpretation. If we follow Taylor's account of Herder as opening our minds to an important area of value, hitherto overlooked in our ethical thought and understanding of human life, then we can see the espousal of authenticity as an ideal as a profoundly challenging corrective to prevailing moral assumptions—the putting in place of something that had been left out. That is to say that authenticity values are a part of morality such that recognition of them involves important changes in our moral understanding as a whole. Subsequent developments have stressed a kind of contact with oneself, yielding important self-knowledge to help one to work out what kind of being one should strive to be. This kind of authenticity is perhaps best thought of as a high level, or very general, virtue. If so, it is a virtue with both moral and epistemic ingredients: a counter-example, perhaps, to contempor-ary claims that moral and intellectual virtues are to be crisply distinguished even though their connections and similarities should be explored. (See the collected papers in DePaul and Zagzebski, 2003.) There is an untidiness here, but sorting things out could be an educationally fertile exercise.

Authenticity is threatened by pressures to conform, to guard against which the modern culture of authenticity has, in recent decades, talked much of goals like 'realising my potential', 'self-fulfilment' and 'doing one's own thing'. As noted, Taylor believes that much of the original and admirable ideal of authenticity has thus been degraded. Many cultural critics join Allan Bloom in seeing these developments as undermining moral commitment and discouraging hard thinking. Yet the moral fervour with which people hold to these positions remains powerful. Anyone who has taught philosophy knows how often students respond with amazement and even moral outrage when one suggests that there just may be such things as objective moral truths.

We are now in a position not just to resolve the paradox that Peters rejects authenticity as a value while Elliott commends him for displaying it: we are also able to recognise something very important behind it. Taylor helps us to see that Elliott is talking of authenticity as something recognisably close to Herder's ideal, something a writer might exemplify with or without striving for it. Peters, however, has encountered and been troubled by modern versions (or degradations) of authenticity and their powerful presence in modern culture. So behind the paradox are matters of cultural malaise, as well as ideals, to which many philosophers rightly address themselves. Taylor's analysis has the virtue of showing that the distinction between the two authenticities is no simple black and white affair. There are continuities and discontinuities in each as well as strengths and weaknesses. Philosophers must carry on trying to sort through these if they hope to cure the maladies and nurture the ideal. Elsewhere I have discussed ways of teaching philosophy likely to favour the development of student authenticity (Degenhardt, 2003, pp. 47–50). But many contemporary educational policies seem more likely to foster moral and intellectual fragmentation and perhaps stagnation. It is natural to doubt whether philosophers can really be very effective in correcting powerful cultural movements. But if philosophers and related theorists helped to created the maladies that afflict education, then there can hardly be any *a priori* reason for denying that we can also help to put things right. And since authenticity is very much to do with how we learn to conceive ourselves, and to live in the light of this, then philosophers of education should be even more involved here than they already are.

REFERENCES

Bloom, A. (1987) *The Closing of the American Mind* (New York, Simon & Schuster).

Conant, J. (2001) Philosophy and Biography, in: J. Klagge (ed.) *Wittgenstein: Biography and Philosophy* (Cambridge, Cambridge University Press).

Cooper, D. (1983) *Authenticity and Learning: Nietzsche's Educational Philosophy* (London, Routledge & Kegan Paul).

Degenhardt, M. A. B. (2003) Should Philosophy Express the Self?, *Journal of Philosophy of Education*, 37.1, pp. 35–51.

DePaul, M. and Zagzebski, L. (2003) *Intellectual Virtue: Perspectives from Ethics and Epistemology* (Oxford, Clarendon Press).

Elliott, R. K. (1986) Richard Peters: a Philosopher in the Older Style, in: D. Cooper (ed.) *Education, Values and Mind: Essays for R.S. Peters* (London, Routledge & Kegan Paul).

Hadot, P. (1995) *Philosophy as a Way of Life: Spiritual Exercises from Socrates to Foucault* (Oxford, Blackwell).

Janik, A. and Toulmin, S. [1973] (1996) *Wittgenstein's Vienna* (Chicago, Ivan R. Dee).

Peters, R. S. (1964) *Education as Initiation* (Inaugural Lecture) (London, Evans Brothers for The University of London Institute of Education).

Peters, R. S. (1973) *Reason and Compassion* (London, Routledge & Kegan Paul).
Peters, R. S. (1974) *Psychology and Ethical Development* (London, Allen & Unwin).
Peters, R. S. (1977) Ambiguities in Liberal Education and the Problem of its Content, in: *Education and the Education of Teachers* (London, Routledge & Kegan Paul).
Taylor, C. (1991) *The Ethics of Authenticity* (Cambridge, MA and London, Harvard University Press).
Thomas, K. (2009) *The Ends of Life: Roads to Fulfilment in Early Modern England* (Oxford, Oxford University Press).
Trilling, L. (1972) *Sincerity and Authenticity* (Cambridge, MA and London, Harvard University Press).

14

Vision and Elusiveness in Philosophy of Education: R. S. Peters on the Legacy of Michael Oakeshott

KEVIN WILLIAMS

Richard Peters responded very positively to the re-statement of the tradition of liberal education in the second half of the 20th century elaborated by Michael Oakeshott (see Podoksik, 2003, pp. 222–3). Readers may well be surprised to learn that aspects of Oakeshott's writing on education still retain quite an influence on work in the philosophy of education. In *Education and the Voice of Michael Oakeshott* I draw attention to the tendency of philosophers of education (for example, Rene Arcilla and Maxine Green) to continue to draw on his *oeuvre* (Williams, 2007, pp. 2, 10, 11, 102, 81). Since the publication of the book, at least two extensive pieces have appeared addressing Oakeshott's philosophy of education, one on his conception of civic education (Engel, 2007) and the other dealing with the role of tradition in his theory of liberal learning (Alexander, 2008). Equally significant is Oakeshott's more general impact on thinking about the educational project. For example, in a recent extensive and searching study of the role of religion in education in the USA, Marc O. DeGirolami (2008) draws substantially on Oakeshott's work in the elaboration of his framework of educational theory.

Despite his very positive response to Michael Oakeshott's educational vision, Peters is also judiciously critical, demonstrating that it is possible to maintain scholarly distance from a philosopher whom one admires. His criticism is always nuanced, selective and discriminating and his appraisal of Oakeshott's philosophy of learning on the grounds of its 'systematic elusiveness' (Peters, 1974a, p. 433) on crucial issues is particularly subtle, fine grained and illuminating. Peters is also critical of features of Oakeshott's philosophical style. Oakeshott writes in the grand style of English prose, but unfortunately his rhetorical virtuosity can lead him to present the ideas of his opponents in the form of unjustifiable, tendentious parody. Peters takes him to task for a tendency to be provocative and to make statements that are designed to offend the culture of *idées reçues* regarding education. For example, in one of his essays, Oakeshott sternly affirms the need for teachers to confer absolute priority on what they have to teach rather than on the

Reading R. S. Peters Today, First Edition. Stefaan E. Cuypers and Christopher Martin.
Chapters © 2011 The Authors. Editorial organization © 2011 Philosophy of Education Society of Great Britain. Published 2011 by Blackwell Publishing Ltd.

interests of children (Oakeshott, 1981, p. 306). Peters directs particular criticism at his explicit and unfashionable rejection of the role of pupils' interests in fostering the motivation to learn (Peters, 1974a, p. 436). This criticism, along with several other aspects of his critique, shows that Peters is not an educational or political conservative as he is sometimes perceived.

This chapter opens with a brief account of the nature of education in Oakeshott's thought, and this is followed by a review of some aspects of Peters' criticism that can be rebutted. The main part of this chapter considers Peters' justifiable critique of three features of Oakeshott's work. These are (1) the rigidity of his distinction between vocational university and education, (2) the lack of clarity and accuracy in his philosophy of teaching and learning, especially the under-conceptualisation of the role of example in teaching, (3) the over-emphasis on tradition in moral and civic learning. In order to make sense of Peters' criticism of Oakeshott, it is necessary at the outset to say something about the nature of the educational vision that Peters found so congenial.

OAKESHOTT'S EDUCATIONAL VISION

Oakeshott argues that a capacity for a specific kind of learning lies at the heart of what it is to be human and that only through this activity of learning can we come to acquire facility in any of the practices or languages that make up what he calls a 'conversation' (Oakeshott, 1981, pp. 197-247). 'Conversation' is Oakeshott's central organising metaphor and it refers to the special conversation constituted by participation in a cultural inheritance into which education offers an initiation. The languages of this conversation offer themselves to us in terms of discrete and autonomous modes of experience: the mode of practice or practical living and the modes of scientific, historical and aesthetic experience. Philosophy has a somewhat ambiguously situated role in respect of these modes (see Williams, 2007, pp. 18, 202–4). Oakeshott's conception of education is based on the rigid distinction that he draws between the practical and the other modes of experience. He considers that genuine education, i.e. as conducted in schools, colleges and universities, consists in the initiation of young people into the metaphorical conversation made up of the languages of human understanding (including that of art) that are rigorously disjoined from the world of practical experience. Coming to acquire a facility in using these languages of human understanding is for Oakeshott the characteristically educational endeavour. Free then from all considerations of instrumentality or extrinsic purpose, genuine education is undertaken in an institutional arena that is a 'place apart' (in Fuller, 1989, pp. 69, 71–72, 76) from the rest of life and 'the distracting business of satisfying contingent wants' (p. 28). Accordingly, for Oakeshott, genuine education is of necessity liberal. It is liberal in that it is conducted in this arena that is free from intrusion by the demands of the language of practical activity, the 'language of appetite' (p. 41). But education is also liberating or emancipatory in that it liberates us from the grip of this language: it emancipates us from servitude to the world *sub specie voluntatis*, 'from the here and now of current engagements' (p. 37).

The metaphor of conversation is developed in terms of a distinction that Oakeshott makes between what he calls the 'language' and the 'literature' or 'text' of a mode of thought (Oakeshott, 1981, pp. 308–9). This distinction, considered at some length by Peters (1974a), allows Oakeshott to distinguish between different kinds and levels of education and should be considered more a conceptual tool than an epistemological truth. By 'language' he means the 'manner of thinking' appropriate to a particular mode of experience, and by a 'literature' or 'text' he means 'what has been said from time to time in a "language"' (Oakeshott, 1981, p. 308). The literature consists in the facts, information, discoveries, conclusions or disclosures provided by the appropriate explanatory language. A textbook of geology, for example, contains some part of the current state of geological knowledge, but this compilation need make no reference to the way in which geologists came to establish this knowledge. The textbook represents the literature or text of geological knowledge, while the investigatory procedures whereby geologists have established this knowledge represent the language of the discipline. Oakeshott believes that learners need to be familiar with the literature of human understanding before they can master its languages. Facility or fluency in the language of any skill must be acquired by trying to speak or practise it rather than by studying dictionaries or grammar books about it. Much of this learning takes place within the context of a personal relationship between teacher and learner on an apprenticeship basis. In his pedagogy Oakeshott lays particular emphasis on the personal nature of the educational transaction.

Before addressing the three aspects of Oakeshott's thought that are subject to the most sustained critique from Peters, it is necessary to make some general points regarding Peters' response to his ideas.

A Defence of Oakeshott

Several of his criticisms either neglect remarks of Oakeshott's or else do not reflect his later work, particularly as it has been developed by commentators in recent years. For example, as noted previously, Peters is quite correct to be critical of statements by Oakeshott denying the need to take into account the interests of children. But this is qualified in the light of the more sensitive attitude that he displays in his account of the teacher/learner relationship (see Williams, 2007, pp. 165–6).

Peters is uneasy with Oakeshott's attitude to the issue of access to education or educational opportunity (see Peters, 1974a, p. 436). In Oakeshott's essays he identifies a neglect of socio-economic factors on access to education. Oakeshott's invitation to join in the educational conversation can appear to be extended pre-eminently to the advantaged. Yet careful reading of *On Human Conduct* (Oakeshott, 1975), as well as recent scholarship on his work, shows that Oakeshott's political philosophy can be interpreted in such a manner as to accommodate extensive and radical change (see Williams, 2007, pp. 189–228).

Peters takes Oakeshott to task for his neglect of the necessity for assessment in teaching and learning and, indeed, he finds that Oakeshott is inimical to its role in university. But this criticism neglects a comment in a less well known article, 'The Definition of a University' (Oakeshott, 1967), that Peters does not seem to be aware of. In fairness the essay in question repeats material found elsewhere but it does contain some original arguments. In this essay Oakeshott displays an awareness of the need for assessment in education. 'Although', he writes, 'there may be ways of discovering ... the relation between ... abilities and ... ambitions, these devices will not be infallible, even if the criterion itself remains uncorrupted' (p. 140). The criterion in question is the aptitude for and the 'willingness to submit to the discipline of academic study' (ibid.). Given the status that society confers on accomplishment in the academic spheres, it is perfectly understandable that many have ambitions to enjoy this acknowledgement. What Oakeshott says is that it is not enough for a student merely to aspire to academic achievement but that she must give evidence of ability at her studies and also be prepared to do the hard work required.

THE THREE CRITICISMS

The main part of this chapter is concerned with three features of Oakeshott's philosophy of education that Peters is right to challenge. The first of these is the rigidity of the distinction between university and vocational education.

The Distinction between University and Vocational Education

Peters takes issue with the rigidity of Oakeshott's distinction between the respective nature of vocational and university education (Peters, 1974a, pp. 436–8). In his account of the relationship between the two forms of education, Oakeshott makes use of the distinction between the 'language' and the 'literature' or 'text' of a mode of thought (see Oakeshott, 1981, pp. 308–9). In vocational education, as Oakeshott represents it, students learn only to read the literature, most usually of science, whereas in university education they learn to think scientifically, that is, to speak the language of science (see p. 309). Unfortunately Oakeshott fails to expand on this distinction, but the following elaboration is probably true to his intention. In designing a bridge, engineers use the findings about the tensile strength of different materials that scientists have established, but they need not know how these conclusions were arrived at, nor need they know why it is that the materials have these particular qualities. Developing this metaphor, it could be said that engineers learn only to read the language as represented in particular texts, but they do not learn how to write or speak the language concerned.

But Peters challenges too sharp a distinction between vocational and university education in his long essay on Oakeshott (Peters, 1974a) and also in *Ethics and Education* (see Peters, 1970, pp. 29 and 85) as well as in such papers as 'Ambiguities in Liberal Education and the Problem of its Content' (Peters, 1977a), 'Dilemmas in Liberal Education' (Peters, 1977b) and 'The Place of Philosophy in the Training of Teachers' (Peters, 1977c). As David Carr notes, Peters has provided searching analyses of the difference between the classical conception of liberal education with its pursuit of knowledge for its own sake and 'studies devoted to the achievement of certain occupational ends' (Carr, 2008, p. 347). Peters' work in this area provides a context for his challenge to the usefulness and plausibility of Oakeshott's language/literature distinction to discriminate between vocational and university education. The claim that all the literature used in vocational education consists in findings, conclusions, or results derived from enquiries within the disciplines is incorrect. In the respect of most vocational skills, as indeed Oakeshott himself points out, there normally exist what he calls 'technical literatures' (Oakeshott, 1981, p. 319) by which he means texts containing practical theories or guidance for aspiring practitioners. Such technical literatures consist in inductive generalisations derived from successful practice within the activities concerned. Texts of technical literatures might have such titles as 'The Art of Teaching', 'The Art of Nursing', 'The Practice of Accountancy', or 'Engineering Skills'. Whereas the aim of theorising within the terms of the explanatory languages is to establish true propositions, the aim of the theories found in these technical literatures is to help the individual to practise the relevant skills.

Yet again, though, it must be said that in the less well known article, noted previously but ignored by Peters, Oakeshott would appear to qualify somewhat the exclusiveness of the language/literature distinction. In this essay he acknowledges that students learning a vocational skill may recognise that the literature that they are using is the 'product of enterprises designed to enlarge our understanding of ourselves and the world' (Oakeshott, 1967, p. 136). Still, Peters is correct in finding this account of the relationship between literature and language in vocational education unsatisfactory. The learning involved in vocational preparation for certain occupations requires much more than a mere recognition of the dependence of the conclusions in the literature on achievement within the explanatory languages. Even to read and understand the literature of a subject assumes a significant mastery of its disciplinary language. The information in much vocational literature would just be unintelligible to someone who did not have a grasp of the language from which it is derived. Without a thorough knowledge of the language of physics, for example, a person would be unable to make sense of a textbook on engineering. Moreover, it is hard to imagine that someone could be a good engineer without being able to manage the explanatory language of physics.

Indeed an individual engineer may well demonstrate a greater mastery of the language of physics than a graduate with a degree in the subject.

Peters' conception of the relationship between liberal and vocational learning is more accurate and generous than Oakeshott's. It is possible, he writes, to 'describe a vocational training as liberally or illiberally conceived and implemented' (Peters, 1977c, p. 139) rather than focused narrowly on practical ends. In the case of teacher education, students can be taught to consider not merely the application of psychology or sociology to classroom problems but to enjoy 'a glimmering of the fundamental problems in the disciplines' (ibid.). Indeed given that education cannot be conceived in terms of any set of 'agreed or non-controversial ends' (ibid.), the education of teachers will invariably give rise to philosophically challenging issues.

The next feature of Oakeshott's work that Peters questions is his philosophy of teaching and learning and this is subjected to a detailed and searching critique.

'Elusiveness' in Oakeshott's Philosophy of Teaching and Learning

Oakeshott's philosophy of learning is to be found in different sources and is suggestively rather than systematically presented. To understand Peters' criticisms it is necessary to draw the various strands of Oakeshott's theory together. In elaborating his pedagogic theory, he again makes use of the language/literature distinction. Every human skill or ability, from mowing the lawn and swimming to the activities of the scientist and historian, he explains, can be understood as a metaphorical language of human achievement. Accordingly every skill can also be said to offer a literature in terms of the rules that the skills embody. The literature consists in what might be called the propositional ingredient of knowledge—what he calls 'information' (in Fuller, 1989, p. 51). Every skill, whether of a practical or theoretical nature, is capable in principle of yielding its own 'technical literature' (Oakeshott, 1981, p. 319). The term 'technical literature' embraces what he previously called 'technical knowledge' or 'knowledge of technique' (p. 7) and refers to the rules that govern skills. 'Technical knowledge' in this sense might be better described as disjunctive knowledge since this expression draws attention to the character of such knowledge as disjoined from knowledge in use.

But theoretical activities, which are propositional of their nature, offer a further literature that consists of the results of the enquiries that they facilitate and support. This literature consists of the detachable propositions or items of information that result from enquiries in, for example, science or history. Accordingly, it would include formulae in science or mathematics or dates in history, in short, whatever facts are authoritatively established as a result of enquiries conducted in the appropriate disciplinary languages. Practical activities such as swimming or cabinet-making do not, to be sure, offer a literature in this sense. The purpose of these activities is to realise certain practical goals and not to produce propositions. Care must be exercised not to confuse disjunctive knowledge, that is, the formulated rules that inform an activity and theoretical or propositional knowledge. Rules are propositions that are parasitic on practical activities, whereas theoretical enquiries consist, by their very nature, of propositions.

Oakeshott's distinction between disjunctive/articulate knowledge or information and practical/executive knowledge or judgement is reflected in a further distinction between two kinds of teaching, namely instruction and imparting. The concept of instruction needs closer examination. Instruction is teaching 'in the simplest meanings' (Oakeshott, 1981, pp. 11) of the words, and it constitutes only the 'meanest part of education in an activity' (p. 92). Involving the communication of inert facts as items of information and the provision of directives relating to the performance of particular actions, it is that aspect of teaching to which Gilbert Ryle applies the term 'teaching *that*' (Ryle, 1973, p. 110). What Oakeshott seems to have in mind is what Ryle calls drilling (p. 109).[1] Drilling is a useful term because it communicates the notion of teaching both verbal and non-verbal routines of a mechanical nature. Just as army recruits are drilled in parade ground exercises, pupils are drilled in such routines as reciting the multiplication tables and spellings.

Imparting and the Teaching of Judgement

The notion of making appropriate use of information leads very quickly into the kind of teaching to which Oakeshott applies the term 'imparting' rather than instruction. Rather than the communication of facts, he understands imparting as the communication of judgement. Oakeshott quite rightly maintains that there is no abstract aptitude called 'judgement' that can be acquired apart from the context of its exercise in the performance of particular tasks (in Fuller, 1989, pp. 56–7, 59–62). As it makes no sense to speak of teaching judgement in the abstract, teaching judgement involves therefore the teaching of specific skills. Oakeshott also rejects the idea that to teach a skill we must first convert 'our knowledge of it into a set of propositions . . . and that in order to learn an activity we must begin with such propositions' (Oakeshott, 1981, p. 91). It is hard to believe that anyone would think that, in order to learn a skill, we must begin by learning propositions about it. But here he is no doubt thinking less of a theory of learning and more of a tendency to conceive of teaching and learning as being of this propositional nature. Although formulated rules have a 'pedagogic value' (p. 92), this does not mean that a skill can be taught by instruction in any determinate number of propositions or facts; learning judgement cannot be reduced to the acquisition of 'technical knowledge'.

With regard to the teaching of judgement there is a change in Oakeshott's attitude towards the matter, though Peters does not take this change into consideration. In *Rationalism in Politics*, Oakeshott writes that the judgment embodied in 'practical knowledge . . . can neither be taught nor learned, but only imparted and acquired' (Oakeshott, 1981, p. 11). But later, in 'Learning and Teaching', he writes that '"judgement" may be *taught*; and it belongs to the deliberate enterprise of the teacher to teach it' (in Fuller, 1989, p. 60). But Peters is right to find the account of the manner in which this 'deliberate enterprise' is managed a questionable feature of Oakeshott's theory. Judgement, argues Oakeshott, is acquired by the learner's 'imitating the example' (p. 62) provided by the teacher's performances in 'a concrete situation' (see pp. 60–62 for this recurring phrase). It must, he writes, 'be imparted obliquely in the course of instruction ... . It is implanted unobtrusively in the manner in which information is conveyed, in a tone of voice, in the gesture which accompanies instruction, in asides and oblique utterances, and by example' (p. 60–1). Accordingly he envisages judgment being acquired by the learner following example of a person accomplished in the exercise of a skill. Observing an exemplar at work emancipates 'the pupil from the half-utterances of rules by making him aware of a concrete situation' (p. 62). The essential thesis of Oakeshott's pedagogic theory is that the acquisition of judgement involves the learner's following the example of a teacher. What he proposes therefore is an apprenticeship model of learning whereby the learner works 'alongside the master' (Oakeshott, 1981, p. 33). The master provides him with an 'opportunity not only to learn the rules, but to acquire also a direct knowledge of how he sets about his business (and, among other things, a knowledge of how and when to apply the rules)' (p. 92).

There is something intuitively appealing about this notion of the teacher as exemplar and it has been constructively used by the late Terence H. McLaughlin, a distinguished student of Peters and a successor as professor at the Institute of Education, University of London. Elaborating on Oakeshott's work in analysing the activity and influence of the teacher, McLaughlin shows how this account reflects an attractive vision: 'The wide ranging sorts of influence over pupils that the teacher has to exert in the "conversation between the generations" that constitutes education means that the teacher must be a *certain sort of person* who communicates not only knowledge and skill but also (parts of) him or herself' (McLaughlin, 2008a, p. 225). But Peters finds serious deficiencies in the Oakeshottean vision of the activity of the teacher. He takes Oakeshott to task for elusiveness in his account of how the teacher communicates knowledge and skill and he also criticises crucial elements in his account of the role of example as the human conduit of judgement (see Peters, 1974a, pp. 442–9).

Peters' Critique of Oakeshott's Pedagogy

First, he carefully demolishes Oakeshott's notion of imparting. 'Impart', explains Peters (ibid., p. 443), is an achievement word whose application is not limited to imparting as Oakeshott represents it because it can also be applied to instruction or 'teaching that'. A teacher, for instance, can be described as instructing children in the names of the capital cities of Europe. If, as a result of this instruction, the children can recite the names, the teacher can be said to have successfully imparted this knowledge. Impart is the perfectly appropriate term to describe the result of successful instruction. In fact, Oakeshott would have done better to avoid the term 'impart' and to refer to 'teaching how', which is what is really involved in teaching judgment.

Peters goes on to criticise his failure to makes distinctions between different senses of the term 'judgment' and also between different kinds of skill. He speaks of judgement with regard to the use of any concept that is a feature of all language acquisition. It is the judgement involved in making any discrimination whatever among phenomena, which Oakeshott came to call recognition or identification (see Oakeshott, 1975, pp. 3–6). Judgement also refers both to the judgement necessary to exercise a skill in non-routine situations, the literal paradigm of which is the judgement exercised by a judge in a court of law, and also to the judgement that is necessary in the particularly accomplished exercise of a skill. Accordingly, Peters explains, it is misleading to speak of the learning involved in the acquisition of judgement in an undiscriminating way.

Just as there are different forms of judgment, there are also, notes Peters, different kinds of skill, which is something that is ignored by Oakeshott (Peters, 1974a, pp. 447–9). A distinction can be drawn between skills such as typing, driving, or swimming that have a simple, specifiable goal and those such as teaching, social work, historical research or wood carving that have more complex goals where the notion of success is less definable. It is manifestly at odds with common sense to argue that the judgement required in the exercise of a skill with a determinate goal can be acquired only through apprenticeship to someone proficient in the practice of that skill. For example, people can and do learn to type, to service their motor cars or to swim by the trial and error method of doing it themselves without the mediation of instructors, although they may well have recourse to the 'technical knowledge' inscribed in books and manuals. They will probably learn more quickly and more efficiently with the help of a teacher but the presence of a teacher cannot be said to be a condition necessary to learning such skills although, without the help of a teacher, learners are likely to make serious mistakes.

In acquiring more complex skills such as teaching, diplomacy, or medicine, the opportunity to observe and imitate the practice of skilled performers is obviously desirable and conducive to effective and economical learning. But it cannot be shown that these aspects of apprenticeship are a condition necessary to the acquisition of such skills. However undesirable it may be in practice, there is no reason in principle why, once she has some grasp of what is required, a person cannot learn even such complex skills as these without recourse to the model performances of others. In fairness to Oakeshott, it must be said that he is not unaware that people can teach themselves even complex skills. In 'The Definition of a University', for example, he rejects 'the prejudice which attributes all learning to teaching—especially in a university, where to be a pupil and to be taught is not at all the only path to learning'

(Oakeshott, 1967, p. 132; see also Oakeshott in Fuller, 1989, p. 44). The possibility of self-teaching is also suggested in the observation derived from Aristotle that 'we come to penetrate an idiom of activity in no other way than by practising the activity; for it is only in the practice of an activity that we can acquire the knowledge of how to practise it' (Oakeshott, 1981, p. 101). Strangely enough, in this passage there is no reference whatever to the teacher's role in providing a model for the learner to imitate. Here too, Oakeshott mentions the importance of the notion of practice in learning, but unfortunately he fails to elaborate on the crucial contribution that practice, which Peters quite properly emphasises (Peters, 1974a, p. 446), has in the learning of a skill.

With regard to judgement in the sense of a personal style or idiom, Peters explains that Oakeshott seems to confuse the activity of detecting the style peculiar to a skilled performer with that of acquiring such a style for oneself (ibid., p. 448). In neither case is the actual personal experience of 'working alongside the master' in principle necessary. Though Oakeshott would probably concede this, the point is not clear from his writings. In the absence of a teacher, a learner may very well learn to detect the idiosyncratic style of a historian or a philosopher by reading her books, or learn to identify the personal style of a cabinet-maker by examining work that she has done, or she may learn to identify the style of golf stroke peculiar to a particular player through watching him on television. Subsequently, without the personal intervention of the learning model, by assiduous practice, the neophyte may come to incorporate something of the other's style into her own performance. Yet, as Peters notes, Oakeshott would hardly approve of too much mimetic, of too much assimilation of another person's style (ibid., p. 449). Such imitativeness would be inconsistent with the proper insistence in his conception of education on 'enabling the pupil to make the most or the best of himself' (in Fuller, 1989, p. 47).

The criticisms above demonstrate how difficult a task it is to articulate the role of teacher as a model for learners. It is indeed a task that remains a matter for concern in philosophy of education.[2] As James Stillwagon argues, there is much more to be learned about the relationship between the teacher and the subject-matter and 'student desire', although 'some aspect of the teacher's identity must be tied up with . . . educational goals and institutional practices' (Stillwagon, 2008, pp. 81, 68). Even more recently, Colin Wringe has addressed the complexity of the almost certain 'emotional involvement' that will inform the relationship between teacher and learner where 'real learning is going on' (Wringe, 2009, p. 248). Wringe also argues that it is necessary to acknowledge that 'something resembling the relations of discipleship' (p. 251) will tend to be a feature of rich teaching and learning environments. The view of discipleship that he proposes is very nuanced and sensitive to 'the obligation of exceptional moral vigilance' (ibid.) that teachers must exercise to ensure that learners are not subject to undue and inappropriate influence.

Peters is well aware of these difficulties in accounting for the influence of the teacher and he wrestles with the issues involved (for example, Peters, 1970, pp. 258–9; 1973, pp. 11–12) and the reader gets a sense of this struggle from his writing. For example, in *Ethics and Education* he uses the somewhat strange notion of the teacher as one who 'lures' (Peters, 1970, p. 259) young people into the world of learning. In *The Logic of Education* (co-authored with Paul Hirst), the rather lame observation that that teacher will allow 'glimpses of himself as a human being to slip out and be receptive to this dimension of his pupils' is to be found (Hirst and Peters, 1970, p. 100). In 'What is an Educational Process?' the analysis, however, becomes more nuanced and probing (Peters, 1973). He explains that the difficulty in accounting for the personal influence of the teacher derives from the fact that this influence is related to the acquiring of attitudes and in this process 'so much is caught rather than explicitly taught' (ibid., p. 12). There is an absence of explicitness in what occurs and much depends on 'whether the learners are drawn to the teacher or not' (ibid.). 'And what', writes Peters, 'is more chancy than human attractions?' (ibid.). The influence of chance contributes to making the whole area of the personal dimension in human learning very complex. Probably the most helpful source of insight on the issue is to be found in autobiographies and imaginative literature and in this endeavour the work of Oakeshott provides a rich, suggestive and rewarding starting point (see Davis and Williams, 2003, pp. 262–70).

This leads to the third strand of Peters' critique and it deals with Oakeshott's theory of moral and civic learning. The problems in this area are related in several ways to the general difficulties with his philosophy of learning.

Oakeshott's Account of Moral Learning

Oakeshott argues that generally there will always 'remain something of a mystery' about how moral and civic learning takes place (in Fuller, 1989, p. 151). Despite this 'mystery', he suggests that we come to acquire our moral values in the manner in which we learn our native language by 'the observation and imitation of the behaviour of our elders' (p. 152). He maintains that the 'greater part ... perhaps the most important part—of ... [this] education we acquire haphazardly in finding our way about the natural-artificial world into which we are born' (ibid.). As Peters notes, Oakeshott does not get to grips with the pedagogy involved in the transmission of moral values. In fairness, Oakeshott cannot be taken to task for the parsimony in his account of the mechanics of the transmission of values since it was never his intention to provide a comprehensive account of the matter. Yet in his writings there is a serious absence of elucidation on how facility in the 'language of moral converse' (Oakeshott, 1975, pp. 59, 64) is actually acquired. In his theory of learning, as Peters points out, 'Theories about roles, imitation, or identification are never mentioned' and there is no reference to empirical studies on the transmission of values (Peters, 1974a, p. 449).

Yet it is possible to identify the principal elements of a theory of moral and civic learning in Oakeshott's work. At the heart of this theory is a distinction that he draws between the two different styles of moral life—the ideological and the traditional/ecological. The ideological style represents the 'morality of the Rationalist' (Oakeshott, 1981, p. 35) for whom moral life consists in the self-conscious pursuit of moral ideals and the application of moral rules. These ideals have to be determined in the abstract and defended against contrary ideals before being applied to concrete situations. The traditional/ecological, by contrast, involves participation in an existing practice of moral conduct. Most of all Oakeshott is keen to resist any account of moral learning as the acquisition of an ability to engage in theorising about principles rather than acting morally. Ideally for Oakeshott, as for Shakespeare's (1997) Coriolanus, 'action is eloquence' (Act III, Sc. ii, line 76), and articulated knowledge would usually, therefore, be superfluous. It is this resistance to articulated knowledge that leads Peters to claim that for Oakeshott principles are 'somehow spurious in relation to justification' (Peters, 1974a, p. 451, and see also Benn and Peters, 1977, pp. 317). Oakeshott, writes Peters, is not 'much interested in the discussion and justification of principles' and what 'fascinates him is the judgment required to apply them in particular circumstances' (Peters, 1973, p. 20).

In his later writing, however, Oakeshott shows that this is not his actual considered view. In *On Human Conduct*, he gives a careful account of the different forms that justification may take to rebut the imputation of injustice in respect our actions (Oakeshott, 1975, pp. 68–70). He explains that we may justify an action (1) by relating it to the moral principle that we are accused of violating (2) by pointing to the relationship between the action in question and the duties attaching to an office or role (3) by invoking a principle of a higher moral priority. An example (the examples are mine) of justification of the first form would be where a person argues that his taking another's car keys is not a case of theft or an injustice to the other party as this person commonly drives when drunk and thereby puts at risk his own life and that of others. A doctor offers a justification of the second kind where, to the accusation of professional negligence, she claims that she was precluded on the grounds of professional ethics from disclosing to her parents, without the daughter's consent, the fact of her pregnancy. The individual in the first example offers justification of the third kind where he admits to telling a lie about his knowledge of the whereabouts of the other person's car keys by arguing that his falsehood is justified in terms of the higher moral principle of respect for life. Thus he justifies his action by invoking a principle that can be said to be more compelling because it is of a higher order of moral priority than the one purportedly neglected.

In his considered and mature view, Oakeshott therefore accepts the role of justification in the moral life. Unfortunately, however, he does not significantly develop his theory of moral and civic learning.

Oakeshott and the Language of Moral Converse: The Limits of an Analogy

How persuasive then is the analogy between learning one's native language and learning values? The analogy is first suggested in *Rationalism in Politics* in the course of his discussion of the traditional or habitual form of moral life (Oakeshott, 1981, p. 62). Here he offers the following account of the analogy. As children learn to speak by imitating the example of the adults who surround them, they acquire their moral values in the same way. And as in learning to speak, what they learn is language in use rather than rules of grammar and syntax. The origins of children's moral education lie then in the assimilation of patterns of behaviour, rather than in learning to negotiate and apply moral ideals, rules and principles.

Now this account of moral education is plausible enough up to a point but unfortunately Oakeshott leaves us only with the analogy between moral learning and the acquisition of the mother tongue and does not elaborate further upon how facility in the 'language of moral converse' (Oakeshott, 1975, pp. 59, 64) is acquired. Peters accepts that the analogy does capture the elasticity necessary in the moral life, which 'evolves in the way in which a living language evolves' (Peters, 1974a, p. 450). So what else should be said about the language metaphor? Despite being suggestive and illuminating and catching much of the spirit of moral education, the analogy stands in need of important qualification. Peters identifies three important criticisms of Oakeshott's analogy: (1) to count as being moral conduct assumes a background of principles and the possibility of justification is crucial (2) in the moral life appeal to custom is not enough (3) in teaching moral values explanation is fundamental.

The first criticism concerns the essential place of knowledge of principles or rules in moral education. This knowledge is not required in learning a language—we would say of a person that she has succeeded in learning a language if she can speak it intelligibly without making mistakes. She will, for example, recognise and avoid such incorrect utterances as 'I you love' or 'J'aime toi' simply because they sound incorrect. Formulation of the appropriate rules of grammar and syntax can be found in books but explicit knowledge of such formulations is not necessary in making correct utterances. By contrast, however, a person cannot be said to have learned to behave morally unless she can indicate something of what makes her actions moral. To count as being able to speak a language, all that is required is the production of appropriate utterances in the appropriate context, whereas to count as acting morally a person must be able to understand why she is acting in this way. And this understanding necessarily consists in formulated rules, ideals and principles. This explains Peters' charge that 'Oakeshott's suspicion of principles inhibits moral discussion' and moral reasoning (Benn and Peters, 1977, p. 317). For example a pupil who hands into the school office a wallet found in the assembly hall must understand that she is acting in terms of obligation rather than of expediency and she must be able to indicate something of this understanding in order that we can qualify her action as moral. Or, in owning up to a misdemeanour to avoid a collective punishment being meted out to the whole class, a pupil must have some understanding of the notions of personal guilt and responsibility and must also be able to put into words something of this understanding. In these two examples it is not necessary that the pupils be able to justify an abstract set of principles, it is necessary only that they be able to relate their action to standards that they value. Any attempt at justification must be conducted in terms of moral considerations of a general nature, although the exercise in justification can occur at different levels of generality and of sophistication.

This leads to the second important difference between learning a language and learning to behave morally. In the case of a natural language an individual can respond to the charge of using bad grammar (for saying, for example, 'it's me'), by invoking customary forms of speech as a court of appeal. By contrast, an appeal to what others normally do when asked why one has contributed to a charity will not endow an action with a moral quality, any more than a similar appeal will serve as justification or as a criterion of the moral acceptability of failing to file full and accurate income tax returns. To count as being genuinely moral an individual's actions must express her own personal values, conviction and commitment. If what is conventionally done were to be accepted as the sole criterion of moral value, if it were the case that 'what custom wills, in all things should we do it', the result would be that, to continue with the words of Coriolanus, 'The dust on antique time would lie unswept,/And mountainous error be too highly heaped For truth to o'erpeer' (Act 11, Scene 111, lines 121 to 124). The serious danger with the analogy between learning the mother tongue and learning values is then that it could serve to justify blind, uncritical allegiance to the forms of moral conduct that are customary in a particular society. Reading Oakeshott's writings one cannot help suspecting that he sets a very high value indeed on our traditional patterns of moral conduct. It is, argues Peters, as if the 'only relevant justification' for moral and political decisions 'would be an analogy drawn from arrangements sanctified by custom' (Benn and Peters, 1977, p. 317). Yet the sanctification of what is customarily done as the sole criterion for what should be done is anathema to the spirit of an education that aims to promote critical thought.

The third qualification or criticism concerns the place of explanation in moral learning compared with language learning. It is true that both acquiring command of the mother tongue, and the learning of values are co-extensive with all human learning. Consequently, as some of the later research of Piaget into the acquisition of national and cultural mind-sets bears out, much moral education is acquired informally; it is caught rather than taught.[3] A child learning to acquire the prudential arts of human life learns *pari passu* to observe the moral considerations that pervade these arts. For example, the conventions of good table manners have both prudential and moral aspects in that they prescribe conditions that facilitate the expeditious and hygienic consumption of food in such a manner as to show respect for the susceptibilities of other diners. But it would be mistaken to assume that education in values does, must or should occur in quite the unstructured manner in which children come to learn the mother tongue. Children will usually acquire facility in speaking their mother tongue without any direct intervention by adults regarding the rules of grammar. By contrast, children come to acquire their moral standards and patterns of conduct from those adults, particularly parents and teachers, who are responsible for their upbringing and who are in a position to make moral demands of them in a systematic way. Thus teaching children to behave honestly, for example, involves explaining to them what honesty means and showing them what to do to act honestly.

Contra Oakeshott, Peters is correct to affirm the role of propositional knowledge in the moral life, although, as previously noted, he shares Oakeshott's scepticism regarding rationalistic, in the sense of contrived, programmes of civic and moral education (Peters, 1970, p. 60). Oakeshott is nevertheless wise in insisting on the priority of behaving morally rather than in theorising about it. What we practise is far more important than what we preach. To an extent his account of the moral life is more like that of great novelists such as Jane Austen and George Eliot than that of philosophers or psychologists. Given the Piaget-Kohlberg framework of his moral developmental psychology, it is hardly then surprising that Peters is uncomfortable with Oakeshott's non-Kantian account of moral conduct and moral education conceived as embedded in practices. This practice account is not inhospitable to articulated principles but it can appear that these are only begrudgingly accommodated. Peters' attitude to Oakeshott's views is consistent with the general thrust of his response both to the latter's general pedagogy and to his account of moral education.

CONCLUSION

There is a serious sense in which the elusiveness in Oakeshott's pedagogy is due to the literary, almost poetic, quality of some of his writing. His philosophy of education lends itself to being captured in literary images as well as through conventional philosophical discourse (see Williams, 2007, pp. 4–5). One reason for this is that when he writes about education, Oakeshott draws greatly on his own experience. As he put in a letter to me: 'In most of what I have written about education I have had my own schooldays in front of me' (Oakeshott, 1983). This autobiographical dimension is reflected in his intuitive approach to philosophising about education. Indeed, the experiential and intuitive spirit of some of Oakeshott's essays on education could be said to be close to that of D. H. Lawrence's writing on the subject.

By contrast, although experience plays a role in the development of his educational vision (see McLaughlin, 2008b, pp. 304–13), Richard Peters is a very systematic analytic philosopher who philosophises with an exemplary intellectual rigour. He has also an acute awareness of the value of empirical evidence in educational enquiry that, as he notes, is absent in Oakeshott's work (Peters, 1974a, p. 449). It would not therefore be unfair to describe Peters, as does Podoksik, as a more 'analytical' philosopher than Oakeshott (Podoksik, 2003, p. 222). Podoksik's claim is largely true but it stands in need of qualification in the light of Peters' later work. Yet even in 1974, in 'Subjectivity and Standards', Peters states his intention to eschew the 'current analytic manner' and to write in a 'more synthetic and hazardous ... older style of philosophy' (1974b, p. 413). It is also clear from the same essay that Podoksik's claim that Peters 'advocated rationalistic education' (Podoksik, 2003, p. 222)—the term 'rationalistic' is used in the sense of exclusively concerned with intellectual development—must be qualified. 'Subjectivity and standards' defends a much broader conception of the educational endeavour where Peters argues that education 'should, above all things, sensitise us to the predicaments in which we are placed as human beings, to the possibilities it presents for joy and despair, ennui and excitement' (Peters, 1974b, p. 413). In *Education and the Education of Teachers* published in 1977, as Paddy Walsh notes, Peters re-affirms this expansive view of education (Walsh, 1993, p. 125). It is a view fits well with his perception of life as an 'awesome spectacle of human beings trying to make some sort of sense of the world and trying to sustain and cultivate a crust of civilization over a volcanic core of atavistic emotions' (Peters, 1972, p. 87). The vision of life and of education reflected in these quotations has an imaginative resonance that is informed by a very wide notion of rationality. The rich educational aims that support this vision are consistent with the commitments that underpin the educational engagement articulated by Michael Oakeshott. Despite some justifiable criticism of Oakeshott for his elusiveness, these aims reflect the compatibility between the educational visions of Richard Peters and Michael Oakeshott.[4]

NOTES

1. Ryle's essay was published in the same collection of essays, edited by Peters (1973), in which 'Learning and Teaching' first appeared.
2. This concern is reflected in the special issue of the *Journal of Philosophy of Education* entitled *Philosophy of the Teacher* (Tubbs, 2005).
3. For a useful summary of this research see Paul, 1984, pp. 6–16.
4. This chapter has benefited from the comments of Stefaan Cuypers, Christopher Martin, Paul Standish and William Ryan.

REFERENCES

Alexander, H. (2008) Engaging Tradition: Michael Oakeshott on Liberal Learning, in: S. Gough and A. Stables (eds) *Sustainability and Security within Liberal Societies: Learning to Live with the Future* (New York, Routledge), pp. 113–26.

Benn, S. I. and Peters, R. S. (1977) *Social Principles and the Democratic* (State. London, George Allen and Unwin).

Carr, D. (2008) Review of *Education and the Voice of Michael Oakeshott* by Kevin Williams, *Journal of Philosophy of Education*, 42, pp. 345–47.

Davis, A. and Williams, K. (2003) Epistemology and Curriculum, in: N. Blake, P. Smeyers, R. Smith and P. Standish (eds) *The Blackwell Guide to Philosophy of Education* (London, Blackwell).

DeGirolami, M. O. (2008) The Problem of Religious Learning, *Boston College Law Review*, 49, pp. 1212–75.

Engel, S. M. (2007) Political Education in/as the Practice of Freedom: A Paradoxical Defence from the Perspective of Michael Oakeshott, *Journal of Philosophy of Education*, 3, pp. 325–49.

Fuller, T. (ed.) (1989) *The Voice of Liberal Learning: Michael Oakeshott on Education* (New Haven and London, Yale University Press. [This collection contains most of Oakeshott's essays on education.]).

Hirst, P. H. and Peters, R. S. (1970) *The Logic of Education* (London, Routledge and Kegan Paul).

McLaughlin, T. H. (2008a) Philosophy, Values and Schooling: Principles and Predicaments of Teacher Example, in: D. Carr, J. Haldane and R. Pring (eds) *Liberalism, Education and Schooling: Essays by T. H. McLaughlin* (Thorverton, Exeter and Charlotesville, VA, Imprint Academic), pp. 222–38.

McLaughlin, T. H. (2008b) Israel Scheffler on Religion, Reason and Education, in: D. Carr, J. Haldane and R. Pring (eds) *Liberalism, Education and Schooling: Essays by T. H. McLaughlin* (Thorverton, Exeter and Charlotesville, VA, Imprint Academic), pp. 304–31.

Oakeshott, M. (1967) The Definition of a University, *Journal of Educational Thought*, 1, pp. 129–42.

Oakeshott, M. (1975) *On Human Conduct* (Oxford, Clarendon Press).

Oakeshott, M. (1981) *Rationalism in Politics and Other Essays* (London, Methuen. [Originally published in 1962 by the same publisher and now available in an expanded edition edited by Timothy Fuller, Indianapolis: Liberty Press, 1991.]).

Oakeshott, M. (1983). Photocopy of Letter from Oakeshott to Kevin Williams, 23 June 1983, on the Character of Present-day Schools. Available at: library-2.lse.ac.uk/archives/handlists/Oakeshott/Oakeshott.html—3k Accessed 7 March 2009.

Paul, R. W. (1984) Critical Thinking: Fundamental to Education in a Free Society, *Educational Leadership*, 42, pp. 6–16.

Peters, R. S. (1970) *Ethics and Education* (London, George Allen and Unwin).

Peters, R. S. (1972) *Reason, Morality and Religion. The Swarthmore Lectures 1972* (London, Friends Home Service Committee).

Peters, R. S. (1973) What is an Educational Process?, in: R. S. Peters (ed) *The Concept of Education* (London, Routledge and Kegan Paul), pp. 1–23.

Peters, R. S. (1974a) Michael Oakeshott's Philosophy of Education, in: *Psychology and Ethical Development* (London, Allen and Unwin), pp. 433–54.

Peters, R. S. (1974b) Subjectivity and Standards, in: *Psychology and Ethical Development* (London, Allen and Unwin), pp. 413–32.

Peters, R. S. (1977a) Ambiguities in Liberal Education and the Problem of its Content, in: *Education and the Education of Teachers* (London, Henley and Boston, Routledge and Kegan Paul), pp. 46–67.

Peters, R. S. (1977b) Dilemmas in Liberal Education, in: *Education and the Education of Teachers* (London, Henley and Boston, Routledge and Kegan Paul), pp. 68–85.

Peters, R. S. (1977c) The Place of Philosophy in the Training of Teachers, in: *Education and the Education of Teachers* (London, Henley and Boston, Routledge and Kegan Paul), pp. 135–50.

Podoksik, E. (2003) *In Defence of Modernity: Vision and Philosophy in Michael Oakeshott* (Thorverton. Exeter and Charlotesville, VA, Imprint Academic).

Ryle, G. (1973) Teaching and Training, in: R. S. Peters (ed.) *The Concept of Education* (London, Routledge and Kegan Paul), pp. 105–11.

Shakespeare, W. (1997) *The Tragedy of Coriolanus in The Norton Shakespeare Based on the Oxford Edition* (New York and London, W.W. Norton and Co).

Stillwagon, J. (2008) Performing for the Students: Teaching Identity and Pedagogical Relationship, *Journal of Philosophy of Education*, 42, pp. 67–83.

Tubbs, N. (2005) *Philosophy of the Teacher*, Special issue of *Journal of Philosophy of Education*, 39, pp. 183–420.

Walsh, P. (1993) *Education and Meaning: Philosophy in Practice* (London, Cassell).

Williams, K. (2007) *Education and the Voice of Michael Oakeshott* (Thorverton, Exeter and Charlotesville, VA, Imprint Academic).

Wringe, C. (2009) Teaching Learning and Discipleship: Education Beyond Knowledge Transfer, *Journal of Philosophy of Education*, 43, pp. 239–51.

Index